UNSETTLING EUROPE

UNSETTLING EUROPE

EUROPE

Jane Kramer

Random House New York

The material in this book, excepting the introduction, originally
appeared in *The New Yorker*, in slightly different form.

Library of Congress Cataloging in Publication Data
Kramer, Jane.
Unsettling Europe.
1. Europe—Social conditions. 2. Aliens—Europe.
3. Alien labor—Europe. 4. Refugees—Europe.
5. Migration, Internal—Europe. I. Title.
HN377.K7   304.8′34   79–4763
ISBN 0–394–50433–X

Manufactured in the United States of America
24689753
First Edition

for Vincent Crapanzano

CONTENTS

INTRODUCTION

The four parts of this book are about Europeans whom Europe never expected to accommodate. Some of these Europeans are old colonials come "home" to die with the empires they had supported. Some are Third World refugees, migrant workers, Communists out of a *compromesso storico* with reality. All of them are people who have had at least as much to do with what we call "modern Europe" as the young technocrats and the bland new having-and-spending *bourgeois* who usually get the credit (or the blame) for the changing quality of European life. I began the first of these stories, "Les Pieds Noirs," in 1971, about a year after *The New Yorker* started sending me to Europe. It was a portrait of a family of French-Algerian refugees in a Provençal village—a family nearly deranged by war and loneliness—and writing it became a kind of private antidote to the public rhetoric I kept hearing about Europe, my respite from the windy idioms of most European politics. A few years later, when Idi Amin expelled the 27,000 Indian settlers who, for all purposes, had built the country he took over, I wrote the second of these stories, "The Uganda Asians," which turned out to be another portrait of a family in exile—this time about a family of Muslim traders who had fled the Uganda bush to a London workers' borough. Then, in 1975, I began "The Invandrare," about a Yugoslav peasant who had been working for nearly eight years in Swedish factories, trying to earn the money to finish building a house in his native village, a house that was never really going to justify his sacrifice. And finally, in 1979, I finished the story about an old, bickering Communist couple in the Umbrian countryside and their *dottore* son—I have put it first, here—called "The San Vincenzo Cell."

W e are all susceptible to easy abstractions about uneasy or complicated facts of life. And so we tend to talk in abstractions about Europe. We talk about the Left, the Right, about Eurocommunism and Eurodollars and—my own favorite—the Economic Miracle. We confront, with piety, the idol of the Swiss Franc and the Amazing Mark. Europe, for us, becomes a message written in code with words like Social Democracy, *Gastarbeiter*, Yves Saint Laurent, Terrorism, the State, the Breadbasket, *la miseria*, the Crillon, the Pope, and High Culture. Scandinavia is a word for social contract and social boredom. Germany means the Recovery and Autobahns and Ulrike Meinhof. Switzerland means gold bars and Arab ski chalets, Italy means good leather and lost letters and the Brigada Rosa and vines terraced down a Tuscan hill, and England is strikes and stately homes and an Irish Problem. Not surprisingly, a Europe described in newsmagazine cliché and conference jargon did not mean very much to the people in the stories I was writing —which may be why I began to suspect that these stories belonged together, that they had more in common than my own pleasure in the eloquence of a few supposedly ordinary people. I saw that what the people in them really shared was a kind of instinctive subversion of that narrow rhetoric which either claimed to include them or inadvertently ignored them. They were too complicated, too contrary, too bitter, for the rhetoric. They did not fit the exhausted conventional categories of European life. They were unwelcome and unwanted, and merely by being themselves they managed to sabotage the image most other people held of Europe, but it was their labor and their various loyalties which had supported that image in the past, and which support it now—and which will certainly have a lot to do with Europe's future.

Europe obviously has been transformed since the Second

World War—by the war itself, and by the disintegration of vast
empires, the ruin and then abandonment of so much of domestic
rural life and economy, the export of southern labor to northern
industry, and, finally, the vast and probably unprecedented recruitment of the working poor into the protective network of
new, "Western," Communist power. It seems to me now that the
people in the four families that occupied so much of my time
over the last nine years were both casualties and survivors of
this transformation. A friend calls them "people who fell into
the cracks of history." They had to do with policies and ideologies that had changed a world but neglected, somehow, to engage them honestly in the process. They were all, in their way,
beside the point of modern Europe—the leftovers of failed na-
tionalist and economic structures, the human data everyone
forgot to program. But they have survived the failed promises
of an old order—*and* of a new one—and they have also survived
the rhetoric of that survival, making their own odd, angry, and
almost always exasperating adjustments to a Europe that had
always gauged the worth of strangers (and its own outsiders)
by the distance they observed, the discretion with which they
kept away.

By now, I tend to see Europe through the eyes of these four
families that have settled, and unsettled, what once for me
was a familiar landscape. Because of them, I have had to relearn
Europe to include London's grimy outlying "coloured" boroughs,
France's hidden resettlement villages in the mountains, Sweden's
cold apartment blocks for foreign workers, Italy's odd *comuni*
where the Communists rule but the Catholics still reign. And I
know now that their vision of themselves as Europeans is much
more compromised and ultimately much more troubling than the
description of experts whose job it is to explain them to everybody else. The pathos of their longing is that it is so often merely
for belonging, for some corroboration by the world around
them. Their confusion is at least as deep as the values and quali-

ties that set them apart. None of them will ever really accept the fact that they were necessary to Europe once, but only cere- monially noticed—in a way, even Italy's peasants went un- noticed by the society they served—that it was their remoteness, the remoteness of class and protocol as much as distance, that preserved whatever myths of status they had. Now that they want to—or have to—share Europe, they are out of place.

Akbar Hassan ("The Uganda Asians") grew up thinking of himself—with a pride right out of Kipling—as a loyal and ser- viceable British subject on permanent duty in the hinterlands of Empire. The Martins ("Les Pieds Noirs") thought of them- selves as French until they actually left Algeria and came "home" to the *métropole*. Predrag Ilić ("The Invandrare") and Mario Cecchi ("The San Vincenzo Cell") are Communists— Predrag by birth and Mario by conversion—and they both hold their Party mythologies about the future, but mainly their long- ing is for the real world, the world around them now, and they measure themselves by its values. The villa that Predrag Ilić is building, year by year, in a faraway Serbian village is more his statement about success as a Swedish worker than as a Yugoslav who had to emigrate. Yvette Martin's Parisian husband is a vindication of her own defiant and abused citizenship. Akbar Hassan did not buy his used Mercedes to impress relatives in the Bay of Kutch or even to revive images of lost power in Uganda as much as to consecrate his years as a "big capitalist man," English fashion. Mario Cecchi's friends, with their co- operative dairy and their dance combo for the local Festa dell' Unità, are less concerned with Communist notions of property than with the dignity of being one's own *padrone* in Italian country life.

Europe is cynical in ways that foreigners, and especially Americans, have trouble understanding. This was true when Henry James was writing, and it is true now, a hundred years after *The Europeans* was published. Europe plays with identity.

When necessary, it can arouse identity. Its elegant manipula-
tions, its style and sophistry, have to do with the myths of
Nation and Citizen it has mastered. And despite the lessons of
Naziism and then Stalinism, it has gone right on with causes and
ideologies that are still never really expected to threaten the
complacency within its borders. But now outsiders—native and
foreign—have broken the mold of European life by the sheer
force of their helpless and extravagant difference. They are part
of a new mold. They are a social and political and certainly an
economic fact of life, and they have made of Europe a more
polyglot, more various sort of place. But Europe has yet to
settle on an ethic, or even an appearance, appropriate to its new
reality.

Europeans have never been known for an excess of tolerance. Affection in Europe has rarely traveled well from one
village to another, let alone from *métropole* to colony. The
French—left and right—with 55 million people, can talk about
"achieving" a population of 100 million by the year 2000 and
still suffer from a kind of chauvinist claustrophobia that neither
includes nor acknowledges as properly French the old *colons*
whom they have manipulated to be "French" by conviction if
not by *pays*. Refugees like the Martins inhabit as much of a
shadow world in France as the foreign workers do in Sweden or
Switzerland or Germany. None of them are part of the common
reality of Europe, as the rest of Europe seems to understand it.
The stubborn European landscape does not seem to want to
receive them at all—although by now there are certainly towns
in France that are recognizably "French" because of the Portuguese and the North Africans eating lunch from paper bags on
construction-site scaffolds; towns in Sweden that are recogniz-
able Swedish because of the Turks and Greeks and Yugoslavs
hanging out at the train station; towns in Italy where the land-
mark is the new Casa del Popolo on the main piazza, not the
church, but where the people like Mario Cecchi who use that
Casa del Popolo can never really feel at home.

Europeans have argued for years about the implications of

colonialism, of industrialization, of the left and social revolution, but they have rarely posed the simple human question of what being "European" in a changing Europe means. What, for instance, does it mean to be part of the huge white colonial population—settlers and workers, merchants and engineers and colonial civil servants—that arrived in France and England, in Belgium, Portugal, and Holland, with the dissolution of Europe's empires? In France alone, there are over a million French-Algerian refugees like the Martins, along with a million *pieds noirs* children born since the end of the Algerian War. There are another 250,000 from what was once French Morocco. Belgium and Holland have managed to absorb some 100,000 of their old colonial settlers from Africa and Asia. But a country like Portugal, bankrupt for years by colonial war and revolution, has not been able to offer much in the way of a welcome for the 600,000 Portuguese who came home over the last ten years from Guinea and Mozambique and Angola. By the time all of these refugees arrived, a million poor mainland Portuguese had already had to leave home and were trying to survive in France.

Then there are those other refugees—colonials themselves, like Akbar Hassan and his family—in racial or political exile, or in economic flight from the new poverty in Europe's old colonies. Consider the 10,000 Indonesians in Holland. The 35,000 Indochinese in France. The Jamaicans and Indians and Africans in England. England alone has had to make room (and grudgingly) for 1.5 million New Commonwealth citizens (New Commonwealth being the current official British euphemism for "coloured") since the end of the war and the independence of its important colonies.

Now add to this the people we call migrant workers—Yugoslavs like Predrag Ilić, Turks and Greeks, Portuguese and Spaniards and Italians, Arabs and Berbers from the North African coast, even Finns who cross the border into Swedish factory towns to work. They call themselves "the niggers of Europe." They do its dirty work. They come from countries that cannot, or will not, offer them any alternatives besides emigration or poverty, and by now it is impossible to count them all. Some, like the Italian migrant workers, can travel freely across Common Market borders without the visas and the permits which would identify them more precisely to the OECD bureaucrats who keep the migrant labor statistics. Others bring their wives, and their wives have children, and those children, growing up, are not likely to return willingly to the poverty of their parents' old farms and villages. Millions more—"cousins"—come for a week or two and stay illegally and are, of course, unregistered with anyone. But even the official figures are enormous—more than 10 million migrant workers in the industrial states of northern Europe. And they have managed to hold out, despite legislation against them, despite an oil crisis and the labor cutbacks and social backlash that crisis produced. Taken together, they amount to a kind of migrant nation of their own, much bigger than some of the countries whose base labor they supply.

Finally, there are western Europe's Communists, families like the Cecchis—Eurocommunists or Stalinists or Revisionists or Closet Democrats, as the mood moves them and the people watching them. Nearly two million Communists are registered in the Party in Italy, one million in France, hundreds of thousands more in every other western European country.

What does "Europe" mean, then, if these 19 or 20 million people are not included in the word?

None of this counting says very much in the end. I wrote about the particular people in this book because I liked them (or at least most of them), because they moved me, because they had what seems to me more and more to have been a remarkable kind of courage. A professor of the genre that usually refers to itself as "neo-Marxist" pleased me the other day by complaining that my "sociology" of Italian Communism fell away (he meant apart) when the Communists themselves took over the narrative of "The San Vincenzo Cell" and distracted me with their rich and eccentric histories as "people." I do not believe much in sociologies. In a way, the people in this book are my analogue to what my friend would probably call "alienation." And the often ordinary details of their lives, the dramas that absorb them, would be *their* answer, I imagine, to the hypocrisies of armchair class analysis. Alienation can be another way of saying lonely or desperate or exploited or excluded. A good part of modern Europe may be alienated from itself, but this does not really seem specific enough, or warm enough, to describe anyone. It seems to me that the rhetoric of master and slave, ruler and subject, capitalist and worker, can be equally cold.

It is the triumph of these private people over their public "sociology" that interested me. This is one of the reasons I changed their names and in some cases the names of towns or villages connected with them. They were never public people, however they saw themselves or wanted to see themselves. I hope that no one takes their anonymity for unimportance, that the lives they shared with me survive and, in a way, celebrate that privacy.

I have many people to thank. The Cecchis in Italy, the Martins in France, the Hassans in England, the Ilićs, who at last report were still in Sweden. Then I would like to give my loving thanks to William Shawn, for the guidance and the remarkable kindness that have been my education as a writer. To William Whitworth and Pat Crow, who edited these profiles at *The New Yorker*, and to everyone else at the magazine who helped with them. To Jason Epstein at Random House, who waited so calmly and encouragingly for the book, to Gary Fisketjon for all his help in putting it together, and to Alexandra Halsey for her help. To David Fromkin for a title. To Jay McInerney for research. To Eleanor Mefford for countdown patience and countdown typing. To Ester Wilson for looking after me and my family. To my daughter, Wicky, who traveled with me to France in a backpack over eight years ago to find the Martins and has since helped out on every one of these expeditions. And finally to my husband, Vincent Crapanzano. He introduced me to the Europe in this book, and it is dedicated to him.

JANE KRAMER
Zurich

THE
SAN VINCENZO
CELL
(1979)

No one sang the "Internationale" at the Festa dell'Unità in San Vincenzo last summer, and some of the old-timers in Mario Cecchi's cell were horrified. Mario's neighbor Domenico Spina—a staunch *compagno* whose tinted photograph of Joseph Stalin hangs in the milking room of the San Vincenzo dairy cooperative—complained loudly about people forgetting the Revolution. So did Carlo Benetti, the farmer who lives across the road from Mario Cecchi, still sharecropping a few hectares for one of the valley's big landowners. Carlo Benetti said it only proved that people were getting lax and muddleheaded, what with all the talk these days about a "new" Communism. Carlo is eighty-one, the oldest *compagno* in the cell. He has not missed a night of L'Unità since Italy's Communists came out of clandestinity in 1944 and started having their enormous festivals, and this was the first time he could remember that San Vincenzo had neglected the "Internationale."

Normally, when the Communists in the Umbrian village I call San Vincenzo held their summer festival, they hired a combo through the local Party secretary, and the secretary, whose nephew led the combo, saw to it that the "Internationale" was played before the dancing started and that every family had a mimeographed copy of the words. The difference this year was that Mario Cecchi and two of the other San Vincenzo men had put together their own combo. It was a triumph for the village, since there are fewer than three hundred people in San Vincenzo and the farms around it, and most of the men are old Communists, like Mario Cecchi, who have been working the land or herding cows or sheep day and night all their lives and have never had the time or the money for making any music more complicated than a tune on a shepherd's pipe or a harmonica. Mario himself is a shepherd—a "retired" shepherd, as he puts it. He spent sixty punishing years looking after sheep, and it is

unlikely that in all those years he ever imagined that at the age
of seventy-one he would be climbing onto a bandstand out behind the village bar-and-grocery-store—the *spaccio*—to start
playing dance music on a trumpet. Mario plays the trumpet
because his son, Alfredo, happened to buy a trumpet in Perugia,
and after a couple of months of seeing it around the house
Mario got curious and picked it up. Young men like Alfredo
travel nowadays, and make money, and spend it on things like
trumpets. They go to high school in the hill town that overlooks
San Vincenzo's valley and is the seat of the township—the
comune—to which San Vincenzo and most of the other villages
in the valley belong. They go to trade school in big provincial
cities like Terni and Perugia. A few of them—clever and ambitious boys, like Alfredo Cecchi—study at universities with the
sons of counts and senators and capitalists, and become *dottori*.
The rest leave to work in shops or studios in town—or in the
big textile mills in Prato or the factories in Milan or Turin or
even Germany. But every August all of those boys come home.
They arrive with gifts and booty for their families, and the result is that San Vincenzo has gradually acquired (along with its
television sets and refrigerators and Fiat Cinquecentos) Mario
Cecchi's trumpet, one used electric accordion, and a full set of
rock drums from a bankruptcy sale at a Frankfurt strip joint.
The drums completed the trio that called itself the Compagni di
San Vincenzo—three old Communists whose politics did not
prevent them from instantly signing up for the local Socialist
festival and the Christian Democratic festival along with the
Festa dell'Unità and the First Communion of Domenico Spina's
only grandson. In fact, the Compagni were so exhilarated by the
prospect of their first season, and so busy practicing the songs
they heard on the *spaccio* jukebox, that they never thought of
the "Internationale"—not even when the red flags of the Communist Party of Italy went up around the yard, behind the
spaccio, that doubles as the village boxing ring and dance floor,
and the straw fence along the road was hung with bright-red
posters of Antonio Gramsci's earnest face. They opened the

festival this year with their own oom-pa-pa arrangement of "Cherry Pink and Apple Blossom White," and to Mario Cecchi's mind they made a splendid music. Children began jumping up and down in front of the sawhorse bandstand. Husbands fled to the bar, inside, before their wives could shame them into dancing. And Domenico Spina, remembering the "Internationale," signaled desperately to Mario Cecchi—who took his comrade's raised and waving fist as a tribute to his new musicianship, and waved back, proud and shy and smiling.

M ario and his wife, Anna, argue a lot about the Communist Party. Mario is devoted to the Party. For Mario, the Party is a kind of miracle that can take the cell of querulous old men who meet in the Cecchis' kitchen on the first Saturday night of every month—and always end up drinking too much wine and losing at cards to Anna—and connect it to a source of pensions and loans and health-insurance checks as beneficent as the Virgin Mother. It is nearly forty-five years now since Mario abandoned the mountains to settle down in the valley and court Anna, and perhaps he has simply lost a native skepticism about valley people and their institutions. He knows that the Italian Communist Party is one of those institutions, but he is also certain, beyond any doubt, that a famous German philosopher named Karl Marx, whom Alfredo is always quoting, has had a great deal to do with the fact that there is a big electric refrigerator with a freezing unit and an icemaker in the Cecchis' kitchen. Refrigerators always figure in the Cecchis' arguments about the Party—mainly because their own refrigerator stands just opposite the kitchen table, where they sit and fight. Anna will point to the refrigerator, and an angry flush will start at the base of her throat and spread up across her face, mottling the skin on her fine brown cheeks. And then she will shout in her raspy *contadina*'s voice that it was she, Anna Cecchi, and not some dead German—not, for that matter, some big Party *capo* like Palmiro Togliatti or Enrico Berlinguer, either—who starved

and slaved and did without for years so that the Cecchis could
have an electric refrigerator to keep the milk from spoiling in
the valley heat.

Anna has a way of arguing—with her black eyes wrinkled
into slits and her finger jabbing at the air like a *vipera*—that
amounts to a kind of malevolent composure. Even Mario is a
little in awe of Anna when she starts shouting at him across a
table full of fruits and cheeses and salamis and dusty litre bottles of Carlo Benetti's homemade wine. She curses the Party as
if Communism were a pretty younger woman down the road or
a filthy, secret habit, and she always ends these denunciations
by pounding her chest and thanking God that she never went to
school and learned to read the books that have confused her
husband all these years, and have even made her *dottore* son,
who is a town councilman and should know better, so ludi-
crously cheerful about the human race. Illiteracy is Anna's last
stand against the Communist gospel that has taken hold of San
Vincenzo since the war. Her only concession to the written word
is the crabbed signature she has mastered. She needs a signature
to cash the disability check that the government sends her every
month for what she claims is a crippling case of rheumatism in
her knees, a disability no one else in the family seems to notice.

Mario has given up trying to convert Anna, but her fierce,
unrepentant ignorance shames him, and he feels a kind of duty,
as a Communist, to defend himself against it. He tries to tell
Anna that she will never know the left from the right so long
as she refuses to know her left hand from her right hand. It is
his only pun, and he is pleased with himself for having thought
of it, because it seems to him that if Anna took the trouble to
educate herself, she would have to come to the conclusion that
Palmiro Togliatti and Enrico Berlinguer had a great deal to do
with her refrigerator—more, even, than Alfredo, who put the
down payment on it.

Mario is not obsessed with the Party. He is the least inclined
of anybody in his cell to spend a Sunday afternoon peddling
memberships or a warm spring evening listening to politicians

making speeches, and the only time he ever campaigns for a Communist candidate is when Alfredo, who is halfway through his second term on the town council, is running. Mario is shy. He has habits of solitude from years alone in the mountains with his sheep, and now that he is old the company of too many people at the same time makes him nervous. But Mario's loyalty to his nearly two million comrades in the Party is as deep and easy and complete as his thirst for a *caffelàtte* in the morning. It is a fact of nature—and it has nothing at all to do with his distaste for politicians or his suspicion that most of the Communists who stood in line for jobs when the Party took over the *comune* some twenty-five years ago have got as indolent and as unloving as the Christian Democrats who came before them. The Party has transformed his world—it has taken the fatal span of a poor Italian life and added the sweetness and the edge of possibility, and for this Mario will be loyal until he dies.

There are moments lately when Mario will suddenly shake his head and shrug his small, bony shoulders, and his eyes will fill with tears, because of the surprising fortune that has landed the Cecchis in a fine cement-block house with a *dottore* son and his delicately bred wife living in the house next door. Mario often opens his kitchen door at these moments and squints through his wire-rimmed glasses until his teary eyes focus on the stone farmstead, abandoned now, a quarter of a mile down the road, where he and Anna lived in poverty for nearly thirty years and raised four daughters and a son—the farmstead where they worked with a couple of kerosene lamps for light and a pail for drawing water from a village well, and fell asleep to the sound and the stench of sheep and pigs in stalls below their room. The sight of his old house seems to reassure Mario. He cannot tolerate much strangeness. Long ago, in the war, he was taken from home and put on a train and then a ship and finally left in a bunker in Sardinia. He spent a year in the bunker, sick with terror and shellings and malaria, never really knowing where he was or why, or, finally, which side he was even fighting on. And since that year—aside from one all-night bus trip, with a group

of Communist pensioners, to watch the changing of the palace
guard in Monte Carlo—he has avoided going anywhere un-
familiar.

It never occurred to Mario to build his new house out of sight
of his old one. He says sometimes that the story of his life is
written on the road they share. That road begins as a footpath
on the mountain where Mario summered a flock of sheep when
he was just a boy. It winds a good way down the mountain, and
when it reaches town it widens into the shady piazza, where
Alfredo Cecchi goes for his council meetings and the local Party
secretary has an office. Eventually, it cuts across the valley, past
San Vincenzo and the Cecchis' old and new houses, and joins
the provincial highway just beyond the dairy cooperative, where
Mario Cecchi likes to look after the cows a few afternoons a
week now that he has sold his sheep and retired. The town is
one of those high, walled Umbrian towns like Assisi and Spo-
leto. A dark town, with cobblestone streets that climb and cross
and knot like vines, with close, overhanging houses, and stalls
where carcasses swing from buttress beams and fruits and vegetables are hawked in a kind of medieval tableau that, as it
happens, has been the inspiration for a profitable postcard business run by the local Christian Democrats. It is still their town
—these Catholic clerks and merchants and *dottori*. Twenty-five
years of Communist power has not intimidated them at all, and
most Communists who come to town still have the uneasy feeling of being foot soldiers on unwelcome bivouac among a cap-
tive gentry. Even the children of the town, in their skinny jeans
and fake American-college T-shirts, playing the pinball machines at "disco clubs" that have been carved out of ancient
vaulted stalls across the piazza from the town hall, seem to
mock the Communists' respectability.

Some Communists, of course, live in town. There are Communist doctors and lawyers and teachers with houses there, or
apartments. And the town beauty is a young Communist architect who arrived from Turin a couple of years ago in a silver
Alfa convertible and stayed to open up an office. But old Com-

munists like Mario come to town only when they have to, and they leave as soon as their business at the town hall or the bank or the public hospital is over. It was these old Communists who petitioned the *comune* in the nineteen-fifties to widen and pave the road as it ran out the lower gate of the town walls and down the mountain and on across the valley. They believed then that one fine, curving sweep of tar was going to cut the psychic distance between town gentry and valley peasants like a sword. What they got, with their road, was only a shorter trip that aggravated their differences. Gradually, the Communists began to build their own town—a new town just below the old-town walls. And once the Party had started to broker building loans with low interest rates and twenty years to pay, it was only a matter of time before this new town was a thriving marketplace, with 2,000 people and a wide, shady avenue of farm-machinery stores and showrooms, a cooperative grocery, a movie theatre, three cafés, and a Casa del Popolo, where all the important Party meetings are held now.

Mario thinks of the new town as his children's town—part of a future that he will miss but his grandchildren will inherit. Alfredo shares a big office there, with land surveys of the province hung in Lucite on the walls, calling cards on the desk, and a brass plaque on the door to tell clients that he is a "Specialist in Cooperatives." And a lot of Alfredo's old grade-school friends—boys and girls born into indenture to a *padrone* and his land—are plumbers and electricians and hairdressers in the new town now, with plate-glass storefronts where their parents can read the family name in letters a foot high. Mario likes visiting the new town. He does not seem to notice that most of those stores and houses were cheaply, quickly thrown together, that the materials the builders used are already worn. Other people—people from town—consider the new town shabby and insubstantial. They say there is something unreal about this *borgata* that spreads its grid of little houses down the mountain and then ends abruptly at the railroad tracks that mark the beginning of the valley—returning the land to a green and

brown and golden patchwork broken only by the old villages of
the *comune* and the scattered sharecroppers' farmsteads that are
as much a part of the landscape as the fields of wheat and maize
and olive trees. But Mario thinks that the new town is beautiful.
He likes to ride there on his moped on Thursdays, which are
market days, and watch the young men in their trucks and the
young women pushing strollers, and otherwise enjoy the commerce and the bustle of modern life.

Still, a kind of nostalgia often draws Mario back into the
mountains. He hitches a ride in a truck or a jeep as far as the
road goes, and then he walks, stopping at shepherds' huts along
the way, looking for pastures where he used to graze his sheep,
collecting the herbs and roots with which he treats the cows at
the cooperative. He says that there is one spot, high in the
mountains, where he can stand late in the afternoon and just
make out the long aluminum barns of the cooperative—so
many miles away in the valley—shimmering as the sun hits them.
He likes to tell Anna, after one of his trips, that, thanks to the
Party, a life that began in poverty in those mountains is going to
end in dignity and comradeship. And then another argument
begins because Anna will say that something Mario ate in the
hills, or a touch of moon fever, has made him senile. She tells
him that the San Vincenzo dairy cooperative was not built out
of any deep concern for Mario Cecchi's dignity. It was built
because their son, Alfredo, went to school with a boy named
Pietro Gaspari, who grew up to be an important Party function-
ary in the province and controls a lot of farm credit, and this
meant that Alfredo was able to finance the cooperative with a
gift from the province of 100 million lire and a loan of another
100 million—and with the region contributing a good deal of
the interest, thanks to the fact that someone from the Party's
regional secretariat was married to Pietro Gaspari's first cousin.

Anna Cecchi is a cynic. She knows that her own good fortune
probably involves someone else's misery, and that a dairy cooperative for a cell of old Communists means less land and less
cattle for the Christian Democrats. Common sense and her own

past tell Anna that in Italy there can never be enough for every-body—enough money or food or power, or even hope. They tell her that politics, at its best, is a successful protection racket, played by ancient Italian rules of indenture and reward, that whatever the politicians have to say about socialism and prop-erty, the Party is doing well because Palmiro Togliatti was smart enough to present it as a kind of *gran padrone* to a whole class of people—shepherds, like Mario, and peasants and fac-tory workers—whom no *padrone* had ever bothered to solicit. She is a shrewd old woman, but in all these years of nagging Mario about the Party it has never occurred to her that she, more than anybody else, is the person who holds their cell together. Alfredo Cecchi says that his mother cheats at cards. A round of *briscola*, which is a kind of barnyard bridge involving three-card hands and a lot of distracting chatter, can inspire Anna to lyric heights of dishonesty, and if the old-timers of the cell rarely miss their monthly meeting in the Cecchis' kitchen, it is not because Mario's simple devotion has inspired them but because of a kind of collective determination, nurtured over years of failure, to catch Anna at some sleight of hand and see the evening's take end up, for once, in someone else's pocket.

Officially, Mario's cell is not the only cell in San Vincenzo—officially, there should be a cell for every ten or so dues-paying Communist families. But Mario's is the original cell, the one that met secretly at night back in the nineteen-thirties, the one that brought the news of a workers' state in Russia to hun-dreds of incredulous *contadini* in the valley, the one that still meets regularly despite the fact that the Party has not been in-terested in its cells, or in hearing from the people in its cells, for years. Mario and Carlo Benetti and Domenico Spina have been comrades in the Party since those first clandestine meetings—three young men, terrified of the police, terrified of each other, huddled in one of the dark stalls of an abandoned farmhouse deep in the valley, listening intently to Radio Moscow's Italian broadcast on the village schoolteacher's shortwave radio. The schoolteacher is dead now. He died in 1942, fighting with the partisans, and a lot of the old sharecropping families whose sons once met in that dark stall to plot a revolution that never happened have left to work the land in other valleys and ceded their places in the cell to new families. But the cell still carries a kind of respect and authority that none of the other Communists in San Vincenzo have. The fact is that people in Mario Cecchi's cell—the old ones by habit and the younger ones by a kind of association with habit—work harder at being good Communists than all the other *compagni* in San Vincenzo put together. The habit comes from years when every man, woman, and child in the cell set out by foot or bicycle on Sunday mornings to sell the Party newspaper, *L'Unità*, at farmhouse doors. Roberto Filippini, who farms a couple of hectares near the Benettis', still bicycles across the valley on Sunday mornings with a knapsack full of papers—exactly the way he used to as a boy, during the years of Mussolini, dodging Black Shirts and spies and, later on, German troops, risking his life to bring the Party's news to the valley farmers. But Roberto is a bachelor and is apt to be lonely Sundays. He likes stopping at people's houses, and he usually gets invited to stay for dinner somewhere. Besides, as the best long-distance "middle-age class" bicycle racer in the *comune*, he has to keep pedalling to defend his title.

By now, though, most of the *contadini* in the valley have cars or scooters, or, at least, bicycles. Anyone who really wants to spend his Sunday mornings reading *L'Unità* can get to town, one way or another, for a copy, and this means that the cell has been able to drop its paper route. Domenico Spina works Sundays digging and filling the foundation for a Casa del Popolo for San Vincenzo. And he has taken it on himself to spend a few evenings every week recruiting "volunteers" to help him. Domenico is the cell haranguer—a noisy, florid man of violent enthusiasms, and a true believer in the gospel of a Communist apocalypse at which the faithful will inherit a valley where the rain falls precisely thirty inches every year, and the wheat holds, and the pigs gain steadily, and the three white bulls at the dairy cooperative have the energy and the inclination to mount a hundred heifers every day. Domenico was not able to get his Casa del Popolo built in time for this year's Festa dell'Unità, but he is determined to have it ready next year. He has sworn to the Virgin Mother (whom he repudiates) that he cannot in conscience dance at another festival at Emilio Vanni's *spaccio* —Emilio Vanni being a local entrepreneur of uncertain politics but sound commercial instincts who discovered some years back that by rolling a coat of cement across his dirt yard and calling it a "dance pavilion" he could turn a small village festival into an occasion for the whole *comune* and make a fortune selling beer and whiskey and wine to several thousand thirsty Communists.

Carlo Benetti, for his part, "travels" for the Party. He has a red tie, with a hammer and sickle printed on it, and a set of fine false teeth from the government, and he is ready to march in any demonstration, cheer at any rally—ready to join the tens of thousands of militants who will spend ten or twelve hours in a hot, lurching bus so that Berlinguer has a proper audience for one of his speeches or Luciano Lama, the Communists' labor boss, gets a good turnout for a strike. All that Carlo asks of the Party is that it pay his bus fare. He is so inventive and so exuberant as a militant that once he even made the national evening news on television, releasing a sack of San Vincenzo piglets on the steps of Montecitorio, the Italian parliament, during an agricultural workers' protest. Carlo has lived through two world wars and fought in one of them, and now he is worried that he may not live to enjoy the revolution. He wants to fight for freedom the way the Russians fight in the movies that the Party sends around the valley during membership drives. Three years ago, at one of these Russian movies, Carlo climbed on his chair and waved his bottle of wine around and demanded that everybody go home and get a gun and storm the town hall— and Alfredo Cecchi had to remind him that the *comune* had

been safely Communist for over twenty years. That was the
night Carlo Benetti became a Maoist. The Maoists, he instructed
his old *compagni* at the movie, believe in a revolution that never
ends.

Alfredo himself was a Maoist once, at the University of
Rome—he puts it at sometime between his four months as a
Situationalist and his week and a half as a Trotskyite—but
now that he has settled down and become a politician in the
Party he calls himself a "creative Communist." He works hard
for the Party. He says that the Party should be responsive, and
so he drives his Cinquecento around the valley nearly every
night, stopping at villages and farms and listening to people's
problems and giving advice. His father says that, with Alfredo
around, the entire Cecchi family should be exempt from paying
Party dues, since Alfredo can be said to donate himself to the
Party in place of money, and with no practical return on his
investment. As for his mother, Anna thinks that Alfredo should
keep his office in the new town open nights and charge for his
attentions, and now, to comfort herself, she has stopped hand-
ing over a cut of her *briscola* winnings to the Party, thus break-
ing a venerable cell tradition. Alfredo claims to love the life he
leads as a creative Communist. Besides, he has been working
the valley in one way or another since he was a student at the
university and had to come home for five or six months every
year to earn his spending money; he talked his way into a job
selling insurance for a Roman promoter who had figured out
how to double his premiums income with special "retirement"
plans for sharecroppers. Alfredo is thirty-three now, and certainly the most important Communist in San Vincenzo, but his
head is still full of ideas about popular democracy and grass
roots, from his days as one of the chief theoreticians of the occupation of the university cafeteria, and he hustles those ideas
with the same gallant, ingenuous persistence with which he once
hustled overpriced insurance. He likes to say that he is working
not for the Party but for the people in the Party. It is one of the

things about him that old-timers like Domenico Spina consider a little subversive. His mother merely says that too much education has made her Alfredo simple. Once, a couple of months before this year's Festa dell'Unità, Alfredo nearly broke up the *briscola* game in Anna's kitchen by demanding that the festival do something "useful." He said that it was time the cell thought about the valley's Catholics, that it was time to start a Catholic-Communist "dialogue." He talked about cancelling one of the dances for an open meeting on women's rights and abortion and divorce—which caused Anna to disappear with the only pack of cards for thirty minutes. He talked about turning over another festival night to the village children, who would present a play or a dance of their own invention on the subject of the *compromesso storico*. He went on and on, and for a while the old-timers in the cell let him have his say because, for a while, it was really rather pleasant to be addressed by someone who was *dottore*—even if he was only Mario and Anna Cecchi's boy. They listened to Alfredo's talk as if it were a kind of solemn, exhortatory entertainment, like a sermon, and did not bother much with what he said. When the big festival bulletins went up on stone walls and telephone poles and barn doors across the valley, the schedule ran pretty much as always, with dancing every night and a beauty contest for the local girls and nothing more egregiously Communist than a new movie from the Party secretary, called *Soil of Hungary*. It was exactly the sort of L'Unità festival that brought the Party money, and brought the men and women who had worked so hard all year—and often for so little—the solace, and ideology, of nights when the wine flowed and the dancing never stopped and the pork turned, pungent and crisp and dripping, on oak spits over smoky open fires. Alfredo, in keeping with his position as *consigliere del comune*, was listed as referee for the Fifteenth Annual San Vincenzo Middleweight Championships—a boxing match, out behind the *spaccio*, that always involved one professional from Perugia going a round apiece with a lot of local boys while

mothers shrieked and fathers preened and girls giggled and the
Party made book.

The Italian Communist Party is the biggest Communist Party
in the West, and the most important. Nearly two million
Italians belong to the Party. Twelve or thirteen million Italians
always vote for the Party. And fifty-five million Italians can be
said to have depended on it at one time or another for their government, since from 1974 until early in 1979 it took a Communist parliamentary abstention to keep any of the various Christian
Democratic governments going at all. No one in or out of Italy
seems to agree about what, precisely, Italian Communism is,
although there is quite a market in experts lately, and the American ambassador, for one, carries around a thick embassy scrap-
book of clippings from the Party press which he likes to read
out loud at meetings and diplomatic afternoons. It is usually
what Americans mean when they talk about Eurocommunism
—something not quite European, not quite Communist, something so incontestably and perhaps uncontrollably present that
they need to give it a new, friendly-sounding name before they
can even begin to discuss it calmly. Americans say "Eurocommunism" the way primitives say "Grandfather" or "God" or
"Great Big Bird" for the boom that fills the sky during summer
storms and makes the children howl. The Italians themselves
say that *their* Communism has very little in common with the
Communism of the other two "independent" European Parties
—French Communism being a Jacobin affair, vindictive and
sour, and Spanish Communism being isolated in *its* country by
strong memories of betrayal that date back to the Civil War.
The Party in Italy is at the center of its country's politics. It
takes the place that in the rest of western Europe belongs, almost by definition, to Socialists, and, in fact, it owes that place
to a kind of mass default by Italian Socialists, who in the sixties
and early seventies had twelve years in a "center-left" government and in those twelve years showed no capacity for any

activity but profiteering. The Communist Party grew to respectability on the back of Socialist scandals. Palmiro Togliatti's
"giraffe"—which is what the old General Secretary used to call
it, because the Italian Party seemed to him such a strange animal, with no reasonable explanation for existing—became the
popular party of the Italian left, the party that cut through
ideology and class to reach a third of the country's voters. By
now, it is Italy's "other" party—a coalition of interest groups
and attitudes which in breakdown looks less Italian, in a way,
than American Democrat. People in Italy with real contempt
for the Catholics and their party are voting Radical now, by
way of national protest, but if they want to take over a town or
a province from the Christian Democrats, they still usually vote
Communist. The Communists are so respectable in Italy today,
so established and uninspired, that their main problem, with the
voting age at eighteen for most elections, is persuading the
young to vote for them. One reason the Party lost votes, for
the first time in thirty years, in the last parliamentary elections
was that a million or so boys and girls—at the polls for the first
time—considered it too humiliating to pull the same levers as
their parents.

Communist mayors run Bologna, Turin, Florence, Naples,
and even Rome. Communists control six of Italy's twenty regions, forty-five of its ninety-four provinces. They win elections
at the indulgence of the middle class, and if none of the local
militants look respectable enough as candidates, they fill their
lists with "independents"—lawyers, say, or professors who
might never have thought of taking out a Party card but who are
unlikely to refuse the favors of anyone with the perspicacity to
choose them. The Communists govern their towns and provinces with a kind of shrewd and autocratic civic piety—offering
up as "Communism" their lists of illustrious *dottori*, their day-
care-center budgets, their plans for free public buses and gar-
bagemen who arrive on time, and even hose the streets behind
them. They know that it is the country's new *borghesi* who have
almost doubled the Party's vote since 1946, when Italian Com-

munism was still mainly a matter of factory workers and *contadini* and wartime partisans, and the rhetoric was revolution.
The only revolution they would dream of preaching these days
has to do with getting the country a moderately honest government—which is not to say that a Communist boss will hesi-
tate any more than a Catholic when it comes to passing out the
jobs and the credit and all the other spoils of office but that the
Communist is often likely to expect some work and some competence for his favors instead of a deposit in his bank account
across the border in Lugano. The rhetoric toughens for big
public occasions like Party congresses, when Marxism-Leninism
is dusted off for the workers from Milan and Turin, who, despite
the evidence of their *scala mobile* and their seaside villas and
their ten-thousand-dollar cars, still consider themselves the pro-
letarian vanguard of a revolution. But in reality the Italian Party
has never been very revolutionary. Communists in Italy do not
even talk about nationalizing production. It is the Christian
Democrats who have preserved the bizarre national-socialist
structures (and the spoils) of Mussolini's rule. The Communists, who have a survival interest in a healthy economy, have
often ended up, *faute de mieux*, as champions of progressive
market economics and competitive private enterprise. They say
that Gramsci, as their first native theoretician and philosopher,
provided them with such specifically Italian analyses of Italy's
problems that the Party was bound to be unorthodox. The years
of clandestinity—Gramsci writing on his prison cot, partisans
hiding in the mountains, peasant cells marching out against
Fascist soldiers—gave the Party a valorous, romantic past.
Since then, its strategies have been resolutely pragmatic and its
leaders much more interested in dealing with people in power
than in exciting people without it. The Party has had to gauge—
and gauge accurately—the perimeter of its influence (and its
discipline), and by now a Communist like Berlinguer knows
that he has very little to offer the millions of Mezzogiorno poor
or the southern emigrants in shantytowns around the big northern factory cities or the million college graduates who cannot

find work and who drift in and out of ennui and petty crime
and often, lately, terrorist violence. Berlinguer's social contract
with the bourgeoisie depends on the satisfaction of four million
factory workers. He has to answer to those workers—they are
his leverage, his base, his muscle, and they are no more interested in underwriting a new lumpenproletariat at their own expense than they are in subsidizing the prosperity of a lot of
Christian Democratic pols with wage freezes and no-strike
policies.

Actually, it is liberal "issue" groups like the Radical Party
that see terrorism as a sign of Italy's immense distress—something to be cured. The Communists tend to regard terrorism as
a plot to discredit *them*—which to an extent it is, also. Certainly
middle-class Italians have tended to vote Communist as a kind
of hedge against terrorism, assuming that the Communists, as a
"people's" party, could discipline the people's problems. This is
what the Communists promised, and the fact that the Party lost
middle-class voters along with young voters in the last national
elections had less to do with the success of any plots to associate the Party with terrorism than with the feeling of a lot of
frightened middle-class people that the Communists were doing
badly in their job as Italy's political policemen. Those people
voted Communist in the past because the Party, with its promises of clean streets and postal clerks who came guaranteed not
to steam the stamps off their letters, reassured them—stood, as
it were, between respectable Italians and the mess they had
made of their country. And they voted without ever really
knowing what they were voting for. Even now, they cannot
seem to decide whether the Party is truly different from the
Antichrist of their grammar-school textbooks or treacherously
hypocritical. They still vote for its local skills, and one reason
Berlinguer and his friends on the Central Committee are not
very enthusiastic about cells like Mario Cecchi's is that old
Communists meeting in groups to talk things over tend to raise
questions of ideology which frighten voters. Berlinguer is a
power broker. The fact that no one knows precisely what he has

in mind when he makes his moves gives him the freedom he
must have to deal adroitly. If Togliatti, who was a much more
doctrinaire Communist than Berlinguer seems to be, could
calmly betray the other lay parties in 1947 by signing a consti-
tutional agreement to renew Mussolini's old concordat with the
Vatican (and, with it, the Vatican's tremendous power in Italian life), then it is not surprising that Berlinguer also prefers the
Catholics' party, which has something to offer in return for his
concessions. Italy's postwar salad days are long gone—the days
when the government could make jobs for three-quarters of a
million new "schoolteachers" at election time and dispense
enormous pensions to its special friends; the days when one
enterprising Minister of Posts actually put fourteen thousand of
his neighbors on the federal payroll in a month's time. No one
believes any longer in the myth of a "modern" Italy with spoils
for everyone. There is no money now for the lavish, larcenous
patronage of the nineteen-sixties. There are no new jobs to offer,
no new pension funds to raid and squander. The fact is that
there has never been "enough" for everyone in Italy, and it
would probably be out of character for Italy to change now.
Anna Cecchi is right in fighting her family's balmy optimism,
right in suspecting her neighbors, right in saying that in Italy
one family's luck means another's sacrifice. When the Communists took over the Cecchis' *comune*, a lot of Catholics were
suddenly out of work and out of money, and even out of friends
to count on. And when Alfredo's old classmate was able to
channel 200 million lire to the San Vincenzo dairy cooperative,
it meant that Christian Democrats who wanted loans for *their*
farmers had lost precisely 200 million lire worth of access to the
provincial credit lines.

This is the real *compromesso storico*—a compromise with
Italy. It goes on cynically, typically, whatever the Central
Committee has to say about Russia or NATO or the Yugoslavian succession, whatever its arguments about the virtue of
sharing power in a Rome government when mainly what remains to be shared is not the Christian Democrats' power but

the blame for their incompetence. Certainly the Communists have no intention of governing Italy alone, even if Italy were offered. Berlinguer is not a zealot. He is a cool practitioner. He has a lot of the power he wants already, and he is not going to be left presiding over someone else's disaster. He knows that Russia could not—and, at any rate, would not—underwrite Italy's Western standards, and he also knows that a Communist Italy would lose the German and American credit that underwrites those standards now. The most that Berlinguer can do is use his odd mandate as a Communist leader in a parliamentary democracy to play off rhetoric against reality, Eastern authoritarian instincts against Western ties, opposition against engagement. He counts on the Party's remaining, in effect, two parties —the public party, dealing out of Rome, and the remarkable institution called the Italian Communist Party. It is the institution that plays *padrone* to the nearly two million militants who pay their tithes and carry their cards with a Communist's rights and duties listed on the back like a new catechism, and it is the institution that mollifies twelve million voters so that the Berlinguers and the Lamas are left alone.

Berlinguer, in fact, depends on this state of no accountability for his policies—offering instead accountability for his services. He depends on an enthusiasm for following—for belonging, and for accepting and even reifying power—which is not, after all, surprising in the country that produced the institution of the Catholic Church. The Party calls this native instinct to acquiesce "democratic centralism," and makes it sound as if it were a kind of orderly process having to do with correct interpretations of Lenin, when in reality it has to do with ancient habits of a deeply Catholic country. Communists like Mario Cecchi are militants by an act of faith, a suspension of skepticism. They credit the authority of the Party over daily life the way in another time they would have credited papal power. Like the Pope and his Church, the Party seems to pose a kind of pure, federal notion in a country of local passions and fallibilities and corruptions. This, perhaps, is another reason the Com-

munists deal so much more easily with the Christian Democrats
than with the Socialists, say, or the Radicals or any of the other
lay parties. They share with the Catholics a hierarchical mys-
tique, a doting susceptibility to the trappings and rituals of
power. They do not know what to make of the fractious indi-
vidualism of a democratic left. They do not really understand
people who live a good part of their lives away from politics.
The Party, for Communists, is not a function of election time.
It is a language that describes their world, a master plan for
reality. When their sons get restless, it occupies and diverts
them, the way it diverted Alfredo a few years back, when he
started complaining to the Party secretary in town about the
mayor's being "unresponsive to the base." In no time at all, the
mayor had arranged for Alfredo to be put in charge of "preparing the base" for elections to local *consigli di frazione*—little
popular assemblies that had already been introduced in a few
Communist *comuni* in Tuscany, and that Party people were
talking about introducing in their towns in Umbria. This made
Alfredo much happier with the mayor. Alfredo started canvassing the valley, house to house, talking to people about local
government and grass roots and popular democracy, settling the
inevitable arguments about which brother or son would be a
family's candidate for its assembly. He divided the *comune* into
seven districts, and everyone he talked to was excited because
some eighty people were going to get to call themselves *con-
siglieri* and carry smart white cards printed up, compliments of
the Party, by the town stationer. Alfredo himself got to spend
every night for three or four months advancing the cause of *il
popolo*—during which time the mayor divided up the power on
the town council, the Party's local committee passed a resolu-
tion supporting, in advance, whatever the major supported at
the next Party congress, and Alfredo was too busy with his
canvassing to protest, or even notice. It has been nearly three
years since then, and Alfredo is still waiting for an election date.
From time to time, he asks the Party secretary about it—or the
mayor, or his friends on the town council—but everyone seems

to have decided that the *comune* is not quite ready for people's power after all.

Mainly, what the Party expects from its local secretaries and its mayors and councilmen is this kind of "capacity"—as Party jargon goes—"to rally the base" to decisions made in Rome. Party leaders talk about "the base" now the way they used to talk about "the cell" and "the action unit" back when the Party was small and determinedly in opposition—when it could afford to give its ordinary militants a voice, because in those days Communists shared a clear idea of purpose and an idiom of revolution and a simple, combative perspective on every Italian who did not belong. Two things were certain then—that the Party in Italy existed to challenge the Catholics and their class and the privilege their class represented; and that it existed in the world beyond Italy to add its numbers to the Communist International and to safeguard and spread the revolution in Russia. These were the imperatives that defined "socialism" for a village cell like Mario Cecchi's—and, in fact, amounted to its ideology.

The great irony of Italian Communism is that the lively and inventive freedom of the little groups that built the Party was contingent on their faith in this sort of strict and conventional Leninist wisdom. Certainly, as the Party began its complicated *compromesso*, aiming at government, at a bourgeois vote, at respectability and consensus, those cells had to be discouraged. Italy had its own *événements* in 1968. Alfredo liberated his cafeteria at the university, and hundreds of thousands of students shut down not just their schools but their towns and cities —and only then did the old Party bosses seem to realize that it might not be as easy as they had imagined to rally *this* base to a new policy of maneuvering and accommodating in the world of real power. The riots and strikes and occupations of 1968 presented the Party with its first proof of a new, young left in Italy —a scrappy, rebellious left, respecting no conventional authority—and its response was the classic Communist response of undermining a rival left, and even its own dissidents, by making

its separate arrangements with the right. By now—with the col-
lapse of Italy's postwar boom economy in a decade of social
violence and retribution—the Party may have no choice but to
honor those arrangements. Berlinguer still wants the Communists to share power in an emergency government. This policy may be necessary, from Berlinguer's point of view, and even
wise, but as policy it leaves out a lot of ordinary Communists,
like Domenico Spina, whose attitudes were shaped by short-
wave-radio propaganda, and who have no aptitude for the sort
of logic that leads a Berlinguer, say, to cheerful thoughts about
the Common Market. Old militants like Domenico and Carlo
Benetti believe in Stalin and Lenin and the Revolution not because of any sophisticated deductions about reality but because
those words are a kind of code—a comforting, simple code—
for their identity as Communists. Those words give them confidence in who they are, and if they scold and shout and make a
nuisance of themselves at Party movies it is out of an immense
confusion at hearing the words that once explained everything
contradicted now by leaders they have always loved.

Today, of course, the Party as an institution has less to do
with people sharing ideology than with people sharing influence
and jobs and money. It is a machine for patronage, a kind of
overseer of the spoils of a fragile truce between the old workers
at its base and the new bourgeoisie that votes its candidates into
office. A lot of the Party professionals are young men and
women who have been enjoying Party salaries and a certain
technocrats' power since the student riots of '68 convinced the
Party that it was better to try to preempt their disaffection with
titles and offices and important-sounding projects than to risk
losing them to the Lotta Continua or the Autonomia or any of a
dozen other groups on the fringes of terrorism. But practical
power still belongs to the local bosses, with their talent for
sottogoverno—for maneuvering in those ancient networks that
have kept Italy functioning through centuries of abuse by its
official rulers. Those old capi, in their time, had to judge—and
judge accurately—what Fascism and Nazism and Stalinism

were going to mean for the Party and for the country. The few who are left on the Central Committee of the Party are skeptical of what Berlinguer is up to, and they have never much liked the kind of *compromesso* that lets Giovanni Agnelli, the chairman of the board at Fiat, make the rules and gives the Party the job of keeping its people calm in exchange for handouts. They say that whatever small reforms the Party claims to have achieved—a rise in sharecroppers' percentages, a minimum wage, a *scala mobile*—are accommodations to the status quo, not changes in the social order. They complain that the Party now is an object lesson in the power of capital not so much to corrupt as to pacify.

What the Party is, in fact, by now is a kind of shadow government. In Rome, planners and economists and would-be ministers prowl the halls of the Party secretariat with their charts and ledgers and proposals. Each of the country's regions has a secretariat, too, along with its own Party leader and committee and technicians. So does each of the provinces, and each of the *comuni* within a province, and each *comune* is itself divided into "sections," as the Party calls them, with the same hierarchy. None of this is very far from what Lenin had in mind when he talked about a vanguard party, or postulated the somewhat stretched principles of democratic centralism. It is structure, in the end, more than points of doctrine, that makes the Italian Party "Communist"—structure, and the notion of an élite so acute in its judgments that those judgments must be taken to express what everybody else would think if everybody else were smarter.

Alfredo says sometimes that cells like his father's were probably doomed the moment the Party came out of clandestinity and under public scrutiny. He says that maybe a cell, by definition, is better suited to the energy of grand and illegitimate causes—like revolutions hatched in the barracks of Lourenço Marques or the shantytowns of Oran—than to peaceful, ordinary times when there is no risk to discipline emotions. Formally, of course, Italy's cells exist. There are seven cells in San

Vincenzo's section of the *comune*, but by now their bonds are
familial and social, and have as much to do with the long experience of neighbors as with politics. Alfredo has tried to inspire his father's cell with football games for the children and
grandchildren and plans to pool everybody's contributions to
the dairy cooperative, but the cell survives mainly because, of
all the cells in the *comune*, it is the only one with some of the
old energy of a cause to fight for—even if that cause has turned
out to be beating Anna Cecchi at *briscola*. Domenico Spina and
Carlo Benetti and Roberto Filippini and even Mario himself
would have to agree that there are few ideas as powerful as a
Saturday night in the Cecchis' kitchen, with everyone talking at
once, and sweet cakes and homemade wine on the table, and the
Cecchis' new color-television console backed into the unused
hearth as if a match could ignite it, sending images of soccer
stars and weather girls and comics up the chimney and out over
the fields to the darkened stall where San Vincenzo's brave
young men once met, full of terror and enchantment, to dream
their revolution.

M ario Cecchi says that in San Vincenzo only the very brave
or the very rich or the very intelligent—*dottori* like the
schoolteacher who founded Mario's cell and died a partisan—
could afford to think about fighting openly against the Fascists.
Domenico Spina, in his way, fought them. Spina was in the
Italian Army in Sicily in 1943, looking after wagon mules and
meeting secretly behind the base saddle shop with a group of
Bolognese recruits, and the Bolognese, seeing that Domenico was
a country boy and gullible, persuaded him that he could get away
with setting the base on fire. Domenico set his fire, and was
caught, and spent a month in the base prison before the Allies
invaded Sicily and let him out, but still, officially he was a
soldier in a Fascist army, not a partisan. Mario says it never
occurred to anybody in the San Vincenzo cell except the schoolteacher to actually run away to the partisans or to refuse a

Fascist draft call. A lot of the important Communists had already fled to France or Russia by 1941—which was when Italy started fighting—to direct the partisans from abroad. And the idea of fighting without them, or for them, was inconceivable to a timid shepherd with a wife and four children to keep and the first sheep he had ever owned feeding in his stable. Courage was a luxury in Fascist Italy, like honor; a little bravado was often the most that poor people like Mario Cecchi could contribute. Even now, Mario's sort of moral triumphs have to do with health and cleanliness and a night's rest—with the fact that, finally, in his old age, he can look forward to the fresh, cool feel of clean underwear in the morning.

Mario never had much underwear when he was growing up. Washing clothes was a long and complicated ritual, and no one in his family had any clothing he could do without. Mario remembers laundry day in the mountains. Dirty shirts and towels and homespun sheets went into a big clay pot with a draining faucet near the bottom, and when the pot was almost full his mother covered them with jute and then with a layer of cinders and began pouring boiling water over everything. All day long she kept the water kettle on the fire, and at night she plugged the faucet and left the clothes to soak till morning, when she would rinse them in a stream, pounding them on rocks and finally laying them out on the banks of the stream to dry. It was a tedious job, and if it rained, she had to start over, but it was easier for her than for most of the mountain women; Mario's family made charcoal for a count with land in the mountains, and they always had plenty of wood to keep a kettle hot. They were *mezzadri*, just as Carlo Benetti and Roberto Filippini and some quarter of the families who work the land in Mario's valley are today—bound by one of Italy's ancient arrangements between a landlord and the family that tills his fields, chops his wood, or tends his sheep or his cattle in return for a share of the yield or (more likely now) of the profits from the yield. *Mezzadria* was a punishing system. Contracts ran for a year, from August to August, and any landlord with a mind to it could turn

out a family on the last day in July, with no notice at all. People
lived with a kind of congenital humiliation that came from gen-
erations of never really knowing how long they could keep the
only work they knew, the only land they knew, the only home
they were ever likely to find. Big landowners in Italy are a class;
their ties are familial as well as economic, and they have always
kept a code among themselves that no *padrone* takes on a
sharecropper whom his friend or cousin or neighbor has turned
away. The conditions of *mezzadria* have changed a lot since the
Second World War. Communists and Socialists have organized
the sharecroppers into farm workers' unions. They have had
their strikes and their boycotts, and now, by law, a landowner
who fifty years ago could claim as much as three-quarters of
his farmers' harvest gets less than half. Actually, there is no
such thing as a *mezzadria* "contract" anymore. Montecitorio
abolished the contract system in 1964—and in practical terms
this means that no new contracts can be made and no old ones
can be cancelled. Those old contracts are good, now, for a
peasant's lifetime, and his children's and grandchildren's life-
times, though it is unlikely that anybody's grandchild will ever
have to claim one. Bills to transfer parcels of agricultural land
to the peasants who work that land and want it have been
circulating in the parliament for years, and eventually one of
them will pass, and people will be able to rent or buy their land
at prices set and subsidized by the government.

Mario's parents, of course, never worked a particular piece of
land for very long. They covered their mountain over years,
gathering kindling for the charcoal they made in little earthen
mounds around their campsites. But their house belonged to the
count who owned the forest, and their kitchen garden, which
was not much more than a hectare, had to feed thirty people—
Mario's parents and his seven brothers and sisters, along with
two of his uncles and their families. The house, like the garden,
was much too small to support so many Cecchis, but none of
the men or the older boys could leave unless the Army took
them, because in those days a landowner could cancel a family's

contract if a son or a brother who might be serving him left to work for someone else. The only people who left were the small children—if their parents could find a place for them with relatives who had more food or more room or more money, or who simply wanted an extra worker of their own. In 1915, when Mario was seven, one of his aunts from a village on the other side of the mountain asked to borrow him while her husband was away in the Army. She worked in a little chestnut-flour mill in the village, but her husband had been a shepherd, and she wanted Mario and one of his brothers to tend the sheep while he was gone. Mario had just finished his first month of school when his aunt came to collect the brothers. It turned out to be the end of school for them both. Mario stayed with his aunt that winter, and that summer he pastured twenty sheep on the mountain near her house. After that, he and his brother lived the life of transhumants, driving their aunt's sheep down from the mountain every year for winter grazing in the valley. They lived with a peasant in winter, sleeping on a mat on the warm wood stove in the peasant's kitchen, paying their room and board with pails of sheep's milk. When his brother died of a fever during their third winter in the valley, Mario began to make the trip alone. He saw his own parents twice a year in those days—once on his way down the mountain in the fall, and again on his way up the mountain in the early summer. He was at home, though, when his father died, at forty-six, of pneumonia, and when his oldest brother, whose name was Franco, came back from two years at sea with news of a people's revolution in Russia and a stack of pamphlets by a man named Lenin. Mario couldn't read, but he knew that whatever was in those pamphlets cost his brother a life at home. Their landlord's foreman on the mountain decided that his *padrone* would be better served without a headstrong boy spreading tracts about the overthrow of the ruling classes. He refused to renew the family's contract unless Franco left, and so Franco went north to Milan and took whatever odd jobs he could get until he found steady work, cleaning trolleys.

Mario spent fourteen years on loan to his aunt. He stayed
through the war, and then he stayed on after the war, because
his uncle came home shell-shocked and was not much use for
anything but carding wool. Mario does not talk much about the
way he felt through that strange, solitary childhood. It is not
that he is too old now to remember. It is just that he had so
little time as a child to store up feelings to examine later on. In
fact, Mario must have been a very bright child. He taught himself to read, alone in the mountains with his sheep, studying
from the pamphlets his brother left and from the old newspapers, used for wrapping cheeses, that he found in shepherds'
huts. At the age of seventeen he bought a set of Dante with the
only pocket money he had ever had, and read straight through
The Divine Comedy. But mainly his memories from the age of
seven or ten or seventeen have to do with the details of a
shepherd's life—the towns he passed, the streams and roads and
railroad tracks he used to follow, the music of pipes and
ocarinas played by shepherd boys who danced by torchlight in
the long meadow grasses, the steady, sinister hiss of vipers
coupling on summer nights in the mountains. He remembers
the day, once a year, when the village cobbler came to his aunt's
house and, for five lire and a hot meal, made new shoes for the
family. He cannot say anymore whether or not he liked his aunt,
but he can describe the way the old cobbler carved the wooden
clogs and, softening and shaping a piece of leather with some
pig's grease, hammered the leather to the wood with little nails
he held between his teeth. Or the way his aunt and her two
young daughters would drape the kitchen beams with long
skeins of homespun cotton, roll it onto wooden spools, and
finally, slowly, weave it into bolts of blue-and-white ticking
called *rigatino* for the family's clothes. Mario says that in those
days a poor Italian could spend his whole life in *rigatino.* That
rough striped cotton was a uniform of class as surely as the soft
gray riding gloves of a *gran padrone* or the silk of a contessa's
gown.

No one actually told Mario when he was free to leave his

aunt's house. But over the years his uncle got stronger, and his
cousins got bigger—and one day it was simply accepted that he
would go. There was nothing for him to do at home for his
mother. He watched his family making charcoal—stripping the
trees, shaping their clay mounds, smoking the tinder till it
crumbled—but the work and the life seemed foreign to him
now. He was fixed in the rhythms of a shepherd's life, and even
at home he slept at noon and woke at three o'clock every
morning—which was when he used to get up to milk his sheep
and turn them out to pasture and hang his aunt's big pot of milk
and rennet over an open fire to heat for cheese. He did not
especially want to be a shepherd. He envied the young men he
had seen so often in valley towns, drinking in their cafés, playing bocce Sunday mornings, walking out at night with pretty,
vivid girls. He wanted to find a life that would give him some of
the gaiety of those young men. He dreamed about a fine job
with the province. He was going to spend his evenings in a
bright café, watching the women hurry by on their errands,
talking with smart new friends about socialism, about the political trials in Rome, about the Black Shirts who had taken over
Italy and were starting to frighten the *contadini*, demanding
their grain or their pigs or chickens for protection. Mario says
that he was determined to educate himself. He started night
classes in the nearest market town. He had never sat in a room
with so many women before. The smell of all those women
sickened and aroused him, and on his first night at school he
fled outside, behind a tree, and vomited. But he stayed in school
all summer. He was promoted to the third grade right away.
"Don't forget, I was no beginner. I had a month of school at
seven," he likes to say when he tells the story. He practiced
writing and learned his multiplication and division tables, and
so he could not believe it when in September, after all his work,
he was turned down for a job building roads for the province
because he did not carry a Fascist Party card. He says now that
he would never have lasted on a road gang anyway. He already
missed the mountains—the quietness there, the strange excite-

ment he had felt as a boy alone at night, lighting fires against
the wolves. The little town where he went to school seemed
crowded to him now, in his disappointment—dirty and corrupted—and a few weeks after he lost his chance to join the
road gang he became *mezzadro* to an old Maremma count
whose foreman had passed through town looking for a new
shepherd for the count's sheep.

Mario worked for the count for the next seven years. He
spent his summers in a hut in the mountains, living on polenta
that he made from chestnut flour, on ricotta from the big cheese
pot, on the meagre onion soup that shepherds like to call *acqua
cotta*—cooked water. There were hundreds of sheep to graze
and gather every day, and the ewes had to be milked twice a day
for the seventy-five pounds of Pecorino that their milk yielded.
It took three people to tend them. Mario. One older shepherd of
thirty or thirty-five, who was called Romeo and who hated
sheep and roared and cursed whenever he had to milk them.
And one fat, exceptionally lazy boy of twelve, who rode down
the mountain on a mule each morning, carrying the Pecorino to
market, and rode back up each night with onions and bread
and, on great occasions, beans. The ewes conceived in the
summer. In the winter they grazed in big fenced pastures on the
count's Maremma ranch and delivered by Christmastime. Mario
says that in the winter he would wake up every morning to the
bleating of thirty or forty new and hungry lambs. He is proud
that his sheep were healthy in the Maremma—which is such a
raw, swampy stretch of coastline—and delivered well. He liked
his life there, at the sheep ranch. He even liked the count. He
had a kind of wistful admiration for the way the old nobleman
rode around the ranch on his bay hunter and counted sheep with
little taps of an elegant leather crop. But over the years Mario
saw the men around him getting married and producing sons
for the fine new world that—drunk, nights, in the foreman's
kitchen—they would vow to build as soon as Mussolini was
overthrown. Mario himself did not think much about a fine new
world in those days. He did start thinking about a wife, and a

warm bed, and hot meals served in a kitchen of his own. It was
the influence of farmers, he says now.

Mario married Anna that winter. He had found her buying
salt in a *spaccio* that belonged to a rich San Vincenzo peasant
by the name of Renzo Strocci—a peasant who had made money
and bought property, and, in fact, had just hired Mario on his
way from the mountain to the Maremma and sent another
shepherd to the count in Mario's place. In those days, Anna
looked a little like a gypsy, with her warm, high color and her
furious black eyes and the bright, tattered shawls and dresses
that she always wore—she was so ragged and bad-tempered,
Mario says, that he was sure even a penniless shepherd like
himself would have a chance with her. Actually, Anna was an
orphan from the valley, and she was working for day wages at a
tobacco farm near the *spaccio*, sorting leaves as they came out
of the curing ovens to be stacked and bundled. Renzo Strocci
and his wife used to give her food. They took care of a lot of
villagers like Anna, because Renzo considered himself a Communist of sorts, having been *mezzadro* in his time and made
miserable by a few *padroni* of his own. He particularly liked to
sit on a stool behind the counter of his brand-new *spaccio* and
tell *padrone* stories. Everybody in San Vincenzo had heard from
Renzo about the peasant who helped himself to a couple of
bunches of table grapes from his *padrone*'s vines; the *padrone*
had searched and searched till he found grape seeds in the
peasant's dung heap, and then he stood with a gun while the
peasant picked them out and ate them. Then, there was the story
about a vain old baron who owned a lot of land in the valley.
The baron had a fine stable, and he liked to take his guests
out riding and amuse them by ordering the peasants they came
upon in the fields to climb, naked, up some of his red-ant-
infested trees. Renzo always ended his gruesome stories cheerfully. *"Il enbe del padrone non passa il gomito,"* he would say—
meaning, roughly, that the rich were not likely to have got
that way by their own elbow grease. The fact that he himself
was becoming one of the biggest landlords in San Vincenzo—

with four big fields and six hundred sheep and six families *a mezzadria*, not to mention his *spaccio* and a bakery and a little leather factory—did nothing to dampen his pride in himself as a radical. At the end of one year with the Stroccis, Mario collected less money than he had ever collected from his Maremma count, but he says that the count would never have given him a wedding supper, the way the Stroccis did, or a house of his own, or a new chair for the kitchen every time Anna had a baby—or introduce him to a man like the village schoolteacher, a revolutionary and a secret Communist with his own cell. While Anna was busy having daughters—in six years, Pia and Sofia and Angelina and Teresa were born—Mario started going to the schoolteacher's secret meetings. He had never really planned to join the Party, never really foreseen a day when he would solemnly tape a Communist Party card inside his shepherd's boot. He became a Communist because the teacher told him that it was the proper thing for a poor young man in Italy to do, and, thinking it over, he decided that the teacher was right. He says that even then the idea of the Party gave him a kind of faith in a decent future for his little girls. Renzo Strocci had always given Mario his yearly share on time. He had never demanded gifts or eggs or chickens or refused Mario something important for his house, like whitewash for the walls or tiles to patch the roof. He even gave the Cecchis wine and meat on Sundays for their big dinner of the week. But Mario believed now that a Communist should be a free man. He wanted his own sheep, and he told Renzo, and toward the fall of 1941 he took his share from the sale of that year's cheese and wool and lambs, and walked seventy miles to a big sheep auction he knew of in another valley. When he came home, nearly two weeks later, he was leading thirty-nine sheep and six lambs and a big white dog with a tail like a question mark. Mario was thirty-four years old and had just grown a mustache, and he looked so prosperous and pleased with life on his long walk home that a young shepherd he met along the way had asked to leave his own ten sheep with Mario when the Army called him.

Mario, in fact, was getting known in the valley. He had skills and an instinct for animals which few of the valley shepherds had—not really being shepherds anyway but peasants who happened to be looking after sheep. He knew the right grasses and the right water for keeping a young lamb healthy. He could talk any *contadino* into opening his landlord's fields to Cecchi sheep at night, because the cheese he would give the *contadino* in return was always finer and fresher than anybody else's. He knew which streams to follow. He was the first to think of renting a narrow strip of land along the railroad track. He walked his sheep in single file on the twenty "free" inches of grass on each side of a public road. People began to say that Mario Cecchi knew every spare blade of grass in the province. He was still a timid, solitary man—not the sort of person that querulous valley people, with their suspicion of mountain habits, usually took to—but the neighbors liked Mario, and Mario saw to it that there was always a glass waiting for them at the stone farmhouse he had just rented on the old *comune* road. He had a year in that house before the Army called him. Teresa was three days old, and Mario had just bought ten more sheep with the year's profits, when he found the draft notice on his doorstep. He says it was the worst moment of his life.

"At first I thought I could hide. But where? *Dove?* The Fascists were everywhere. The foreman at the big tobacco farm —he was a Fascist, and he beat the peasants until they spied for him. The postman was a Fascist, too. And the butcher. Once when I was taking my sheep along the road, a big truck full of Black Shirts followed me, and I saw the butcher with them. *Mi ricordo bene. Bene.* He had a gun. They all had guns. They followed me for a mile, laughing and shouting and shooting their guns in the air to scare my animals. They said they were giving me a warning. They knew for a fact that when Mussolini came here and everybody had to stop work and line the roads to salute him—they knew I was one of the ones who had not saluted. Even good people—poor, good people—told the Fascists what their neighbors did. It was because they could make money and feed their children by going to the police and saying, 'Beat up So-and-So. Follow Mario Cecchi, who did not salute.' Sometimes there were massacres of families. One village would come to fight another. There were five brothers here in San Vincenzo who almost died. They were Socialists, some people said. Others said no, they were Anarchists. Maybe they were even Communists. No one knew. Not me. Not anyone. The only Communists I knew for sure were Benetti, Spina, Filippini, the schoolteacher, and the others in my cell. But I knew which men to trust. I knew which men, in their hearts, were with the left. And I trusted the brothers. *Bene.* One day a dozen Fascists came to beat up the brothers. The brothers were prepared, because they had been beaten before. They had been beaten and forced to drink bottles of castor oil, and so this time they had guns and chased the Fascists away, and afterward they left to join the partisans in the mountains. But the next day a hundred and fifty Fascists came, looking for the brothers. They lined up all the men from the village on the road and said they were going to burn down our houses. It was a reprisal, they said, because no one had helped them catch the brothers. They started to light a fire, but there was one *mezzadro* in the village —we thought he was with us but now he came forward and said, 'Help! I am a Fascist. If you burn the other houses, mine will catch fire, too.' So the Fascists went away, and for a while no one bothered us, but then the notice came saying that I was to go by train, third class, to Perugia. I didn't expect that. I was too old. I had sheep, babies. I was the *capo* of a big household, and there was no other man to take my place. But I had no time to prepare papers so that I wouldn't have to go. All the young men had already gone, and they were calling the *classi vecchie*, not giving anyone the time to protest. I said to my wife, 'Don't worry. I won't be sent to war. They will see that I am thirty-five and can't fight.' But when I got to Perugia there were fourteen hundred men like me—thirty-five, forty years old—waiting for trucks to take them away to training camp. Fourteen hundred old men. Fathers. Even grandfathers. They said it was clear that

old men like us would only be going to the Coast Guard. But I
knew that they were wrong. I had never had an injection before,
but now, at the training camp, every day for ten days I had injections. I had to hold a grenade. I had to climb a rope a
hundred feet into the air—into nothing. I had to crawl through
the grass with people shooting over me. But I was better off than
some. One man was so fat that he could never do the exercises,
and the officers would kick him in his stomach. Another man
didn't know his left from his right, and they beat him. He was
just like Anna. All he could remember about left and right was
that he was against the right. After a month, they sent us home
and told us to say goodbye to our families. And then we had to
march to the nearest train station, singing Fascist songs. I
walked for miles, and every few minutes someone I knew would
come out of his house and fall in line and start singing. Some
of my neighbors were crying, because they didn't want to leave
their wives or their mothers, or because they were *compagni*—
Communists—and they were ashamed, singing those songs, the
way I was ashamed."

Cattle cars took the men from Perugia to a big port town.
Mario had a fever by then from his injections, and he was
nauseated by the stench and the heat of the crowded cattle car
and by his own fear that this was not the kind of transportation
Mussolini would have provided for a company of future Coast
Guard officers. And, in fact, all the men on the train with Mario
that day went with him to the bunkers in Sardinia. They were
marched to the docks, singing, and into a convoy of captured
tourist boats—and for a day and a night and the better part of
the next day they were shut belowdecks, retching and moaning
and with nothing to eat in all that time but two toast sticks
apiece, an ounce of tinned corned beef, and a cup of water.
Three days—and two more trains—after his boat landed, Mario
was sharing a bunker with four homesick strangers on the far
coast of the island. He says that there were bunkers like it every
thousand feet along the Sardinian coast, that he knew soldiers
who fought and sometimes killed each other just for a chance to

get out of those bunkers and drive the company mule cart to the
supply depot for the bread and rice and moldy pasta that were
their only food. After a while, he says, people in the bunkers
even lost track of who was bombing them. His first company
commander came from the Fascist High Command and told the
men that the bombs were English and American. Then, in July
of 1943—with Mussolini arrested and in prison—a general arrived who told them to stay in their trenches and fight Germans
in the name of King Victor Emmanuel III. And then, when the
Germans rescued Mussolini, that general ran away and a new
one came, to say that they were fighting again for Fascism.

"All that year, we wanted to throw down our guns and run.
But we didn't know how to leave. There were no boats, no
trains, no food. We were eating only once a day, and finally
there was no rice or pasta—just a hundred and fifty grams of
bread a day to keep us alive. There were thirty thousand Germans on the island, taking whatever food there was, killing for
it with their machine guns. We begged our officers, 'Please! Let
us go. Send us home to our families.' But no one wanted to let
us go, and then there was no bread left, and the *miseria* began.
We had to make flour out of melon and zucchini and red beets.
We dried them, and pounded them into flour, and made soup
from that, but no one wanted the soup. It gave you diarrhea.
And the water gave you malaria. There was no medicine—not
for so many soldiers. There were three hundred and eighty
thousand soldiers on the island. That's what they told us. And
there were always more coming—coming from Corsica, from
all over Italy, from every town the Allies held. Finally the
officers had to close our bunkers because so many of us had
died that they were worried about a plague. We camped in
stables—I slept in the straw in a farmer's horse stall—but I had
malaria by then, terrible malaria, and finally they took me to an
infirmary and gave me a bed, my own bed, for four days. After
that, I was lucky. I cured a sheepskin for the farmer whose
stable I had used, and he gave me three lire for it and I was able
to buy a little food. But then there was nothing again. Only

wild garlic and a few tiny wild lemons on the whole island. The officers called a meeting. They said anyone who wanted to leave was free to go with them to the mainland. We said, 'Who has won this war?' But they wouldn't tell us, and after that no one wanted to go with them. We thought they were tricking us again, sending us to another front. So they had to take us by boat to the mainland and turn us loose. I started walking south, with about a hundred other soldiers, and it was somewhere near Naples that the Americans found us. The Americans told us that the war was not over. They said they had no room left in the prison camps for us. They could send us back to the Fascists, they said, or let us stay and work, loading trucks for the front."

Mario stayed. The soldiers gave him chocolate and bread and sugar, and they tried to feed him tinned mutton—he says the Americans had never heard of a shepherd who did not eat mutton. After a month the Americans even gave him money, from a stack of dollars. One night that spring Mario heard on the radio that the German line—*la linea gotica*, people called it—retreating north, had finally passed his valley, and that night he simply walked out of the war. A truck heading north took him about a hundred miles on his way, and then he bought a used bicycle from a farmer with his dollar bills. A few days later Anna found him at the door to their sheep stalls, counting his animals.

Mario measures the cost of the Second World War by the sheep he lost. Fifteen of his own sheep and three of the young shepherd's had been seized by the Germans for food when they held the valley. Only collaborators' houses, with their doors marked LIBERO, had been safe from plunder. And the sheep that the Germans had left in Mario's stalls were weak and scouring from fetid water, because his green and brown and golden valley had become a swamp. The Germans, retreating, had blown up bridges to stop the Americans from advancing, and then the Americans had dammed the valley streams with rubble to get their tanks and their trucks across. Water drained into the fields and flooded everything. Wheat fields that in summer were usu-

ally toasted dry were covered with as much as three feet of
water. Everybody's animals were sick, and there was typhus
around, and typhoid, and cholera. Two of Mario's little girls
had typhus when he arrived, and he says that families ferried
their sick and their dead on homemade rafts and rowboats to
field hospitals on dry ground—that the valley looked just like
the painting of hell, with all the dead souls wailing on their
barca, he had once seen in the town church. Mario made a big
raft and ferried his sheep to a hamlet in the foothills, and he
camped there for a month in a farmer's house, waiting for the
water in San Vincenzo to subside. Finally, he left them there.
He hitched a ride home with an American Army doctor who
was making house rounds on an outboard, and after that Mario
often traveled with the doctor, helping to treat his neighbors'
animals. Slowly, over the winter, the ravaged valley was un-
covered. Mario brought his sheep home. When the old cell—
what was left of it—started meeting again, people got in the
habit of using the Cecchis' kitchen, because all the other Communist houses, from the railroad tracks up to Carlo Benetti's,
had been hit by bombs.

"The Party was already organizing when I came home. It was
like the old days, except that now everything was open and we
had a perspective that was better, from the war. We had a
vision of a better life. We were mostly illiterate. It was not so
hard to convince us. But some of the *contadini* were frightened. They thought we wanted to destroy the churches and get
rid of the priests—they thought they would go to hell if they
joined us. You see, there was propaganda against us. The
Church made a Madonna and paraded her through the valley on
Sunday nights, saying, 'Drive out the Communists! Vote Christian Democrat! Save your immortal souls!' They marched at
night from village to village, and the peasants lit their way with
torches. But we Communists kept on. We talked always of the
struggle of the *contadini*. We told them that only Togliatti could
help us all. And we met and met—in those days, every week we

had a cell meeting. And we went to the big Party meetings in town, too, and later, when the market grew, in the new town. We went to those meetings where there were always men who knew more than we did. They explained, and we listened. Sometimes we replied, but not often, because those important men from the Party told us that for the Party to grow and be strong and make the right decisions it was necessary for people like us, who were poor and uneducated, to take the advice of people who *knew*. What they said was true. There was no liberty before. There were still *padroni* who would knock on your door on the last night in July and if you didn't give them your garden vegetables and your wine and olive oil or offer your wife to clean their villas—you were out on the first of August with nowhere to go. But the Party changed that. They saw that the *mezzadria* laws were changed. And the laws about children working. Now a boy can stay in school for eight years and no one has the right to take him out. There was Alfredo, born in '46. A shepherd's son, and now he could be anything he wanted. I told him, 'You can be a pharmacist if you like. You can be a clerk in a big bank. Or a veterinarian, like Domenico Spina's son-in-law.' Thanks to the Party, my son is *dottore*, like the son of a millionaire. The Party has made them brothers. It has made us all brothers. I worked for twenty-five years after the war. I had eighty sheep to sell in order to buy this land and build this house. I made one million five hundred thousand lire from the sheep, but it was not enough, and I thought I would have to beg at the bank for a loan. It was my friends in the Party who saved me. Benetti, Filippini, Spina. They said, *'Basta!* Enough of banks. We are your brothers.' And they lent me more than a million lire. Roberto Filippini took some of the money he was saving for when the law tells him he can buy his land from his *padrone* —you see how Filippini lives, like a pauper, but he has ten, maybe even twenty million lire in his mattress, and he took some of that money and gave it to me, and charged me only five percent interest on the loan. Benetti didn't charge at all. Spina

charged nine and a half percent—but it was on principle, he
said, that he charged me. He said that since all ownership was
wrong, it was really for the government to pay for a new house
and let me use it. *Libero*. In Domenico Spina's Communism,
everything is free."

It has been ten years since Mario sold his sheep. He would
have liked to keep them, he says. They were good sheep, and
beginning to bring in money, but Alfredo was at the university,
there was no one to help him, and a new law said that sheep on
the road at night had to have two shepherds—one in front of
them with a lamp and one behind them. Besides, Alfredo believed that the father of a future *dottore* should not be working
in his old age. Alfredo bought the furniture for his parents'
house with some of the money he had made selling insurance,
and he told Mario to sell the sheep. He said that Mario had a
son, now, who could pay for everything. Still, Mario misses his
sheep. He wanders up and down the road, tracing his old routes,
talking to farmers he knows along the way, helping out with
their animals. Once when all the cows in the next village died,
and not even Domenico Spina's son-in-law, the veterinarian,
knew why, Mario discovered that the grass they grazed was bad
grass—bad from a winter under stagnant water—and he led the
cows and calves from the dairy cooperative, and all the other
San Vincenzo animals, to an abandoned pasture where he knew
the grass was safe. He helps with all the calvings at the co-op.
Every summer, during the month of heat that Italians call the
soleone, he kills a serpent with a stick and saves its blood in a
bottle, and then when a calf or a lamb is sick he pours a drop on
the sick animal, like holy water, and the animal gets better.
Lately, he has been mixing the fodder for the cooperative, too,
adding his mountain herbs and just the right amount of salt so
that the cows are never swollen. And if a cow is feverish—in
Mario's opinion, the Czech and Hungarian and Polish cows that
the Party is always sending are prone to fever, not nearly the
equal of the hardy local breeds—he slips a sliver of *erba nocca*

under the skin just beneath her tail, and a blister rises that draws away the fever when it bursts. He still talks about buying back some sheep, for company, but he has sixty rabbits in a hutch behind the house, and turkeys and ducks and geese and chickens to look after, not to mention a garden full of eggplant, zucchini, tomatoes, carrots, onions, peppers, and six different kinds of lettuce. The doctor tells him his heart is weak, and Mario will admit now that a shepherd's life might be a little strenuous for him—though surely not the life of a busy Compagni di San Vincenzo trumpeter.

Mario could go the *spaccio* every day if he wanted to. He has his social security, which amounts to 80,000 lire a month, and Anna's mysterious rheumatism brings in another 75,000 in national health insurance. Mario could certainly afford to sit all day at one of the fancy umbrella tables that Emilio Vanni put outside the *spaccio* when he bought the place from Renzo Strocci's widow. He could talk and gossip and drink with Carlo Benetti and the other old men who spend their afternoons at the *spaccio*, but the truth is that he has no aptitude for idleness. He would rather be hosing down the bright white tiles at the cooperative, keeping an eye on the heifers that low and drowse underneath the long fluorescent lights, waiting to drop their calves.

Lately, Mario has been hearing rumors about Alfredo's future. People tell him that the Party has chosen Alfredo as the next mayor of the *comune*. They say that Alfredo has been seen in the best restaurant in Perugia, eating lunch with Party dignitaries from the province, drinking Scotch whiskey and ordering imported lobsters. Mario has to dry his eyes when he hears those stories. Even now, he does not know what to make of the strange life he is ending—of a splendid cooperative filled with cows that arrive in trucks from friends he has never met in countries he has never heard of, or of a son who eats in restaurants he has never seen, making plans to run a *comune* of

twenty thousand people. It makes him shy, Mario says sometimes, like a pretty woman, or the thought of God.

Tourists driving through the valley on their way to see the
town church or the notable town walls have been stopping
at Anna Cecchi's door lately to ask about the abandoned farmstead down the road, where Anna lived for nearly thirty years of
childbirth and war and recovery. The tourists want to know who
owns the house, and it pleases Anna to pretend not to remember
the history of the place or the name of the family that was her
landlord. She knows that with most of the old, empty houses
in the hills already sold, rich young couples from Milan and
Rome and sometimes as far as France and Germany have
started coming to the valley. They have started spending a hundred million lire to "restore" a ruined San Vincenzo farmhouse
for their children's summer holidays or their fall shooting—and
their enthusiasm for these old houses seems like mockery to
Anna, because to Anna a *casa colonica* like the empty house
across the road means rotted beams and moldy walls and a
leaking roof. It means foul stalls, and sheep and pigs grunting
for their feed, and all the other emblems of what was once her
poverty.

Mario tries to persuade Anna to forget this mad sensitivity of
hers that makes so many of the smiling and polite young women
hurry back to the children waiting outside in their Alfas or
Mercedes, convinced that they have seen a witch. He tells her to
relax this vigil she keeps against other people's pleasure, to take
some pleasure in the life she has. He says to consider the family
up the road who slaved in the fields for forty years to be able to
build a house as important as their landlord's villa. They broke
their health and their hearts working, and now that they have a
villa that is faithful to their landlord's—from the brass knocker
on the front door to the crests and vines and cherubs carved on
the dining-room sideboard—all they can feel is the bitterness of
an unacknowledged revenge. But Anna does not care much

about acknowledgment. Her own new house is a very private kind of victory, like the music Mario makes on his new trumpet. Life has astonished them both by being kind, and the difference between them is that Anna does not trust kindness. She thinks of it as a ruse—a trick of fate to put her off her guard for some deep, final disappointment—and so she is determined to be vigilant.

When the Cecchi girls were still unmarried and needed chaperons, Anna used to go out evenings. She would visit the neighbors with her girls, or gossip outside the *spaccio* with the other village mothers while their children sat in the dark inside, holding hands and watching Emilio Vanni's television. She even took some trips alone in those days. When the priest in the village of Fontana di Sàngue—which is just across the valley from San Vincenzo—organized an excursion called Churches of Umbria, Anna was the first woman on the bus, and although she did not have much to say for the churches, she did manage to buy a Father Christmas costume in Assisi, which she still puts on every year for her grandchildren. After that, she went on Communist trips—the kind the Party paid for to get people to its big festivals and rallies. She says that she saw Livorno, Cattolica, Parma, Grosseto, Ravenna, Rome, Pisa, Venice, Capri, Naples, Sorrento, Pompeii, and a couple of other cities she can't remember, and the only problem she ever had was in Ravenna, where she got lost and couldn't find her bus and, on top of everything else, tripped on a cobblestone street and broke the vase with Togliatti's picture on it that Domenico Spina's wife, Elena, had wanted her to buy. But once Anna set foot in her new house, it took a calamity to move her. She stopped going to the Festa dell'Unità, and she refuses to change her mind even now that her husband plays the trumpet. In fact, the only reason she agreed to go to her son's wedding at the town hall, she says, was that she could leave the Benetti women in her kitchen, helping with the marriage supper. Anna is literally convinced that if she leaves her house for very long it will disappear —or that she will come home to find a family of strangers in her place, that she will be turned away, helpless, at her kitchen door. This is why, when Mario put on the light-brown suit he had bought in 1960 for Pia's wedding, strapped his trumpet to the handlebars of his moped and headed for the *spaccio*, Anna sat alone in her kitchen, the grim custodian of her small share of Karl Marx's material world.

Anna says sometimes that she must have lost her trust in people with her mother's milk. She was six months old when her father and then her mother died of a sickness Anna usually describes as tuberculosis, and she claims that not one person in their village had the courage or compassion to approach the the house where her four brothers and sisters were slowly starving on a diet of olive oil mixed with cinders, and Anna herself suckled from a tethered goat. "*Dica! Dica!*" she will cry whenever she discovers Mario standing at the kitchen door, looking up and down his road and getting teary and sentimental. "Tell me, where was the Party then, when five little ones were starving?" And it is useless for Mario to tell her that in 1913 Gramsci himself was not much more than a boy, that the Russians hadn't even had their revolution. Anna's parents were *mezzadri* to a town doctor who had inherited a small field in the country. The land was poor, and it could not support them. The only money the family ever saw was a few lire that the church sent when Anna's parents first took sick. Gino, the oldest boy, was nine when they died, and Anna says that her brother had to run to the village, weeping, to beg the priest to send someone to the house to collect the bodies and then, on the priest's instructions, to burn all the clothes and bedding that their parents had used. It was Gino, finally, who broke their quarantine and found his way to the village where their grandmother lived. Their grandmother rescued the children, but they were sick themselves by then, and she was already too old to look after them very well. She tried to leave them at the orphanage in town, saying, "They will die, the little ones. They are full of pus." But the orphanage refused to take them, and eventually the four older children were placed in local families as servants, working for their food. No one wanted a baby Anna's age. She stayed with her grandmother, getting strong and scrappy, helping in her grandmother's garden, feeding the three chickens in her charge. She was finally classified as an orphan on the public dole, and got some money that way which paid for a tile roof to replace the thatch. What was left of the money bought her a uniform to enter a convent school that was guaranteed by the Mother Superior who ran it to prepare a little *contadina*—in only four years' time—in everything she would need to know for her life on earth, serving Christ and the Italian aristocrats whose money kept the Superior's order comfortable. But Anna says that at seven she was as determined to avoid cluttering her mind with catechism as she is to avoid cluttering it with Communism now. She refused to stay in school. She preferred to spend her time scavenging in the village, near her grandmother's cottage. She would stand at the neighbors' doors—barefoot and wearing a faded, tucked-up smock that had been her grandmother's apron—waiting for scraps. She would hide behind the village ovens while the baker tested the heat with flat little pieces of bread called *focaccia*, and then scramble for the pieces when he took them out of the ovens, burned black, and tossed them away. She would make a stop, always, at the local *mulino d' olio* —carrying a big empty wine jug, begging for the dregs of the olive oil, begging, if there was nothing else, for just a drop of oil on her scrap of bread.

There is no doubt that Anna was resourceful. By the time she was six, she had organized a gang of little girls from the poorest families in the village; the girls would sneak out together early in the morning, before the sun rose, with big sacks for collecting wheat and grasses from their neighbors' fields, or straw and hay from their neighbors' barns. Once, the village priest found them stealing wheat from a parish field. He denounced Anna and her friends in church that Sunday. He called Anna to the altar and told everyone to look hard into the eyes of an unrepentant sinner—and then, when she spat at him and ran home shrieking, he sent the police to arrest her. But the policeman

who found Anna, under her grandmother's bed with the chickens, gave her candy and said it was the priests of Italy, not the
children, who needed handcuffs. And though Anna has nothing
good to say about the Communist Party, she often claims to vote
Communist in honor of that policeman—who, she has decided,
was the first Communist she ever met. He and her grandmother
are the only people from her childhood whom she wants to
remember.

"If I have good memories, they are of the sea. Nothing else.
No one else. For seven years I went to the sea. It was because
of a charity for orphans. Every summer they came to collect the
orphans, and then they took us to Perugia and from Perugia to
the sea. Five or six hundred orphans and the sea. I do not know
where. No one ever told us, but it was good—oh, very good. We
were like *gran padroni* there. Every morning the trucks arrived
with fruits and vegetables and meats. There were women there
just to comb our hair—to delouse it with petroleum and then to
wash and comb it. We slept in tents, big tents for sixteen girls.
And then there was a beautiful big house with a kitchen and
machines for washing clothes. Every day, they came from the
house and changed the sheets on our beds. Twice a day they
changed our clothes. Twice a day we were showered and dis-
infected, and there were sprays in the showers, wonderful sprays
like waterfalls, but if you shot your spray at the others, you
were punished. You had to peel potatoes. I had to peel potatoes
often. I was wild then. I was not nice. I used to hit the others,
and then there was no sea that day. I would have to go to the
pine tree and sit under it without bread, without fruit, without
my 'four-o'clock.' There was always bread and jam at four
o'clock, just like the bread and jam rich contessas had. And
there was water, good fresh water—never wine, like children
who are poor have to drink at home. You see, they weighed us,
they examined us, they gave us medicine. We were healthy. We
were fat and strong. And then one day the buses would come,
and they would take away our wonderful clean white smocks
and our hairbrushes, and dress us in our old clothes and send

us home. What do you make of my childhood, eh? *Dica.* A
month by the sea, a month in heaven every year, and then, for
the rest of the year, sick and filthy.

"I was eight when I went to work at the tobacco farm. Every
day I worked from dawn until the sun went down and it was
too dark to see anything. I carried tobacco from the farmers'
carts to tables where the women sat and packed it into bundles,
and the women would scream and hit me. You see, they were
paid by the weight of what they packed. They needed to bundle
a hundred pounds a day, at least, and so they wanted the dark
leaves at their tables because the dark leaves were heavy.
But I was small and thin and so tired—I would choose the
light leaves because they weighed less, and then the women
beat me and boxed my ears. Finally, I was *intossicata.* I was
poisoned, breathing all that tobacco powder, and I turned green.
Vero. I had to be purged with oil. That was my childhood.
Green and poisoned all year long, and fat and brown and strong
for a month in summer."

Anna says that she had no intention of marrying anyone—
that by the time she met Mario at the *spaccio* she would rather
have joined a nunnery, the way one of her sisters did, than wait
on one more human being for her supper. Her family had been
reunited, after a fashion. Gino, her brother, had found a good
job on the railway, and then a wife, and he had added a room to
his grandmother's cottage and was already acting like the family
capo. Anna's second sister was at home, too, a disgrace to the
family—pregnant by a blacksmith who was engaged to so many
women at the same time that when she finally delivered she had
to share a room at the charity hospital with two girls who were
also giving birth to the blacksmith's babies. Anna was so sick of
men by then, she says, that she told Mario he would be better
off throwing his kisses to her pregnant sister. She did not know
how bashful Mario was. The only shepherds she had ever talked
to were the wild Sardo boys who grazed their sheep near the
sea where she had gone in August—boys who would lure the
older girls to the woods with candy and throw them on the

ground and rape them in unspeakable ways and leave them bleeding and beaten. Now, though, it was Gino who beat Anna when he saw that a shepherd was hanging about outside their house after supper. He said that he was cursed with a family of crazy, wicked women, that Anna would surely end up like her sisters—a whore or a nun. But then Mario talked to Gino, and asked properly for his sister's hand—the way Renzo Strocci had told him it was done. And Mario and Anna walked to the village church that Sunday, ate a marriage feast of chicken and pasta at the Stroccis', and, by way of a honeymoon, took an hour's stroll before it was time for Mario to gather the sheep for their evening milking.

Anna has no pictures from her wedding—she says that there was no money for pictures—but she still has the short white dress and the veil she bought for the ceremony. She keeps the dress in her marriage chest, which sits in the bedroom of her new house now, under the imitation-crystal chandelier she chose from the Vestro mail-order catalogue. "My grandmother said to me when I was small, 'If I die, who will make your dowry?' And so she started sewing. She sewed sheets and towels and twelve beautiful white nightgowns. And when I was ten years old the chest was full, and my grandmother said, 'Now I can die at peace.'" The sheets are gone by now, and during the war, when there was not even *rigatino* for making clothes, most of the nightgowns were cut down as dresses for the little Cecchi girls. But Anna still has one of her nightgowns. She keeps it in the chest, and takes it out when her granddaughters come to visit. It is made of rough homespun, but there are pink flowers embroidered on the bodice, and a lovely pink "A," for "Anna," and every edge is finely scalloped. She never wears the nightgown anymore—she has bright brushed-nylon nightgowns now, with sleeves and collars to keep her warm—but she likes to look at it from time to time. She will handle it shyly, the way she sometimes holds the big Spanish doll, with the slim waist and the red satin gown and the black mantilla, that Mario brought back from his trip to Monte Carlo. It is the gesture of a woman who has had some satisfaction in her life, and even some passion, but not much beauty. Anna herself likes to say that the first half of her married life was "cheese and childbirth." She delivered her four daughters hanging on to a cord above her marriage bed. And the only help she had with them was Rosa Benetti, who stood by, boiling water and drinking wine and talking to Anna about women who died in labor. Now Anna has a granddaughter of sixteen—a girl who goes to Switzerland on her school vacations and talks about studying to be an architect— and she has trouble convincing this rosy, petted child that her mother was swaddled in dishtowels, in a house without heat or electric lights or running water, and laid to sleep on the first night of her life in a soft, round heap of ricotta cheese.

Anna was in charge of cheese in her new household. One of the surprising pleasures of married life for Mario Cecchi had to do with walking his sheep across a meadow and knowing that someone else was home stirring the milk for the Pecorino, or heating the dregs for ricotta, or shaping and draining and storing the wheels of cheese to sell. When the war came, Anna had to graze the sheep *and* make the cheeses—with only her grandmother to help her with the babies. She says that she knew the war was coming to San Vincenzo when, one night, their white sheepdog began to howl. In minutes, bombs had hit the railroad tracks and some of the farms around them, and after that whenever the sheepdog howled Anna and her grandmother would gather up the babies and run to a shelter the neighbors had dug behind the Benettis' house. She was in the shelter when the Benettis' house was hit, and Carlo Benetti's mother, who had refused to leave, died under a beam in the rubble. Sometimes when the bombs fell, she was out with the sheep, far from any place to hide. She says that she would walk for miles, that there were no men left in San Vincenzo to keep her out of anybody's pasture—but no men left to protect her, either. While the war lasted she could never stay out to graze the sheep much after sundown. Even so, she managed to save 5,000 lire while Mario was away. She had come upon an abandoned cannon box in a neighbor's field, and she and Elena Spina put it on a cart, dragged it home, and then, with the box and a bicycle pump and some rubber tubing, they concocted a kind of steam engine that served the village women as a permanent-wave machine.

"What did I think of during the war?" she asks sometimes. "To continue. Just to continue. There were no rules. There was no *capo* in any house, no man to divide the meat on Sundays. No one to say, 'Today there will be new shoes for the family. Today there will be sweets for the children.' And the men who were left got funny in their heads. Like Roberto Filippini—his brothers went and he was left. No one knew why. He was a strong boy and only twenty, but he was left behind, and it made him strange. He fell in love with his count's daughter. Think of it—a *contadino* making love to the daughter of his count. They rode together every day. Oh, it was terrible, terrible, seeing them. Every day he brought a horse for her to ride. He should have known that you do not come with a peasant's horse to a lady, but he didn't know anything anymore. What did he know? Gathering olives? Threshing wheat? And to see him gallop across the fields on that peasant's horse, smiling and nodding like a prince. Well, the girl fell one day and hurt herself, and there was trouble. The police came and beat Filippini because he had harmed the count's daughter. They said next time they would bury him alive—the way they had just buried a partisan at Fontana di Sàngue—and the whole village would have to watch. Filippini never went back to the count's daughter. He never married, and now it is too late, because who would want him? Why would a woman marry a *contadino* now? To be a maid for a man like Filippini—who comes with a father to wait on, too? To work like a mule? To stay home and make prosciutto? A woman now can earn money in a factory or a shop. She is not interested that a man has two carts and a new thresher and a dovecote. She is interested in how much money he earns. No—Filippini lost his chance because of the war and the craziness it brought."

None of Anna's girls have married shepherds or farmers. Anna was determined that they would have a kind of release from the land. After the war she took the 5,000 lire from her permanent-wave business, borrowed another 5,000 from Filippini, and bought a sewing machine, to teach the girls to sew. There were agents in the valley then who contracted out piece-work for the big clothing factories in Prato and Milan, and Anna knew that as long as a girl could sew on a machine and take in work—*lavoro nero*—she would have money of her own. It never occurred to Anna to educate her girls. Each girl had two or three or four years at grammar school—depending on how much work there was to do at home—and then Anna would put her in front of the machine, and her lessons in independence would begin. Pia still sews at home in Bologna, where the village boy she married is now a clerk in the social-security office. Sofia and Angelina live near Anna, in the new town, and they sew together in a local factory and have both even married stonemasons, though Sofia's mason is Catholic and Angelina's Communist, and the two men never meet. As for Teresa, she got married to one of the clothing-factory agents and went to live in Rome, and she has stopped sewing and become a lady and complains now when farmers like Carlo Benetti come to demonstrate and block the traffic with their marches, so that she has trouble getting around to all the shops.

Anna believes that she has done well by her daughters. Sofia and Angelina visit every week, and Pia and Teresa come in August with their families—which means that every summer Anna has eleven boys and girls to entertain her, reciting her favorite folk story about the stupid shepherd from the mountains and his misadventures in the big city. Italian children love the story. There are as many versions as there are adventures to invent. But now Alfredo has told his mother that it is much more than just a funny story. It is a parable, he says, about the significance of money, about a pure man in a capitalist world. Anna does not believe Alfredo. She thinks he is a little touched, with all these odd ideas, and while she is proud to be the mother of the next mayor of the *comune*, she likes to tell Alfredo that something must have happened to his head during his long and troublesome birth—something to make his conversation so peculiar. Alfredo was born during the *soleone*, and it was very hot, she says, that year. She had been in labor from five in the morning to seven at night, and still there was no sign of Alfredo —not even after Elena Spina and Rosa Benetti held her for two hours over a pail of boiling water. Finally the women sent Mario for the midwife, who arrived on her motor scooter. The midwife stayed for an hour, Anna says, but then she saw by her watch that if she stayed much longer she would be late for an important meeting of the Party's local committee, and—being an ardent Communist who could not imagine missing an important meeting—she gave Anna an injection and pushed and pounded with all her strength on Anna's stomach. Five minutes later, with Anna shrieking curses at the midwife and at Communists everywhere and their meetings, she had cut and tied the cord and cleaned the baby and was racing toward town on her scooter.

"You see, Alfredo was *born* a Communist. Born in time for a meeting. I vote for my son, and I am proud that he succeeds, but when he is with the group, to me he is another Communist. He is one of them. I remember how his father was so happy, at last, to have a son. He ran to the neighbors shouting, '*Ciondolo! Finalmente, ciondolo!*' And I was already nervous because the men had been waiting for a boy for the Party. I told them, 'Italians! You change your faith anytime it suits you'—because I remembered when half the village believed the Catholics. Well, now everyone is Communist. Alfredo is Communist. He is a good boy, but he believes anything. First, the priests were after him, with their football games. The priests are smart. They make football games for the little boys, and before you know it they have your son in the seminary. And then the left was after him in high school. Not his father's friends from the

Party. Oh, no—he thought that his father's friends were old reactionaries. These were *new* friends he called the left. They were the ones who told him to go to the university. I said, 'No. It is time for you to go to teachers' school or accountants' school—to a school where you will learn something useful and be able to get a job.' But one day I went away to Pia's—Pia was sick, and there were all the children—and when I came home Alfredo was gone. Gone to Rome, to his sister Teresa. He had enrolled at the university behind my back. He said, 'Don't worry, Mama. I am going to study economy and commerce and make you rich.' But one week in Rome and he had changed to philosophy—*political* philosophy. He was already listening to that nonsense. Even now, he believes what his professors told him. He goes from house to house, he talks to the peasants. What does he think? Does he think that in San Vincenzo they are all Communists? They vote Communist—the people here— to get jobs on the railroad, jobs with the *comune*, but when they have a holiday there are two Masses and a procession of saints. Alfredo has enough to do with his office—but for these people he works for the Party and loses time and sleep and money. He even goes to Fontana di Sàngue every day now, and in Fontana di Sàngue they are *all* Catholics. He does the priests' work for them. He takes the children for bocce and volleyball and foot-ball, and the priests are happy because they can rest. *'Basta,'* I say to him. *'Basta.'* I say, 'Your politics don't interest me. They are a joke, like the politics of the other side.' I never went to the Fascists' meetings—not even when all the other women went, with their black vests, and Fascist ribbons across their chests. So why should I go to the Communists' meetings now? I have my house and I want to be a free citizen, and I do not understand all these discussions. When they begin, I do not understand, and by the end I understand less. I say, 'Perhaps I am stupid.' I ask Alfredo, 'What do you solve with all this talk?' First, the Communists come with one kind of propaganda. Then they come with another. Now there is no one coming—there are

only orders. No, I do not see clearly why there is all this fuss.
I will vote for my son, but do not ask me to believe."

Alfredo Cecchi is involved in so many projects these days that
he often sleeps at his office, just across the street from the
Casa del Popolo in the new town. Alfredo is still an enthusiast.
He cannot resist a scheme that looks as if it might help him
along in his life's work of "looking for communism," as he puts
it, and after his rounds of the valley farms and a visit to the
dairy cooperative he usually has to stop at the office to finish
work he has promised someone earlier in the day. Looking for
communism is important to Alfredo. He says that Berlinguer
has stopped looking for communism, and so has Luciano
Lama, whose Confederazione Generale Italiana del Lavoro includes a cooperative-farm union and a union for *mezzadri* and
an agricultural workers' syndicate. Alfredo admires restless,
critical people, like Pietro Ingrao, who was the first Communist
president of the Chamber of Deputies and used to visit the
students in their bars and cafés back when Alfredo was at the
university. Or like Maria Antonietta Macciocchi, the writer,
who went directly to the Italian and French workers and their
families for her politics. "Looking for communism" is an idea
that Alfredo picked up from books like theirs. He reads a lot.
He had read Herbert Marcuse, Dino Buzzati, Ignazio Silone,
Piero Gobetti, and Boris Pasternak, as well as Gramsci, Lenin,
Marx, and Croce, by the time he exhausted the little library at
the Casa del Popolo and persuaded his high-school friends to
quit their Communist Youth group and start a secret society for
talking about the wonderful left to come. Even then, he says,
the Party had got stiff and stale, like a corporation. Even then,
there was a Mafia of Party bureaucrats. A peasant who needed
a contract signed or a birth certificate for his baby had to leave
his fields and his animals and walk—sometimes for ten or
twenty miles—across the valley and up the mountain to town,
and then if he arrived at five minutes past one in the afternoon

instead of one o'clock, he would find the town hall closed for
the rest of the day, and a notice telling him to go home and
come back tomorrow. All the offices of the *comune* are in town;
there is not even a branch in the new town, where most of the
peasants go to shop. Alfredo says that by now, after twenty-five
years of local power, some of the old Communist civil servants
are so confident in their jobs at the town hall—the way the
Catholics are confident in *their* jobs at the federal post office—
that they only open their offices from ten to noon and spend the
rest of the day in the cafés, dealing and politicking.

One of the things Alfredo says he learned from all his reading
was that "looking for communism" meant looking for ways to
give people a sense of pleasure and control in their lives as
citizens, instead of deceiving them with the same old and self-
important hierarchies presented under new names. His experi-
ences with the *comune* have convinced him that a kind of political technician is taking over the Party—that the frescoed offices
of the town hall are filling up with tedious and pretentious men
whose only real contact with *il popolo* is with the porters who
hurry from room to room with balance sheets and planning
charts. Now that the mayor is certain to retire, and Alfredo
has the Party's blessing to take his place, Alfredo is promising
people that by this time next year there will be a branch office
of the town hall in every village.

Alfredo knows why so many important Communists from
Perugia, and even Rome, take him to restaurants these days and
feed him lobster. There are seven men, including Alfredo, on
the secretariat of the Party's local committee, and without Alfredo they are deadlocked. Three of those men are more or less
disposed to Berlinguer and his politics. Three are old appara-
tchiks, like Domenico Spina, whom everyone in town calls "the
Russians." And for the past few months—ever since the mayor
bought a little villa on the Adriatic and started bargaining with
the town movers—they have not been able to agree on any
candidate but Alfredo. It is not that they approve of Alfredo—it
is simply that they are sure that while Alfredo is out planning

football games and cooperative farms and otherwise looking for
communism, they will be free to go about their important business of sabotaging one another. Besides, Alfredo is young, and
appealing, and people like him. All those nights of visiting in
the valley have made him popular—much more popular than
any of the six others. The last time he ran for the town council,
nearly three hundred people wrote in "Alfredo Cecchi" on their
ballots—which meant that they wanted to cast a vote for Alfredo in particular, quite apart from the list that included him.
He is certain to win by a lot more votes than the old mayor did.
Even Catholics in the pious village of Fontana di Sàngue will
vote for him. The Party will get a lot of good publicity, what
with a new mayor who plays football with the priests. And the
old-timers will get to keep on fighting over the *comune*'s
patronage and power.

Alfredo has nearly convinced himself that once he is mayor
he will be able to lead the people against these dreadful politicians, to give them back their cells and their local power, to
inspire the kind of excitement that will prove to them that
Communism in Italy is not "an idea that stopped"—as five
young San Vincenzo Communists who quit the Party this year
in protest wrote to the local paper. He says that his real problem has to do with terrorism and the panic over terrorism and
the kind of paranoia that has started to infect the valley—that it
has to do with a lot of Communists who are going to look at
any complaints he makes against the status quo as a sure sign to
the opposition that they are all halfway into the Red Brigades.

Still, Alfredo takes on project after project, like a *galan-
tuomo*, and one of his charms—a charm evidently lost on his
five friends who quit the Party—is that the most outrageous
schemes that come his way will usually appear "creatively"
Communist to Alfredo, for the simple reason that they involve
him. Alfredo knows his appeal. He is tall and strong, with a
thick neck and curly black hair and his mother's astonishing
dark eyes, and he likes to dress up in a pair of cowboy boots
from a trendy Western shop in Rome. His boots tip him back-

ward when he walks, and make him look as if he were sizing up
something—an opportunity, perhaps, or an opponent. There is
a kind of energy about Alfredo that might seem edgy, nervous,
in a thinner, smaller man. In Alfredo—leaning back, and a little
barrel-chested in his fitted Western shirts—it turns into something amiably ruffled. He hustles himself and his schemes and
his politics with a kind of interchangeable good will. Lately, for
instance, he has been talking a lot about banking. A small, close
group of noble families control the banking in the *comune*, and
Alfredo, doing a little research in the town records, discovered
that their banks—with 20 billion lire in working capital—have
invested some 15 billion lire in industry in northern Italy and
put only 5 billion back into the *comune*, in the form of loans or
credits and investments. He tried to explain this to people on
his nightly rounds of the valley and in his council speeches,
but no one seemed to understand. He says that poor people in
Italy are afraid of banks, afraid, sometimes, just to enter a bank
—they are so in awe of that kind of institution and the power
it represents. Some of the old peasants in Alfredo's *comune*
will gratefully accept 3 or 4 percent interest on their savings at
one of the private local banks, when the interest at any bank
in the nearest city would be 9, or even as much as 12, percent.
Once, hoping to change this, Alfredo applied for a seat on the
board of the richest bank in the *comune*, and then, when he was
refused, he wrote to the Russians at their embassy in Switzerland, outlining a brand-new scheme to open branches of their
State Bank in Italy for Italian Communists. He told the Russians that as a good Communist he was always happy to donate
his councilman's salary, say, to the Party but that business was
business and as a businessman he considered a commission
appropriate. He has not heard from the Russians, but he is
counting on some connections he made in Switzerland through a
friend he met in the summer of 1968. That was the summer he
drove to France with two classmates from the university to see
how the French left was doing with its protests. In the course of
his visit he was seized by the Aix police, who, for reasons they

were never able to explain, took him for Daniel Cohn-Bendit—
and Alfredo became a kind of celebrity by proxy. Alfredo met
his Swiss friend in jail, where they were both waiting to see the
juge d'instruction. His friend was a Trotskyite at the time, but
now he is an important investment banker in Geneva, and while
Alfredo is waiting to hear from the Russians his friend has put
him in touch with an Arab consortium that has placed a standing order for three million hectares of vineyards no more than
seven miles from downtown Rome. Alfredo is trying hard to
convince the Arabs, who like the shopping in Rome, that they
may have a little trouble buying three million hectares of anything seven miles, or even seventy miles, from the city—that,
for that matter, three million hectares is a tenth of Italy. He tells
them to consider something more modest—maybe three thousand hectares or three hundred—and sends them postcards of
the Po Valley and the Chianti Mountains. He stands to make a
lot of money if he finds a vineyard for those Arabs, but more
important than the money, he always says, is their solemn
promise to study his plans for running the vineyard as a cooperative, with the peasants sharing in the profits.

Actually, Alfredo is making a reputation for himself as a
"specialist in cooperatives." Even the office he shares with four
friends is a cooperative, and it has prospered in the thirteen
years since they set up shop under the aegis of someone's big
brother, who was twenty-one and the only man the five boys
knew who could legally register a new business and was willing
to do it. The office then was one small room above the movie
theatre. It was a kind of all-purpose enterprise, which according to the flyers Alfredo handed out would "pay your taxes,
audit your books, administer your payroll, build your house, sell
insurance to you, buy you a new factory or farm, and sell
your old one." Alfredo sold the insurance for his Rome promoter, and the others did what they could to make enough
money for buying books and food and renting rooms for five or
six months a year at their various universities. The sign on their
door said, "All Your Business Needs Are Met Here," but the

business itself consisted of six folding chairs and a couple of wobbly desks begged from the local school board. Today there are Parsons tables and fancy stainless-steel arc lamps and dark-brown Habitat couches in big sunny rooms they started renting four years ago, and the five young men are all *dottori* now and have added a secretary to their collective. In fact, theirs is the first and most important office in the province to concern itself with the planning and administration of cooperatives. The dairy cooperative was their project—and it was certainly an original project, considering that Umbria has never been a very hospitable place for cows. Alfredo took the project to his friend Pietro Gaspari, who was already an important person in the Party, and together they went to the provincial Cooperative Federation for help in establishing what the Italians call a *stalla sociale*.

Alfredo says that cooperative farms are going to save Italian agriculture. The country has been importing close to half its food since the nineteen-sixties, when national illusion had it that Italy, with a little building, was going to be a rich industrial power, freed from the old, punishing rhythms—not to mention the punishing economics—of the land. Everyone ignored agriculture then. The Party saw to it that the *mezzadria* laws were changed, and then it seemed to stop caring. It gave up on the terrible farming problems of the Mezzogiorno. It never arrived at any intelligent national programs for the land, either—for what to farm, or where, or how food should be distributed. Not even the success of the Party's huge cooperative farms on the plains of Emilia-Romagna—farms that, with their enormous capital investment, now amount to one of Italy's major economic institutions—seemed to indicate to the Party that farming was worth much interest or much thought. The Communists concentrated on industrial Italy, on the working class and its demands and problems. And it is probably true that if the Confederazione Generale Italiana del Lavoro had fought for its farmers fifteen or twenty years ago the way it did for its workers —had seen to it that a valley like the Cecchis', bone-dry in

summer but often too wet in winter to hold the wheat, or even
to support the weight of a modern plow or a machine for cutting
fodder corn, got proper irrigation and electric lines and decent,
intelligent rules for land division and land tenure—most of the
young men and women who fled to factories would still be on
the land.

Alfredo's cooperative is the local showplace. It uses land that
once belonged to a farm-machine cooperative—a co-op that
failed because the big landlords owned their own threshers and
tractors and the peasants did better with people like Domenico
Spina, who was saving money for his own land at the time by
hiring himself out by the day, with an old tractor he had bought
on loan. The gifts and the credit that brought the dairy cooperative its land and its long aluminum barns and eighteen stainless-
steel milking machines and a fancy vat to keep the milk at an
even four degrees Celsius—that was only the beginning, Alfredo
says. He and his partners wrote a charter for the twenty families
in the cooperative. Each family would contribute six cows—
cows of its own or cows that it could buy with loans, at 7
percent, from the Federation. And each family that could would
also contribute its fodder harvest to the cooperative, which
would deduct from that family's contribution the amount of
feed its particular six cows consumed and then pay for the rest at
going market prices. Families like the Cecchis, with no land to
speak of, would agree to deduct the cost of the feed for *their*
cows from their share of the yearly profits. Alfredo bought his
parents their cows as a present, just in time for a parade of
proud *contadini* marching their livestock through the village and
down the road to the co-op barns. That day, all the cows were
draped with flowers. Carlo Benetti had saved the money from
two of his pension checks and bought a Polaroid camera for the
occasion. He took a picture of every cow, and those pictures
were duly stapled to pieces of paper and handed out as certificates of stock in the cooperative. That night the members
elected an administrative council, and the council elected a president to call meetings twice a week and be a sort of cooperative

manager and live in the big new house that had just been built for him. And there was a big village party in the barns, too—singing and dancing, and a feast of roasted pig and *tagliatelli*, and the presentation of the three white bulls that had been the cooperative's first purchase.

No one in the San Vincenzo cell expected that belonging to a co-op would be complicated. They seemed to forget, with their stock certificates and Polaroid pictures, that cows had calves and that calves grew into heifers and had their own calves. They never expected the strange, skinny red cows that kept arriving from Czechoslovakia and Poland as part of the Party's cross-breeding program. No one knew how to divide these new animals—how to divide the cost of feeding them, to begin with, and then how to divide the profits from their milk. That was the first problem. Then the cooperative started to make a little money—mainly because the *comune*, being Communist, decided to donate five million lire a year for every hundred of its cows. What this accomplished was to convince a lot of strangers that they belonged in San Vincenzo's cooperative, too. Socialists and Liberals and Social Democrats, and even Christian Democrats, including a nephew of the count who had once been Roberto Filippini's *padrone*—they all came to the cooperative council and asked to join and help Italy build socialism, and the cooperative got a lot of bad publicity refusing them, because the count's nephew told the local newspaper that San Vincenzo's dairy cooperative was part of a Russian plot to keep Italy's milk from the mouths of its Catholic children.

Finally, there was the year that Domenico Spina, who was on the cooperative council, along with Roberto Filippini, Carlo Benetti, and Alfredo's father, decided that the co-op was based on wrong notions of privilege and private property—that a true cooperative would not ask six cows from every family but would belong to all Communist families who wanted to join it, whether or not they had a cow, or six cows, or sixty, to contribute. This time, it was not the *padroni* but the drifters who started to show up at the door to the milking barn—without cows, without grain or fodder or even work of their own to contribute, demanding their share as "fellow-Communists."

Strangers have stopped appearing at the barn now, but Alfredo still spends at least one night each week with the co-op president—a cheerful old man who rattles around his enormous house in an undershirt and a Red Sox cap and has yet to understand, or perhaps divulge, the co-op's peculiar finances. Alfredo goes over the books each week—and the books of a new meat cooperative, across the valley, that takes San Vincenzo's calves in exchange for its own breeding heifers—and he keeps track of whether the three hundred San Vincenzo cows are doing well. But he no longer pretends to understand what the president writes in those big red ledgers with the hammers and sickles on their covers. It seems to Alfredo that the village *contadini* have simply taken their shiny new co-op, with its incubators and tiled barns and all the other paraphernalia of modern farming, and adapted it to an ancient and rather suspect logic that goes beyond the understanding of a young *dottore* sitting at a Parsons table with a pocket calculator.

Alfredo has organized a lot of cooperatives since then, but none, he says, with pictures of people's cows stapled to their stock certificates, and none that have meant as much to him as the *stalla sociale* that got the men of the old San Vincenzo cell to share their work and their money as well as their frustrations and their August parties. The co-op families have, all told, about a hundred hectares at their disposal, but Carlo Benetti and Roberto Filippini, being *a mezzadria*, still have to farm for their *padroni*, and most of the other men in the co-op take outside jobs to help support themselves. Domenico Spina is the only one with enough land of his own to be able to farm exclusively for the co-op. Still, everyone gives at least eight hours a week of his time to work at the co-op barns or on his own farming for the co-op, and there is a month during the harvest when one man from each co-op family is always there cutting and baling straw. So it matters less to Alfredo than perhaps it should that he cannot read the co-op books and has no idea what the co-op owes in taxes—no idea, really, whether the co-op is thriving or is on the edge of ruin, as the president, who believes that paying taxes is against God and the Italian character, likes to complain over his glass of wine. The president knows that as long as the *comune* is Communist, the Party will always rescue him with gifts and credits, because the Party has decided to consider the San Vincenzo cooperative a model for the world.

Actually, the cooperative that seems to be "looking for communism" in ways that please Alfredo most is a weekly paper that he and eleven friends began this year. Most of his friends on the paper are Radicals. They are part of a movement that is new to Italy but has now managed to put twenty deputies in Montecitorio—a movement away from the empty rhetoric of Italian politics to the real issues of Italian life, like birth control and abortion and nuclear safety and civil rights. There are a few Communists on the paper, but Alfredo says it has been the Radicals who have fought for the kind of articles he wants. Alfredo wants articles for farmers, say, or for local businessmen with money problems. He wants the paper to give people advice about credit, about schools, about marketing, about child care and abortion. He has even invited a priest he knows—a young worker-priest with a degree in anthropology—to write about the problems of reconciling Christ and Marx. He says there is nowhere else that people in the valley can get the practical and honest information that they need or see a man like the young priest write openly about the thoughts that trouble them the most. The other Communists on the paper want only comics and cheerful propaganda and advertisements. The paper is losing money, and despite the fact that Alfredo and his friends have each put in three-quarters of a million lire and are asking readers for contributions, the bank that Alfredo once tried to join is charging them 25 percent interest on a seventeen-million-lira debt. The Communists say that country papers in Italy do not survive on the contributions of intellectuals or on advice about telling scarlet fever from roseola. Papers, they say, sur-

vive on advertising money and on the kind of news that makes
the people who read them forget their disaffection.

"There are people in the Party who could pose the same
questions the Radicals pose," Alfredo says. "Questions that
concern *people* and the way they live. But the Party burns men
like that. To get to the top, you have to agree with the Party.
Disagree and you are finished. The trouble is that there is no
self-criticism in the Party, no spirit of self-criticism. I joined
it—but only because the country here is not Rome or Milan,
where you can do something as a Radical or with a *real* communist Party. Here you need a base that people know, that
means something. The left? What is the left to these peasants? It
is nothing. To them it is only long hair and sex, and now terrorism. No—I joined the Party to accomplish something, and
for that the people had to accept me. My friends who quit—
they were valuable people to the Party. If they had stayed, we
might have accomplished something together. Now it is up to
me alone. The Communists will make me mayor, but they will
fight me. They fight me now. They call me a bohemian because
I write for divorce and abortion, and they—well, they usually
take a good stand in the end, in Rome, when it is necessary for
the Party image, but they will never pose the problem first.
Here, for instance, they refused to put a woman on the secretariat. For years they refused. And then when there was pressure—when they *had* to—they went to the nearest factory and
chose the stupidest woman there and put her on the secretariat,
and that way they could say they had found a woman *and* a
worker."

Alfredo considers himself a feminist. He has argued in the
town council for a local branch of the Unione di Donne Italiane
and for a column on women's issues in the weekly bulletin of
the *comune*—both of which the council rejected. He is proud to
be married to a "new" woman, a modern woman—a woman, he
says, "who is rational, like a man." His wife, Lidia, is a lawyer's
daughter from Rome, a dark, lovely-looking girl with the starch
and the quiet fervor of a wellborn radical. They met at the

university, and it seemed to Lidia then a kind of miracle—finding a boy who was not a bourgeois Marxist, like the others, but whose roots were gloriously, enviably popular. The thought of living in Alfredo's valley, near a mother-in-law who cured insect bites with raw potato slices and a father-in-law who talked of herding sheep in the mountains—to Lidia, it was a mission, something pure. She and Alfredo built their house on a little plot of land, next to the Cecchis', that had been set aside for Alfredo, and they furnished it with navy sheets and rheostats and Danish woods, with Picasso and Robert Indiana prints and a wall of books and good German stereo equipment. Lidia had come to San Vincenzo with gifts from her Roman friends, money from her family, and a pale-blue trousseau—and she was tender and amused and never angry when Anna refused to cross the yard and visit because the house, to Anna, seemed odd and plain. Actually, Lidia came to love the Cecchis. Her interest in their lives is genuine, and so is the affection that at first seemed too stubborn, too determined, to last for long. But Alfredo—for all his speeches about rights, and his campaigns to get the village women on the road and marching to the town hall on National Women's Day—drops his clothes all over the house, and talks too much about his mother's cooking, and has yet to wash a pair of his own socks. He disappears for hours without telling her where he has gone, and then he comes home to a drink and a book and a pleasant record on the stereo, and tells Lidia to hurry with the supper. If he promises a favor to a friend—a book bought or an errand run—he sends Lidia into town to do it for him. And he is always promising someone something. One of the reasons he is free to drive around the valley visiting is that he can always leave Lidia in the office with the paperwork, and then she is right there if he decides to spend the night. Lidia admires Alfredo, but she says that the only liberated Italian men she knows are priests like their friend from the paper, who have no women to exploit. She says that whatever Anna claims, Anna was waiting for a son to spoil.

Alfredo, in fact, depends on Lidia. She has shaped his appetites and his tastes and, in a way, his confidence. She has given him the courage of her class to believe in his own image as a maverick. "The Stalinists on the secretariat—they can't control me. They can control the jobs. They can control the men who run the sections. But the base is mine, the valley is mine, and they know it. I have a strength—country children have it. We have lived through troubles, and it makes us different, stronger. With me—it *pushed* me. I wanted to win, always. I began with sports. I believe in the power of sports. I believe in *lo spirito di squadra.* I played football because I knew that if eleven people could get together on one point, could reason together—I knew that was something valuable. My mother hated football. She said it made me late to supper, it made me dirty. But my father understood my ambition. He never said much, but he knew that I was getting the strength of character a boy from the country needs. I had good breath and good sense, and I was the captain. They said that all I needed to be a real football player was technique in passing. That was my dream, you see—to be a football star. I had to go to high school in the city, where I could get the kind of diploma that would let me work and earn money for the university. I was not a rich boy—I could not go to the *liceo.* So I went to the city, and I had to get up at six in the morning. I went by bicycle to the station and then by train to the city and then by bus to the nearest stop, and finally I walked. It was always eight by the time I got there. That was my life for five days every week. But on the weekends there was football. The football field—it was the only place where I felt free. Maybe this is why I organize the football games in Fontana di Sàngue—so that those boys will feel free, too. I consider that village my cell now. San Vincenzo is already Communist, but Fontana di Sàngue is Catholic, and I do not like it when the Party turns its back on the Catholics. The people from Fontana di Sàngue told me that for twenty years there had been no real discussion in the village—and then five years ago we formed our group for football, and we began to talk about things, playing. We began to talk about the village school, about getting elec-

tricity. After a while we got signatures and made a bocce court
and brought electricity to the village, and then public sewers and
a public road. The priests had ignored the people in Fontana di
Sàngue. But it was still the priests they trusted. They did not
trust the Communists until we started our football games and
taught them how to make choices and decisions about their
lives. The Party always laughed at my work there—but one day
the women of that poor, superstitious village marched on the
town hall, demanding street lights, and now the Party listens
when I say that soon the children of those women will be Communists."

Alfredo likes to say that he, too, is a Communist because of
football. He played for the village church when he was small,
but once he was old enough for a bicycle, he started going to the
Casa del Popolo in the new town on Saturdays and Sundays for
a game. There was a vacant yard behind the Casa del Popolo
which made a perfect football field. Alfredo and his friends
liked it so much that they started playing hooky weekdays, and
Alfredo claims that whenever a grownup passed the field, they
fled through an open window into the Casa del Popolo's library
and pretended to be reading. Not many of the boys read much
otherwise—they went to school for as long as they had to, and
then they apprenticed in workshops or garages and ended up as
electricians and masons and mechanics. But a few read everything they could get hold of, and they started reading in that
little library. Alfredo says that soon boys and girls from all the
villages of the *comune* were coming to the Casa del Popolo to
meet. They came, he says, to escape the "suffocation" of the
Party and its youth groups, but evidently the Party also wanted
to escape these critical and irritating children. They were
thrown out of the Casa del Popolo library, and then they had to
make their clubhouse behind a pile of used tires in a local tire
shop.

Two of Alfredo's new-town friends went on to universities,
and they all had trouble of one sort or another—and ended up
as important Communists. Alfredo's trouble had to do with

passing his oral examination in political philosophy. He failed it six times in as many years. The first time, he says, was because he did not know Thomas Hobbes' birthday. Alfredo called the test a "quiz show," and the professor called Alfredo a Communist, and after that every time Alfredo took the test the professor asked him about Hobbes' birthday and Alfredo refused to answer. Finally, in September of 1972, with four hundred students waiting in the auditorium for what had become an annual piece of theatre, the professor bowed out, saying that Alfredo was "irrecoverable" and might as well have his doctorate—and adding, for the record, that Thomas Hobbes was born in 1588.

"The professor was a Fascist. For him, anyone on the left was a Communist. I went, of course, to the Communist student cell. There were a lot of us on the left in our department, and we all went, but I was not inscribed in the Party. I didn't like the red scarves and the hats and the exhibitionism—and I was not at all convinced that the Party was good. But I knew, even then, that it was necessary for the left to stay together. There was violence at the university in '68. There were many groups on the left—good groups, like the Partito Socialista Italiano di Unità Proletaria—but there was a big law school and a medical school, and those students were always on the right. They wanted to fight us. And so we organized our occupation to protect the cause and to protect ourselves. We took over the cafeteria and slept there and drew up lists of what we wanted. We wanted different exams, rational exams—not exams about birthdays. We wanted a say in the curriculum. We wanted better fellowships because, as things were then, only the rich students could afford a good, clean room. I think now that that one year—1968—was more important politically than the twenty years that went before it. It was the year when the left woke up, when we began to understand that the *people* counted—that the Communists were wrong in thinking that only the political class, the Party class, was charismatic.

"There was nothing but politics that year. We wrote tracts.

We traveled. We organized debates, made marches. We took over some of the university accounts. We took turns guarding the university, because the Fascist students were making trouble, destroying everything and telling the public it was us. Finally, we began our contacts with the workers. We had meetings with workers, and talked to them about a new politics, so that by 1969 our protest involved the whole cultural life of a city. There was a moment when we became a true city of the left. And the right was desperate. The riot police came every night, and there were infiltrators everywhere—in our bars and in our classes. Women came to us at night and pretended to be liberated women and offered themselves to us in the name of the revolution, and they were infiltrators, too."

Alfredo can still spend hours talking about 1968. The memory of '68 is exhilarating to him, and, in a way, his running around the valley now—playing football, talking to peasants every night—has to do with trying to recapture some of his old passion. It is very important to Alfredo that no one think of him as selling out the principles of his one moment as a hero. He refused for a long time to join the Party. He let the Party pay for his first campaign for the town council, but he ran then as an independent on the Party list, and did not join until a few years after he had won. He says now that he had come to realize that the left in Italy could advance only through its official numbers, that it was stupid to refuse a Party card, like a spoiled boy. But he is too smart to believe that entirely. He knows he joined the Party under pressure, and this is something it upsets him to admit.

Every Saturday morning lately, Alfredo gets up at six o'clock and bicycles alone, on his ten-speed racer, for thirty or forty miles, thinking about himself and the Party and about what to do with his life—and why. He says that early morning on the road, with the mist rising from the valley, is the best time for reflection. He knows, he says, that socialism is possible, that people can build a kind and functional world in which to live. But when the sun comes up, and the trucks start across the

valley, and the *contadini* begin to work their fields like figures
from an old novel while the rich *padroni*, in their Mercedes,
head for weekend houses on the mountain—then Alfredo suspects that socialism may be as hard to come by as three million
hectares of vineyard in the shadow of the Vatican.

They met at the Cecchis' on the first Saturday night in September—Mario and Anna and Alfredo, Carlo Benetti, Domenico Spina, Roberto Filippini, and a few others from the San
Vincenzo cell. It was the first meeting of the cell since the Festa
dell'Unità. Families had come and gone on their August holidays. The Benettis had just sent their oldest son and his wife
and four children back to Düsseldorf, to a flat in a factory
housing project that Carlo and Rosa Benetti had only seen in
photographs. Anna herself was still putting the Cecchi house in
order after a month of Pia and her family. They had come to
work on the villa they were building for the time—not much
longer now—when Pia's husband would retire from his government job with a nice pension and could bring them home to
stay, and they had camped on air mattresses in the Cecchis'
living room. Teresa, who had been home in San Vincenzo, too,
had settled *her* family next door, at Alfredo's, while Alfredo
and Lidia went to the beach for two weeks with Lidia's parents.
There were still signs of them all tonight in Anna's kitchen—
forgotten toys, a volleyball, and a plastic Kojak in the corner,
and, on top of Anna's new refrigerator, boxes of sticky cakes
from the *pasticceria* which the grandchildren had never finished. Near the door, there was a case of *amaretto* with a couple
of bottles gone.

Anna Cecchi has a weakness for *amaretto*, and she always
gets to indulge it in September, when Alfredo comes home from
the Mediterranean and presents her with a case of the sweet
liqueur as a kind of consolation prize for the vacation she refused to take. Tonight she sat with a big glass of *amaretto* and
dealt the cards while Mario circled the kitchen table looking at

everybody's hand and pouring, and Alfredo made the toasts. First he said *"Salute!"* for his father because the Compagni di San Vincenzo had played so valiantly for the seven nights of the festival that they were already booked for next year. Then he said *"Salute!"* for the Party, which had made more money this time than at the past two festivals put together. And, finally, *"Salute!"* for San Vincenzo's Festa dell'Unità because thanks to the festival there were five new Party members in the village; Domenico Spina's youngest daughter was engaged to the butcher's son from the new town; Roberto Filippini, at fifty-six, had won another silver-plated cup for "middle-age class" bicycling; and one of Alfredo's protégés from Fontana di Sàngue had knocked down the middleweight from Perugia for seven counts.

Domenico Spina drained his glass three times, glanced at his cards, and announced that one day soon the Communists would be taking over Italy, and then France and the rest of Europe. He had spotted three counts and their countesses dancing at Emilio Vanni's *spaccio* on the last night of the festival, and this was a sign, he said, that the nobility—which had a nose for this sort of thing—was already trying to ingratiate itself with its future rulers.

Roberto Filippini added that the group of tourists who had come to the boxing matches had included Clint Eastwood, the American movie star, or Clint Eastwood's brother, or perhaps his cousin or someone just like him.

Anna called *"Briscola!"* She had made a thousand lire while the men were talking about movie stars and movies, and listening to Alfredo's gossip about the great movie director who was in the neighborhood—well, nearly in the neighborhood—at the villa of a beautiful American woman.

Mario watched his wife—an old woman now, with her wispy hair and half her teeth gone—dealing cards to his comrades of more than forty years. He stood there fingering his shiny trumpet, which he kept on the kitchen window sill, for decoration, like a flowerpot or a doll or one of Roberto's silver cups. "I remember fifteen years ago, twenty years ago," he said, "the old house was always full for a meeting."

"It was the television," Alfredo said, grinning. "You had a television set before the others, so they came to watch. Now everybody has a television."

"It was the girls," Roberto said. "Four daughters in a house. With four daughters, you can expect the village."

Domenico growled, "In the old days, there were more people at one of our meetings than at all the speeches of the Christian Democrats."

"People today are too well off," Carlo Benetti said. "They get a little and they are satisfied. They stop fighting." Carlo banged his fist on the table, splashing some of his *amaretto*. "I am for the hard fight. If we are tender now, we accomplish nothing."

Mario shook his head. "No, it is not us. It is the Party. The Party wants to decide everything now. The Party doesn't care if we are red—or black or white, for that matter. The Party cannot be bothered. Those people in Rome—they have lost the habit of listening. What do they want with *us*? With some old men who haven't studied, who know nothing?"

"They wanted us in '48," Roberto said. "They wanted us when the Fascists shot Togliatti. They wanted us then, ready with our guns, ready for the barricades. They wanted us in '49, when the Fascists were burning our Casa del Popolo. I was there, in '49. They came from Rome and asked if I had a stick or a club or any weapon. I said, 'I have a fine stick—a machine gun with forty rounds.' " Roberto always warms to the subject of the Party. It is like a wife, he says. He cannot go to sleep at night angry at the Party. "Let them lead me!" he shouted now. "I am happy to be led by a brave man like Enrico Berlinguer!"

Mario went on, not paying much attention to Roberto. "I remember when everybody came to a meeting like this. The whole cell came. The women, too, and sometimes neighbors, cousins. It is something I do not understand—that everyone came then, but the vote was small. Now no one comes to meetings, and the vote is huge. I do not understand it."

"I understand it!" Carlo shouted. "We are soft. We have cars, bocce, football, movies. We have television in every house. To give up a night for a meeting—it's practically a sacrifice."

"It is because there is no *order* in Italy anymore," Domenico told him. "Look at Russia. Everything is in order in Russia. There is no crime in Russia. No one throws papers in the street in Russia. No one forgets the 'Internationale.' Ha! If we are soft, the Americans have made us soft. They have said that liberty is cars and television, but the Russians know that liberty is order. Order and a good balance of payments."

Anna won another thousand lire, from Domenico.

Carlo was excited. "We used to be called the Little Russia here." He thought for a moment. "No, the Russians are getting soft, too. I am for China. I am for calling ourselves the Little China." Carlo chuckled.

"If we continue like this, talking nonsense, we can call ourselves the Little Vatican," Anna muttered.

Alfredo burst out laughing. He was standing behind his mother, studying her cards, her sleeves, her apron folds. He has never been able to figure out precisely how she wins at *briscola*, but he keeps on trying. "Listen," he said finally. "You can change this. You can go to the section, to the *comune*, to the province. You can speak up at the big meetings, at the congresses. You can sign petitions. You can say that the people are angry, that the Party will have to listen, that it is not right for all the decisions to be made in Rome. No, it is not right." Alfredo, who was getting a little drunk, raised his glass. "To the people! *Salute!* To the cell and the people in the cell!"

Mario drank proudly.

Anna shrugged and put her winnings in her apron pocket. "We will see, in a few years, when you are mayor," Anna told Alfredo. *"Vediamo."*

THE
INVANDRARE
(1976)

Predrag Ilić began to build his house in Yugoslavia eight years ago. Predrag was twenty-one then. He had already served his eighteen months in Marshal Tito's Army. He had a steady job loading trucks at the bottling factory just outside his village. And his bride, Darinka, was about to present him with their first child. Building a house was simply what was expected of him next. A house is an important matter for a Serbian villager. Predrag says that a man at home is nothing without his own house—the way he is nothing without a strong, healthy son and a few hectares in orchard for his plum brandy. This was true enough when Predrag's father built a house, but it was quite literally true when the time came for Predrag to build his, since by then nobody in Yugoslavia was permitted to own more than ten hectares, there were no jobs for well over 1 million of the country's 22 million people, and a house was often the only thing that a poor young man from a peasant village, without ties to the Party or any special education, had to show for himself.* It rankled Predrag to be living with a pregnant wife in his father's old wooden farmhouse. Predrag is a tiny man, barely five feet two, and, like many tiny men, he suffered his humiliations keenly, believing as he did that life rewarded taller men. He already had a long list of grievances. In the Army, in Croatia, he had lost the arm-wrestling championship of his barracks to a strapping blacksmith from Macedonia. Back home, he had lost his best girl friend to a tall butcher from the market town. Now he was a married man—almost a father—without a house.

* This is still true, although the official unemployment figure is lower—around 750,000. It is also safe to assume that most of the 820,000 Yugoslav citizens who are working abroad today would be unemployed at home, too.

Predrag suffered enthusiastically, in the best Balkan tradition.
He exhausted himself suffering, and when he was bored with
that, he exhausted himself manufacturing bravado. He took on
outrageous drinking bets with old, seasoned village guzzlers. He
greased his hair, buffed his chewed fingernails, dressed up in
fancy city clothes. He preened himself and strutted around the
village like an agitated bird while Darinka stayed at home, heating the family flatiron to press the ruffled pink shirts that he had
ordered by the half dozen from a Belgrade catalogue. At night
he sat, conspicuous, in one of the village's three cafés and made
mysterious jottings in a schoolboy's copybook, telling everyone
who asked that he was hard at work on a set of complicated
mathematical problems. He wanted his neighbors to know that
he was somebody—a man of great gifts and bitter disappoint-
ments whom an unkind, unjust fate had squeezed into a life and
a body that were too small for him. But his neighbors did not
pay any serious attention to Predrag. The old men outdrank him
every night and took his money, and the young men laughed at
his nonsensical jottings. Predrag's copybook became the village
joke.

Predrag planned his house as if he were plotting revenge. His
house was going to compensate for every indignity that he had
suffered. It would be a modern house, a villa, like the villa of
the foreman at the bottling factory or of the market-town doctor. It would be built of fine cement from Belgrade—not of
wood, like an old Serbian homestead—and it would have four
big rooms, a modern kitchen, a bathroom with a flush toilet,
and hot and cold running water. No one would be able to say
that Predrag lived like a peasant, on wooden floors. His floors
would be American linoleum. His cushions would be stuffed
with fine foam rubber instead of common goose feathers. His
rooms would be brightly lit by fluorescent light bulbs, warmed
by electric heaters. Tall men would be humbled by the sight of
the plastic hose in his kitchen garden. The wives of tall men
would be old at twenty-five, bent and worn from carting water,
but Predrag's wife would stay young and plump, sitting in her

shiny kitchen, pushing the buttons on an imported washing machine.

Predrag does not live in the village anymore. He lives, with Darinka and their three children, in a Swedish factory town called Södertälje, on the Baltic, and he works on an assembly line at Saab-Scania, earning the money to complete his house. He has been in Sweden for nearly eight years now. There was no way in the end, he says, for him to stay at home and build a proper house—not with what amounted to a weekly wage of less than $20, not with the price of almost everything he needed for the house going up each year. And no other sort of house would satisfy Predrag. He had been born a peasant, to a peasant's life, but before he was out of grade school the world had intruded on that life, first with a paved road to the market town and then with a bus that made the long run to Belgrade every week, returning with glossy magazines and catalogues and all the propaganda of material progress—leaving the young men of the village ashamed of themselves, ashamed of their fathers, and desperate for the symbols of a worldly life. Some of them had already left for factory jobs in western Europe at the time Predrag moved to Sweden, and were planning, like him, to save money for their own villas, figuring that once they had their villas they would somehow find a way to live at home. By now so many have left—and so much building has begun—that the village has grown into a small town, a kind of Slavic Levittown, with the ghostly look of having been deserted in haste at various stages of construction. The new streets, unpaved and overgrown with weeds, are lined with the foundations and shells of the villas the young men dream about in the factories of Germany and Sweden, and they are virtually abandoned from summer to summer, which is when the men come home for a month to spend their year's savings on a new floor or a septic tank or tiles for a roof. The village thrives in summer. It is crowded with children rediscovering the southern sun, young couples showing off their foreign money, and a battalion of carpenters, plumbers, masons, and electricians from the market town. But in September

the potlatch ends and there is no one left but old men and
women caring for babies whose parents cannot afford to keep
them abroad.

In August of a good year, Predrag comes home with 10,000
kronor. Augusts, he *is* somebody, a gentleman on holiday with
his family, a gentleman with a wallet full of cash and a 1967
Peugeot. But in a month the money is gone, and he flees—with
barely enough to pay for food and gas on the long drive north to
Södertälje—before the confidence he has shored up over a
month of spending is gone, too. He figures that he will be
"commuting"—a word he learned in Sweden—for five more
years before his villa is finished and he can consider coming
home to stay. The work is slow, because even 10,000 kronor
does not buy much in Yugoslavia anymore in the way of material
or labor. And none of the artisans from the market town will
work on credit; as soon as Predrag goes, they simply stop in the
middle of whatever it is they are doing and wait till the next
summer to take it up again. The walls of the house are up now,
and there is a temporary roof, to protect it from winter storms
that blow out of the mountain range behind the village. The
sitting room has a floor of black-and-white linoleum, and
Darinka has just moved in her dowry furniture, bought white
nylon curtains, rimmed with pink rosebuds, for the windows,
and ordered straw mattresses, so that the family can sleep there
when they come home on holiday this summer. But good linoleum costs so much in Yugoslavia that Predrag has not been
able to lay the other floors, and he still must save several thousand kronor for electric wire and a plumbing system before any
work can begin on the kitchen or the bathroom.

Winters in Södertälje, Predrag lives a kind of half-life. He
says that in his mind he does not live there at all, that in his
mind he is always home. He sits by the kitchen window in his
little flat, listening to Serbian music on a secondhand shortwave
radio, staring at snapshots in a family album that by now is
entirely given over to the villa under construction, nibbling on

chunks of Yugoslavian cheese and sausage that he buys, Saturdays, at the Haymarket in downtown Stockholm, drinking the slivovitz he smuggles into Sweden each September in empty beer bottles. He has grown testy and despondent in Södertälje, like the young man who in the space of a few months lost his arm-wrestling title and his favorite girl. He complains a lot that he is losing his best years in a cold, dark, unfriendly country. But he does not consider the possibility of going home to the country that in his winter memory is always warm, sunny, and abundant. Instead, he broods, dressed up in one of his old ruffled pink shirts, consoling himself from time to time with a new copybook for his imaginary mathematical problems. The fact that most of his neighbors in the enormous housing project that the Swedes, pleasantly, refer to as a *förort*—a suburb—are also foreign and homesick does not console him at all.

There are 10 million foreign workers in industrial western Europe.* They come from abandoned farms in Portugal and Spain and the Mezzogiorno, peasant villages in Greece and Yugoslavia, tribes in the Maghreb, and remote settlements in Anatolia to work in the factories of the north, and together they represent the human matériel with which the great states of postwar Europe have industrialized. Together, in fact, they represent a new kind of European nation—a polyglot diaspora, a vast migrant proletariat, with no precedent in Western history since the days of the Roman Empire. One of every six workers in industrial western Europe today is a foreigner—not an immigrant settling down in a new country but an *homme déraciné*, as the French say, driven by poverty and dreams to hard, demoralizing work in a strange, hostile northern city, where he survives at a bewildering distance from the life around him,

---

* Ten million is a fairly constant, official figure; it is the number of dependents and illegal immigrants that tends to fluctuate.

counting the years, and often the decades, until he can return home to the imagined glory of a completed house, a little shop or café that has been fully paid for, the respect of old neighbors who have stayed behind. He is a symbol, in a sense, for every Mediterrancan village whose isolation has been shattered by a world of high technology and complex economics, a world that the village is powerless to reject and powerless to accommodate.

By now the postwar immigration of labor to the north accounts for the greatest human uprooting that Europe has experienced since the great waves of emigration to America in the late nineteenth and early twentieth centuries, and it has bound the north and the south in an intricate and desperate symbiosis. The new migrants are the labor by which northern industry survives and dominates—and they are, equally, the source of the foreign-exchange capital with which their own countries manage to survive the domination and the unemployment that domination has produced. At the peak of the emigration—it was in 1973, just before the first winter of the oil crisis—19 percent of Switzerland's workers were in fact Italians who spent their salaries in Italy. In France, a million Portuguese workers in the factories of Paris and Clermont-Ferrand were sending home 22 billion escudos a year, making cheap labor Portugal's most profitable export product. Nearly a million Algerians supported their families in the *bled* on French salaries and pensions, sustaining a domestic economy that might have collapsed without them. West Germany, with more than 2.5 million foreign workers, supported 750,000 Yugoslavs—which meant that up to 15 percent of Yugoslavia's labor force went to work each morning in West Germany.* The benefits were ambiguous for both sides. On the one hand, an unlimited supply of cheap in-

---

* At least 300,000 Yugoslav workers in West Germany have been laid off since the oil crisis and have gone home, but there are still about 400,000 of them left—over 600,000 once families are added.

dustrial labor had guaranteed the flashy, shaky successes of western Europe's postwar growth economies; but the growth spiral was already inflationary by the nineteen-sixties, and by the nineteen-seventies, with an oil crisis and a world recession blocking export outlets, most of industrial western Europe was in a state of overdevelopment that it could no longer support. On the other hand, twenty-five years of constant emigration had done a lot to keep the countries of the south underdeveloped. The emigration had a placebo effect on fundamental social and economic problems, offering temporary solutions to unemployment and encouraging illusions of domestic wealth, based on returning salaries that were most often invested unproductively, as the economists say—invested, that is, in houses, cars, and small cafés and garages; in land held for investment and left fallow; and, especially, in goods and materials imported from abroad. It has subverted what was once at least a functioning agriculture, draining the southern countryside of young men until there are now vast farm areas in the south with virtually no farmers. And it has kept the governments of the south from having to make decisions about their own development—decisions already complicated by the fact that businesses and governments in western Europe had little reason to risk investment capital in politically unpredictable southern countries when they could profitably employ the best workers from those countries at home.

Now, with Europe in trouble, the migrant workers are the first to suffer. The thousands who have been laid off since the recession started are returning to countries that are unable to reabsorb them. The millions who have stayed abroad are suddenly usurpers. Ten years ago they were welcome to jobs that no one else wanted; today they are the villains of the recession, feeding their families with money that by rights belongs to decent northern working men and women. Germany banned the importation of additional foreign labor in 1973, France in 1974. Countries like the Netherlands and Sweden enforced

complicated laws and union agreements that read like progressive social legislation but accomplished the same thing.* In
1974 the Swiss actually took a vote on expelling foreigners;
more than a third of the voters came out in favor of a depor-
tation plan.† With jobs scarce, money tight, and all the tensions
of recession high, a backlash that for years went officially unacknowledged is now respectable, in the name of western
Europe's new "crisis economics."

Every country has a name for its foreign workers, and usually
treats them accordingly. The French, calling them *les émigrés*
and sometimes *les déracinés*, keep them underpaid and literally
uprooted, in huge, desolate communities of squatters in the
slums of Paris or in the filthy *bidonvilles* that ring their big industrial cities, looking curiously like sets for a French protest
film about workers' conditions in Rio or Casablanca. The Germans call their foreign workers *Gastarbeiter*—guest workers—
and as workers they are paid well to perform well but as guests
they are discouraged from making themselves at home in Germany and are urged, instead, to take up a sterile, temporary sort
of bachelor housekeeping in corporate dormitories built to keep
them efficiently close to their factories and effectively removed
from Germany itself. The Swedes, however, call them *invandrare*, which means simply "immigrants" and is used in a
welcoming way for everyone who comes to settle in the country.
They pay their foreign workers handsomely, house them com-

---

* The same laws and bans are still in effect in these countries,
  though it is important to remember that they only affect certain
  workers. By charter, the nine member states of the European
  Economic Community share a free labor market and cannot
  restrict the rights of one another's workers within that market.
  Some EEC countries have been offering "capital grants"—cash,
  in other words—to get some of their foreign workers to go home;
  there are clearly very few takers.

† Switzerland has had two more national referenda on expelling
  foreign workers since 1974, with roughly the same result each
  time, and will evidently have another soon.

fortably, encourage them to bring their families, educate their children, study them with the earnest curiosity of anthropologists, chart their happiness with psychiatric concern, fight for their rights, and write endlessly about their problems. And this means that, for all practical purposes, Sweden is the most tolerable—and tolerant—place in Europe for a southern worker to live. There are only 8 million people in Sweden, and more than 400,000 of those people are foreign workers and their families —half of them Finns, who can come and go without restriction because of a common-labor-market agreement among the Scandinavian countries. Until the recruitment of workers from the south was stopped, in 1972—ostensibly as part of a full-employment scheme to protect Swedish jobs and provide new ones for women and for elderly or disabled people—a work contract from a Swedish company was considered a plum by any southern laborer educated or informed enough to know one northern country from another.

Southern *invandrare* came to Sweden in such numbers— 10,000 to 25,000 of them a year in the late sixties and early seventies—that by the time immigration was restricted, southerners and Finns accounted for half the assembly-line workers in most of the country's heavy industries. They came because Sweden, more than any other country in the industrial West, is a workers' state—not a Socialist state (which is the myth about Sweden in America and most of Europe) but a stunning experiment in welfare-state capitalism. It is an experiment, really, in profitable collusion between a few powerful industrialists and the enormous federation of labor unions called Landsorganisationen, which dominates the country's institutions, to nurture the Swedish worker into a state of such extraordinary contentment and complacency that he becomes that perfect industrial servant—a man with no ambition beyond the working class. The Swedes seem to have achieved a society in which the highest good is a new Volvo and a color-television set. The country today is a triumph of materialism, and the Yugoslavs and Turks and Greeks who cross the continent to work there are dazzled

and confused, at first, by the prosperity and the apparent decency
of life around them. They find themselves in a kind of never-
never land where curious notions of the social contract have replaced the old, easy etiquette of corruption by which so much
of life proceeds in southern Europe. There are no workers'
slums in Stockholm, no *bidonvilles*, none of the guilty tensions
of exploitation. Most *invandrare* in Sweden work in clean, progressive factories, and they work, by law, for Swedish wages.
Predrag takes home 1,800 kronor a month after taxes—about
$410—which is more than five times what he used to make in
Yugoslavia. When he is out sick, he automatically collects 90
percent of that salary. When Darinka gives birth, she is guaranteed a paid postnatal leave from *her* factory of up to six months.
The money is dispensed with obligatory cordiality. So is every
service of Sweden's elaborate and bountiful welfare state. The
sort of racist hatred that prompted *soi-disant* respectable
Frenchmen to murder Algerian workers in Marseille a few
summers back would be unthinkable in Sweden. The open contempt of the Germans for their *Gastarbeiter* would not be toler-
ated. The Swedes are appalled at the thought that the Swiss
could publicly debate expelling foreigners for the simple offense
of being foreign. Swedes regard foreigners with a calmer, qui-
eter disapproval. They simply treat foreignness as some sort of
congenital indiscretion—as a kind of psychic social disease that
by rights should embarrass anyone afflicted with it into lying
low until the symptoms have disappeared. The *invandrare* in
Sweden soon discover that they are isolated—and they sense
that, somehow, their isolation goes deeper than the volatile,
defensive separateness of foreign workers in, say, France and
Germany. If those workers are "the niggers of Europe," which
is how they have described themselves lately, then the Swedish
invandrare are a little like the sad, nervous boys in a Strindberg
book—well fed, well groomed, well cared for, but unacknowledged as fellow human beings until they have managed a reasonable approximation of grownup attitudes. The confusion the
invandrare feel is deep and bitter because they have so few

practical complaints to corroborate their eerie sense of being in terrible error by being themselves. Predrag, for all his grudges, says that no one in Sweden treats him badly. The problem, he says, is that no one seems willing to admit that he is really there.

Sweden, of course, is a notoriously provincial country. It has no history of cultural multiplicity and no real tolerance for it, and the stolid conformity that confounds tourists who come expecting a nation of sexy girls and broody, philosophical drinking partners is really a reflection of the Swedes' profound uneasiness with difference. Sweden may produce its Strindbergs and its suicides, but the Swedes themselves seem to regard genius and madness alike as object lessons in the lamentable inability of some people to suppress their eccentricities and become cheerfully, comfortably, the same as everybody else. Most Swedes, in fact, protectionist for centuries and secure by now in a benign but stultifying xenophobia, seem to regard foreignness itself as something insulting. Over the past forty years they have adopted the most liberal and humane refugee policies in Europe. But those policies, drafted in the name of the new social-democratic ideology, were based in large part on their conviction that the Swedish character and Swedish values, being the proper character and the proper values, would instantly convert any foreigner—and that in admitting foreigners they were really adding to their sparse population hundreds of thousands of potential Swedes. They had none of the Americans' hard, practical dread of immigrants, nurtured by long and chaotic experience with melting-pot culture. And they had none of the cynicism about immigrants that a history of colonialism in Africa and Asia had developed in people like the French. The Swedes' only serious colonial adventure in a millennium was a seven-hundred-year occupation of Finland, right next door. They were certainly not prepared for what they got when they began recruiting *invandrare* from the Mediterranean, and what they got they found unacceptable. They are uncomfortable with their new prejudice, which they suspect contradicts their image of themselves as flawlessly egalitarian, and so for the most part they do not express it. They simply defend themselves against the presence of so many stubbornly foreign foreigners with a kindly but invincible disregard.

Even the landscape seems reluctant to admit that there are southern Europeans in Sweden. The modern workers' suburbs, full of *invandrare*, that ring the big cities like Stockholm, Gothenburg, and Malmö and the industrial towns like Södertälje are a bland but effective camouflage on lives and customs that most Swedes find at best grotesque and at worst savage. There are no quarters of Stockholm that would announce to a visitor that Greeks, say, or Yugoslavs lived there—not even the few small neighborhoods where nearly everyone by now *is* a Greek or a Yugoslav. In fact, the only exotic place in Stockholm is a vast, white-tiled subterranean market, underneath the old haymarket —Hötorgshallen—most of which has been gradually taken over by Greek, Turkish, Italian, and Yugoslavian concessionaires hawking native food. All the *invandrare* within a couple of hours' drive of Stockholm show up there Saturday mornings and spend more money than they intend to on expensive imported olives, cheese, and sausages—simply because Hötorgshallen is a bustling, odoriferous place with the sort of cheerful chaos that reminds them of the weekly markets at home. There is not much else in Sweden to remind them of home. Walking through the streets of a Swedish city, they have the furtive presence of a people in mufti—clumsy, embarrassed shadows in a world where rage is confined to the closet or the sanatorium, where drunks are solitary, intimacies are meticulously ordered, and people live by an etiquette of absolute discretion.

It is not really surprising that the Swedes—even the Swedish workers, only a generation or two from their own peasant villages—are so alarmed by these Turkish tribesmen, Serbian peasants, Neapolitan and Sicilian slum children. The *invandrare*, to them, are rowdy, vulgar people, shamelessly devious, unnaturally hostile—and almost everything else a decent Swede is not. More often than not, they are also the perpetrators of a prickly, easily brutal machismo that is exaggerated by life in a country where machismo has no prerogative. Ten years ago in Sweden local jurors, elected by their town councils, used to meet a couple of times a month and rarely heard a charge more ominous than "loitering" or "public nuisance." Today these jurors meet daily, with a full complement of interpreters, and are trying cases that involve ugly street fights, armed robberies, rape, wife-beating, and child abuse. The *invandrare*, by refusing to become Swedish when they crossed the border, have carried the violence of poverty into a country where there has always been more suicide than homicide—a country where neighbors are apt to call the police when a parent spanks a naughty child.*

A thousand years ago the Vikings established Södertälje to protect themselves from foreigners. It stood on a narrow, barely navigable channel that linked a finger of the Baltic to the great Lake Mälaren, where the Vikings had their island capital of Birka, and they made it their habit to keep a few warriors posted at the channel, guarding the entrance to their territory and to their ships, anchored in the lake. Eventually they built a garrison, then a small settlement. By the thirteenth century— Birka had long since been abandoned—Södertälje was a village of a few hundred merchants, artisans, fishermen, and farmers. And it was curiously well known throughout the country—being by then a kind of ecclesiastical depot, supplying goods to the clergymen who used to meet there, arriving by boat from the Baltic coast towns and from the thriving new town of Stockholm and the old bishops' townships that had been established on the lake. It stayed small for the next seven centuries. Sweden, emerging from the Ice Age fourteen thousand years ago, was slowly rising, and the Södertälje channel, rising with it, had been impassable since Viking days. Once, in the fifteenth century, work on a canal was started and abandoned. No one

---

* So many did call that it is now illegal in Sweden to spank your children.

had the courage to try again until some merchants and noble-
men got together in 1806, hired engineers, and sold stock to
finance the construction. The new canal opened Lake Mälaren
to the big boats that sailed the Baltic archipelago, and then to
steamships, and it turned Södertälje into an important town. A
rich new bourgeoisie from Stockholm, aping the German
burghers, with their Baden-Baden and their Karlsbad, decided
that the water in Södertälje, drained from a hill above the town
called Torekällberget—Thor's Spring Mountain—was perfect
for curing the rheumatic aches and postnasal drips of the cold,
wet Stockholm winters, and so they took up Södertälje. They
came summers, by paddle steamer or on the new railroad, which
passed through Södertälje on its way to Gothenburg. They built
elaborate villas on the banks of the canal. They kept little sail-
boats in the harbor for picnics on Lake Mälaren; sponsored
band concerts and arranged marriages; danced in the restaurants
of the new resort hotels. Workshops went up around the town to
manufacture fancy bicycles and coaches for them. In 1891 a
small company called Vabis started to make carriages for the
railroad. Thirteen years later, a factory called Södertälje
Verkstäder delighted the rich summer people with Södertälje's
first automobile.

Fashions in resorts change, and with the First World War the
rich abandoned Södertälje. But the factories stayed, and so did
fifteen thousand people who had settled in Södertälje to work in
them. Vabis acquired Scania, which was then a small bicycle
company in Malmö, and in time Scania-Vabis merged with Saab
to become Saab-Scania, Sweden's second-largest automotive
company, and build the enormous plant where Predrag and
some fifteen hundred other *invandrare* work now. The canal
was deepened again, and its thick, beautiful wooden locks were
replaced, to accommodate ships that carried steel, coal, and
lumber to the region's factories. And the town spread across the
canal and out past Torekällberget, in tidy rows of workers'
cottages.

The new workers were in a sense Södertälje's first immigrants. They were the sons of farmers, regretfully abandoning a life and a land that could no longer support them, and over the next few decades they saw Sweden change from a country of farmers, ruled by a propertied élite—until 1921, Swedes voted in local elections in proportion to their wealth and property, forty votes to the richest, one to the poorest—into a social democracy carefully grooming for development. While most of Europe suffered one world war and mobilized for another, Sweden experimented with what the government called a "survival economy"—an economy based not on the expansion of industry for export markets but on a diversification of agriculture and essential industry comprehensive enough for the country to achieve and maintain a level of peacetime self-sufficiency that in wartime, with rationing and a proper sense of sacrifice, would become total. Sweden's stubborn neutrality depended on it. And so did the fact that in 1945, with the rest of Europe destitute, Sweden entered the world market with the greatest immediate export capacity on the Continent, its factories already producing a full repertoire of sophisticated consumer and industrial products, and its currency sufficiently undervalued to insure its export markets and at the same time discourage Swedes from importing anything themselves.

By 1949 Sweden needed labor. More than a hundred thousand political refugees—Estonians, Latvians, Lithuanians, and Poles, mostly—had entered the country during the war and directly afterward, and most of them had gone to work in Swedish factories, but by the late forties even a steady stream of refugees could not keep pace with the country's development, and Sweden cautiously began looking for *invandrare*. Italians came first; then Finns, once the Scandinavian labor-market agreements were ratified, in 1954. Greeks and Yugoslavs began arriving in the middle sixties, and finally, in the late sixties, Turks and Arabs and drifters from a dozen countries. Industries recruited foreign workers, and the government helped them, setting up labor centers in Greece, Turkey, Italy, and Yugoslavia. By the time the recruitment stopped, Sweden had industrialized

so thoroughly and efficiently that it could export some 50 percent of its factory products and still maintain its nearly total
domestic self-sufficiency. And Södertälje had grown from a
passé resort town of 15,000 people into a small industrial
city with ten important factories and a population of 80,000
people—10,000 of whom were *invandrare* from over fifty-five
countries.

There are 41,000 Yugoslavs in Sweden now.* There are
Yugoslavs unloading cargo on the docks at Malmö, a few
miles across Öresund from Copenhagen; Yugoslavs slicing up
trees in Lapland; and Yugoslavs working the assembly lines of
every factory city in between. Six hundred of them live in
Södertälje. Some, like Predrag, left jobs at home for better ones
in Sweden. Most left because there was no work of any kind
for them at home. They are all, to some extent, casualties of a
single event in Yugoslavia's shaky postwar economic adventure
—Tito's famous Economic Reform of 1965, which officially
converted Yugoslavia from the federally subsidized planned
economy of a rigid state Socialism into a Western-oriented market economy, with factories operating directly under workers'
councils and responsible for their own survival in a free domestic and world market. The reforms were critical for Yugoslavia,
which was going broke supporting padded employment in factories that could not begin to meet their costs, but the result was
that those factories, suddenly on their own and forced to support themselves, stopped hiring. Soon they began to lay off
workers and office employees, and in some cases—unable to
compete profitably—to shut down. Tito, to ease the economic
shock and generate some urgently needed capital, had no choice
but to issue passports to workers and open the country's borders,

* The figure is today 40,000, but that does not include the 4,000
Yugoslavs (many of them children of *invandrare*, but born in
Sweden) who are now Swedish citizens.

which for all practical purposes had been closed to labor emigration since the war. Unlike Predrag—and unlike the *invandrare* from most other countries—the Yugoslavs who lost their jobs, or their prospects for jobs, and had to emigrate were often educated and experienced. At least a quarter of them had finished high school; some had been to universities and were professional people—plant managers and accountants and engineers. They knew Europe in a way that workers from the Mediterranean did not. They knew that German factories paid the best salaries in Europe, and so they went to Germany. They knew that Sweden, whose biggest recruitment drive had coincided with the reforms in Yugoslavia, offered them the best life, and so they went to Sweden, too. Most of them left home surprisingly cheerful, given the circumstances. They had confidence in the reforms that had put them out of work; confidence that they would be back in Yugoslavia within a few years. Even the government reassured them—their official status at home, on the record books, was "Yugoslav workers temporarily at work abroad."

Eleven years later, most of those Yugoslavs are still abroad, with no prospect of finding jobs at home and terrified of losing the ones they have.* German factories laid off 100,000 Yugoslavs alone during the oil crisis of 1973–74. Sweden, having been considerably less greedy and more sensible about development, has been able to keep all its *invandrare* so far, but no one can say for sure what will happen to jobs there if there is another year of world recession. The Yugoslavs in Södertälje complain about staying. Few, though, are still under the illusion that they will be leaving soon—unless, of course, Sweden throws them out. They carry their savings home each summer. Yugoslav migrant workers still account for $1 billion a year entering Yugoslavia, but the cost of living in Sweden is going up by 12 percent annually, which means that they are saving less and less of what they make, and there is an inflation rate in

* Officially, the unemployment rate in Yugoslavia is 11.5 percent; unofficially, it may be as much as twice that.

Yugoslavia of anywhere from 22 to 32 percent—depending on
who is giving out the figures, and why—which means that what
they do save buys less and less for them at home.* They know
by now that it is pointless to talk about "a year or two longer."
They joke about the Finns who come to Södertälje to work one
season and still refuse to learn a word of Swedish after twenty
years there because they remain convinced that they are going
home tomorrow. Most Yugoslavs make a point of learning some
Swedish, but, like the Finns, they have discovered that going
home gets harder with every year they stay away. There are
Yugoslav engineers who make four times the money on Swedish
assembly lines that they made at home as practicing professionals. There are Bosnian and Serbian peasants, like Predrag,
who have discovered color television and good cars and credit
plans for suites of walnut furniture, and by now they are more
committed to their dazzling new possessions than to the Communist experiment in Yugoslavia. When they talk now about
going home, they mean going home to a life that meets their
new Swedish standards. They have had to make the sacrifice of
home, and they believe they would lose face in their villages if
they returned without a good deal to show for it. This alone will
keep most of them in Sweden long after their villas are completed or their foreign cars are paid for. And, never really knowing why, they will spend the better part of their working lives
without roots, without community, and without importance.

The center of Södertälje is a small shopping mall, closed to
traffic and popularly called Gånggatan, which means the
Walking Street. It was built by the town council in 1969, against
the protest of a lot of old Södertälje families, who wanted to see
the early wooden buildings of the neighborhood restored for use
rather than torn down, as some were, or moved up to Torekäll-

* Yugoslavia now claims an inflation rate of about 14 percent. No
one knows for sure how accurate this is.

berget, as the best were, into a kind of Swedish Williamsburg and opened to tourists and groups of schoolchildren. But the council and the local businessmen consulted city planners, and the planners said that a modern mall would be a public service —safe, sanitary, and convenient—and this was what the people of Södertälje got. A Södertälje housewife can park her car in the lot at one end of Gånggatan, deposit her children in the Gånggatan sandbox or on the Gånggatan rocking horses, pick up a newspaper, take a chance on the lottery and buy tickets for the next football matches, do her marketing, hurry to the bank, compare prices at two department stores, order a hot dog at the sausage stand and, if she has a minute, stop to eat it on a wooden bench next to a plant in a brightly painted tub. This is how most Södertälje people use Gånggatan. The mall is busy at noon with shoppers, and again in the early evening, when work lets out and people drive over to pick up food for dinner. Saturday mornings the Salvation Army band plays there, distributing temperance leaflets. Occasionally local students set up tables and solicit contributions for Angola.* But no Swede ever really stops to *enjoy* Gånggatan. The Swedes are a private people, and it is not their style to use the middle of town for socializing. They are scandalized when new *invandrare*, taking the mall for a kind of plaza, descend on Gånggatan for strolling and gossiping and drinking and the kind of amiable loitering that goes on all the time in the middle of a southern European village. The sight of an *invandrare* family all dressed up for a leisurely evening paseo on the mall seems to distress the Swedes nearly as much as the sight of a gang of tough young Greeks or Yugoslavs hanging around at night under the Gånggatan street lamps, on the prowl for Swedish girls—and in their own way the Swedes let the *invandrare* know it. Lately the stores on the mall have hired guards to keep their doorways clear and break up nighttime scuffles. The cafeteria in the department store called Domus, which is owned by the Stockholm branch of the coun-

* Now the tables are for "boat people."

try's consumer movement, has put up signs in six languages
warning people who come to gossip over a cup of coffee that
they are permitted the use of a table for only half an hour. The
Södertälje *invandrare* learn about Sweden by learning, trial and
error, the rules of Gånggatan. They learn that acceptable people
are brisk and courteous, rarely playful, and never truculent.
They learn to approve the old Swedish drunk lying quietly by
the canal, and to decry the Finnish drunk who staggers down
the street, shouting and singing and trying to fight with everyone. They learn that friends in Sweden are inherited, not sought;
that pleasures are familial, not social. And they learn, finally,
that until they have mastered these rules, they belong at home
in their workers' "suburbs"—an easy drive from Gånggatan
but much too far for an immigrant family on a Sunday outing
or an after-dinner walk.

The suburbs are Sweden's New Towns. In theory, at least,
they are the oldest New Towns in Europe because the Swedes
began to worry about things like urban sprawl long before anybody else did. As far back as the eighteen-nineties, the city of
Stockholm was buying up huge land parcels, miles beyond the
bridges that describe the central city, with the intention of building on the new land when the time came and diverting rural
emigrants to settle there. With the ascendancy of the Social
Democrats, in 1932, the New Towns became part of Sweden's
social ideology. Every city in the country, whatever its size or
its population, wanted its own New Towns in the name of modern demographic thinking. And Stockholm was the model because Swedes from the provinces are "second city" people and
tend to venerate Stockholm the way Frenchmen do Paris, con-
fusing imitation and envy. Actually, the postwar Stockholm
suburbs, like Tensta and Skärholmen—Skärholmen alone holds
34,000 people—were planners' dreams and human nightmares.
They were vast concrete ghettos rising out of barren landscapes
next to six-lane superhighways, isolated from the natural growth
and rhythm of the city and, not surprisingly, never developing
into true communities. They were places with nowhere to walk

to, nowhere to go—places aggressively at odds with the sort of human scale that could have made them neighborhoods. And they fixed, physically, divisions of class and caste that belied the surface egalitarianism of the new Swedish state. Södertälje has built seven of these suburbs since 1945—five of them since 1960, when the immigrants started to arrive in numbers. And half the people in the new Södertälje municipality, which gained 20,000 extra citizens over the past few years through the consolidation of surrounding towns, live in them. *Invandrare* like Predrag, being the newest, poorest, and least passably Swedish people in town, inevitably end up in the newest, biggest, and least desirable of the suburbs, which usually means that they are the farthest from the center of Södertälje and the closest to the major factories. Predrag's suburb—call it Vikingabyn, which means the Viking Village —houses 6,000 people in a maze of indistinguishable buildings bounded by parking lots and numbered according to a logic that seems designed to discourage visitors. In fact, the visitors' sections of the lots are generally taken over by Vikingabyn's children, who come home from school in the afternoon before their parents have finished at the factories and wait outside, in little packs, shouting at each other in Finnish, Serbo-Croatian, Greek, and a dozen other languages, and, occasionally, playing together in Swedish. It is hard, though, to find a Swedish name on the directories that hang in the entries of each Vikingabyn building. The Swedish workers who do live there shun the foreigners, and they move as soon as they can to the older, more respectable, "Swedish" suburbs. Vikingabyn itself, despite its 6,000 people and its prowling children and its shiny, cut-rate construction, has a curiously empty tone to it. People keep to themselves there, and when they do meet they are awkward, as if their common foreignness were something embarrassing. They connect by rumors. Rumor that the veiled Turkish woman with five children—the one who lives on the second floor of Predrag's entry—was so badly beaten by her husband for taking a walk around the parking lot that she had to spend a

week in Södertälje Hospital. Rumor that the six Finnish families
in the entry feed vodka to their children. Rumor about the politics of the Greeks on the fourth floor. Rumor concerning unspeakable home movies that the Italian brothers who work at
Saab-Scania and share a flat on the ground floor order from a
sex shop in downtown Stockholm. Rumor that one of the four
Yugoslav workers in the building—Predrag among them—is
paid by his embassy in Stockholm to report everything he hears
or sees about the others.

The Yugoslavs themselves engage in a kind of nodding, outsiders' camaraderie when they meet in the elevator or the lot or
the Vikingabyn supermarket, but, believing the rumors, they are
not friends. There are obviously spies in Sweden watching
Yugoslav workers—very likely not just agents from the embassy, whom everyone expects to find anyway, but conscript
informers, workers who have had a problem with their passports or a run-in with police during their summer holidays and
are let off in exchange for information, which usually turns out
to be information about one another. When the Yugoslavs first
came to Sweden, there was a kind of truce among them. No
other *invandrare* were as odd and polyglot an assortment of
people as the Yugoslavs, but they were sharing an exile, and for
a while they were able to put aside the old divisions of class and
nationality that plague Yugoslavs at home. They tried to get on
with one another. They joined Yugoslav *klubbar* in the big
cities. Slovene intellectuals who worked on assembly lines with
Macedonian peasants invited the peasants home to dinner. Serbs
and Croatians went to discothèques together to look for lonely
Finnish girls. The truce was strained, though, by time and tem-
perament, and it ended abruptly in 1971, when two Croatian
nationalists—members of Ustaša, the party that ran an "auton-
omous" Croatian state for the Nazis during the Second World
War, killed hundreds of thousands of other Yugoslavs, and now
operates as a secret terrorist society—tortured and then murdered the Yugoslav ambassador to Sweden. A year and a half
later, three Croatians hijacked an SAS airliner, holding the

passengers hostage at the Malmö airport until the assassins were released from their Swedish prisons and guaranteed safe conduct on the plane to Spain. The Swedes reacted with quiet horror. The Yugoslav government reacted by enlisting more informers. And the Yugoslav *invandrare* reacted by disclaiming one another. The situation was worst in Gothenburg and Malmö, where most of the Croatians in Sweden work, but even in Södertälje, where there are only a few Croatian families, the Yugoslavs are fearful and withdrawn now, and most of them would rather be lonely than do anything that might attract attention to themselves. They are suspicious of one another and nervous about Swedes, who they are certain will turn against them if there is more trouble, and they generally refuse to say a word about Yugoslav politics to anyone they have not known and trusted for twenty or thirty years at home.

Franc and Ema Mlinarič, who live on the third floor of Predrag's entry, drive Saturdays to the Slovene Club in Stockholm and have a fine time dancing and talking, but the only people they see in Södertälje are other Slovenians. They say they have nothing in common with most of the Yugoslavs in Vikingabyn anyway. They come from families that owned a lot of land once, and Ema is a violinist and Franc a statistician with a university degree. At home, ten years ago, Franc Mlinarič was planning director for a large state factory, but he lost his job when he and Ema had a Catholic wedding—although they had made a point of using a church a hundred and fifty miles from anyone they knew. Two weeks later the reforms started, and he had no choice but to look for work as a laborer abroad. Once, five years ago at Vikingabyn, the Mlinaričs invited Violeta and Nebojša Teodorović, from the first floor, up for a cup of coffee, but the Teodorvićs never returned the invitation. *They* come from Belgrade, and have a certain official status, Violeta being the lively, beautiful daughter of a martyred partisan. Nebojša himself is an electrician. He lost his job in 1965 and couldn't find another, but he and Violeta want to go home and enjoy life when their children finish Swedish high school, and they do not

intend to jeopardize their future by associating with suspect
Slovenians. That leaves the Blaževski couple—Vera and Meša
—and nobody talks to them because they are peasants from
Macedonia, nearly illiterate, and so frightened and suspicious of
everybody that they can barely bring themselves to go to the
Vikingabyn supermarket. Besides, the Blaževskis are never at
home except to sleep. They have left six children in Macedonia
and are desperately saving for a little house. They work at a factory, packing cartons, from seven in the morning till four in the
afternoon; then they drive for an hour into Stockholm, make the
rounds of twenty-one offices there with a mop and a bucket and
an old vacuum cleaner, and get back to Södertälje at midnight
for a quick, meager supper of bread and soup before they go to
bed. The Blaževskis are Predrag's next-door neighbors, but
Predrag himself has never said more than hello and goodbye to
them. He says that they live like pigs and work like dogs and
are precisely the sort of people who give Swedes the impression
that Yugoslavs are animals. In fact, he suspects that Meša Blaževski is the famous informer of Vikingabyn rumor—just as the
Blaževskis suspect that the informer is Predrag.

In moments of sullen humor, Predrag calls his entry "Yugoslavia." He complains a lot about the Mlinaričs. He says that
the Mlinaričs snub him because they come from Slovenia and
consider themselves Austrian by rights and Yugoslav only by
accident, and he imagines that they regret the events that left
them so embarrassingly and indissolubly associated with people
like him. On the other hand, he says that the Blaževskis, being
Macedonians, embarrass *him*. And he condemns the Teodo-
rovićs, who are as Serbian as he is, but "city Serbian," as he
puts it, for spending their last year's savings on a big new Volvo
instead of putting it away for the flat they want to buy in Belgrade—a gesture that suggests to Predrag that they are insuffi-
ciently miserable away from home. Actually, Predrag is jealous
about the new Volvo. He needs a big new Volvo like that, he
says, to get to work on time. He needs it to transport Darinka
and the three children home in summer. And eventually he will

need it back in Yugoslavia, where a Volvo costs more money than he will ever have. He is not satisfied with his 1967 Peugeot, although it has taken him these past eight years in Sweden to work up to it. His first car in Sweden—which was his first car anywhere—was an old Saab that he got for 100 kronor, patched together, and put toward a 1965 Ford. The Ford, plus 1,000 kronor, got him a fairly serviceable secondhand Audi. And 2,000 kronor and the Audi—along with a demolished Volkswagen he picked up at the site of a crash between Stockholm and Söder-tälje—went for the Peugeot he uses now. He has worked a lot on the Peugeot, and he tries to save for a trade-in on the new Volvo that will be as splendid as Nebojša Teodorović's car.

Predrag is Swedish enough by now to believe that the proper car will redeem his life in Södertälje, just as he is still Serbian enough to believe that the proper house will make a man of him at home. Mornings, from his kitchen window, he scans the parking lots of Vikingabyn and draws his conclusions about his status as a 1967 Peugeot person among 6,000 neighbors whom he does not know. The conclusions depress him all day. He spends a good deal of time at the window lately—thanks to a Swedish doctor, who for a small consideration writes gloomy health reports for foreign workers, he has been on official sick leave from Saab-Scania for the past three months. When Predrag first decided to get sick, there was nothing the matter with him except a bad hangover from some smuggled slivovitz. He was cheerful enough then. He tinkered with his car at a local filling station that rents out space and repair equipment for a few kronor an hour, and he even took on some jobs for neighbors who had seen him there. He likes working on engines, having learned something about them in the Yugoslav Army. In fact, when he first came to Sweden, to work in a factory assembling telephone components, he bragged so much about his skill with engines that his foreman finally took him off the line and put him to work in the yard with the company trucks. But a little experience made Predrag touchy. He brought his copybook to work and filled it with strange diagrams. He started

referring to himself as a "mechanical engineer," refused to take
advice from the factory's mechanics, and managed to damage
two expensive trucks trying to find the sparkplugs—whereupon
he lost his job. Having practiced since then on so many of his
own cars, Predrag is getting a modicum of competence. His
neighbors kept him busy during the first month of his "illness"
—which dates from the morning after the people at Saab-
Scania refused his request for a long extension on next summer's
holiday—and were apparently satisfied. But then he ruined the
brakes on a Volkswagen owned by an American draft resister
who lives in Södertälje and works at a local mill, and though
Predrag blamed the car for the trouble—a cheap hippie car, he
calls it—his mechanic's business fell off sharply. The end came
when a group of teen-age boys looking for some distraction
from the tedium of Vikingabyn broke into the trunk of Predrag's
car and made off with all his tools.

By now Predrag has actually made himself sick brooding. But
by now, too, his doctor is under investigation by the health
services and is reluctant to continue certifying Predrag's stomach trouble, and Predrag knows that it is time to work again. He
is trying to talk his way into a job at the filling station—a
mechanical engineer's job. He does not want to go back to Saab-
Scania, where, he says, his talents are unrecognized. He hates
working on an assembly line—the Swedes call it tempo work—
and he especially hates working with other immigrants, most of
all with other Yugoslavs. He wants to work with Swedes now.
He doesn't like Swedes—according to Predrag, all Swedes are
cold and soulless—and he is unlikely to get to know many,
inasmuch as after eight years abroad he speaks only a rudimen-
tary Swedish, claims he speaks Swedish fluently, and is too vain
to take advantage of a law requiring factories to provide two
hundred and forty hours of on-the-job language instruction to
foreigners. Working with Swedes is a matter of pride for Predrag. He does not want to compete with other Yugoslavs for the
approval of a Swedish boss or a Swedish foreman or even a
Swedish worker, and his solution to the problem is to find a job

where there will be no Yugoslavs except him. Once, years ago, at the telephone-component factory, a Swedish worker ordered Predrag to clean up after him at the end of their shift each evening—and the problem, Predrag says, was not the order, which he immediately agreed to, but the fact that another Yugoslav overheard it, cleaned up for the Swede before Predrag finished with his own work, and in no time was the favorite foreigner.

Predrag has had four factory jobs since then, and has lived in three workers' suburbs, and now, at twenty-nine, he thinks of himself as old and used. He says that he never really wanted to come to Sweden. He says that he could have gone to Austria—except that the pay in Austria was nearly as bad as the pay in Yugoslavia. And he could have gone to Germany—except that he hates Germans, out of respect for his father. His father is another cross that Predrag bears, like his small size and his unrewarded talent. The old man is fanatically old-fashioned, an embarrassment in the new Yugoslavia, but powerful still in his village, by virtue of the fact that thirty-five years ago he fought bravely in the war, was captured, spent time in a German labor camp, and finally made a daring escape that turned him into a local hero. The villagers risked their lives hiding him in barns and attics for three years, and so they have a keen interest in maintaining his importance. Moreover, he is the only man for twenty miles around who can repair their plows properly and make the wheels for their wooden horse carts. When Predrag is drunk, he sometimes talks about the life at his father's house in the days before Grandfather Frost officially replaced Father Christmas. He remembers Christmas Eve, when his mother would scatter hay across the floor, and the children would peep and cluck all night, pretending to be baby chickens. He remembers the feast, right there on the hay, which always ended with a special bread that had fortunes baked inside it—basil leaves for health, pennies for riches, beans for a life of good farming. He remembers the priest blessing the house on his father's *slava*, or name day. And he especially remembers Easter: the Easter

pig roasting on a spit in the garden; the sunrise service at the old
church in the woods behind the village; the children singing on
their way home. But he does not like to talk about these things
when he is sober, because he thinks that modern people will
laugh at him.

Predrag likes to talk about modern things—about the new
factories around the village, about state farms, and about huge
forestries that are seeded by airplanes. At home, summers, he
pays his respects to his father as discreetly as possible, and after
a *slava* or a trip to church he makes the rounds of the three
cafés and proclaims himself a Communist. He tends to associate
Communists with airplanes that plant trees—and also with new
villas and trains to Sweden and American movies and everything
else his father disapproves of. When he was a boy—with four
sisters to tend the family's vegetable fields for him and cart water
for the animals and keep the barn clean—he used to hitch rides
on produce trucks to the market town to look at new machinery
and gadgets on display and ride the new buses. Once, when he
was fifteen, he managed to get as far as Belgrade. He stayed
away for four days, sleeping in parks, sneaking into movies, and
watching planes take off from Belgrade Airport, and he returned
home, famished, to a beating. After that, his father took him
over. At sixteen, he asked to go to town to high school, and the
old man promptly sent him to the bottling factory. When he
came home from the Army and found his sweetheart married to
the tall butcher, his father arranged a marriage for him with a
proper wife.

Predrag says that he met Darinka at a harvest dance, walked
with her for a month, kissed her twice, made appropriate in-
quiries about her family, and then proposed. He does not like to
admit, in Sweden, that his father negotiated for a simple girl
from a tiny hamlet—a girl he assumed would know her duty to
the family and never dream of asking to visit Belgrade. Besides,
Predrag *had* seen Darinka at a harvest dance once, chaperoned
by her mother, three aunts, and a couple of married sisters, and
he had dismissed her immediately as plain and rustic. Mr. Ilić,

however, did not dismiss Darinka Jovanović. He was admittedly distressed by the fact that her father was in the Party and had even banished Father Christmas from his household. But Darinka's father also happened to have a few choice hectares in orchard and raised the best pigs in the area, and Mr. Ilić was willing to overlook his politics after the two had discussed the mutual advantages of transporting Jovanović pigs, on private order, in Ilić horse carts. Between them, they produced the best wedding anyone in the village had seen in years. Predrag, in three shots with an old hunting rifle, managed to split the three apples that were hung by kerchiefs from an oak tree in Darinka's hamlet—thereby proving himself to be a manly bridegroom. Darinka tossed a shaft of wheat securely onto the roof of the Ilić farmhouse—proving *her*self to have the character of a constant wife. There were three days of feasting. People danced to the music of a clarinet, a bass fiddle, and two harmonicas. They vied with each other to present the fattest pig, the richest cake, as a wedding gift. In fact, they all had such a fine time at the wedding that only a few guests thought to inquire why the young couple had returned directly from the village clerk, without a detour through the woods to the old church, and those who did ask concluded that Mr. Ilić, with a practical eye to the prize pigs, was keeping peace with Darinka's father and would see to it soon enough that Darinka became a proper daughter-in-law and a pious wife. He saw to it immediately. When Predrag left his bridal bed the next morning, Darinka was already in the kitchen preparing coffee for her new family. From that day on, she cooked and served their meals. She remained standing while the family ate, out of respect for Predrag's mother. And every night, out of respect for his father, she washed Mr. Ilić's grimy feet. She never once asked to go to Belgrade. But she begged to go to Sweden, and now that she is in Sweden she intends to live there until she can live in her own house in Yugoslavia.

Darinka Ilić is not at all plain. She is a small, graceful girl, and she has clear gray eyes and a tender, delicate, round face. She says that she *feels* plain because Predrag talks so much

about the beautiful women he might have married. And she
thinks that she looks plain because to save money in Södertälje
she usually wears jeans instead of the flowered dresses that, as a
married woman, she would wear at home. Actually, in her jeans
and a plaid shirt from Domus, with her straight brown hair
pulled back with a ribbon, Darinka looks more like a young
Swedish student from the country than like a foreign factory
worker of twenty-five who is pregnant with her fourth child. But
there is no one in Sweden to reassure her. Predrag, in his dol-
drums, tells her that she is too simple for him, and he is beginning to complain that without the burden of a wife and children
he would have been able to make something of himself, to save
money and to study—to be a mathematician or a famous mechanical engineer. Sometimes she agrees with him. She makes
1,500 kronor a month after taxes, working at a small factory,
but keeping her two girls at the Vikingabyn day-care center after
school costs a few hundred kronor every month, and the Swedish woman with whom she leaves her little boy, Radislav, insists
that the government does not cover her expenses, and Darinka
has to pay her something every week to make sure that Radislav
gets fed. Darinka would like to find a job that pays more. She
has heard that Astra Pharmaceutical employs a lot of the *invandrare* women in Södertälje, and at higher salaries than the
other factories, but the work at Astra, matching pills and
serums to complicated labels, requires a certain fluency in Swedish, and Predrag refuses to let her sign up for her two hundred
and forty hours of instruction. He does not want to suffer the
humiliation of a wife who speaks Swedish better than he does.
And he does not want her talking to Swedish women, compar-
ing lives and husbands—getting ideas, he says, that he should
help with the dishes, mind the children, degrade himself by
wheeling a baby carriage around the parking lot; ideas that he
should buy her fancy clothes and take her to restaurants and
discothèques and movies. There was a time when Predrag considered taking Darinka to a movie in the Klara quarter, which is
Stockholm's version of London's Soho and does a lively busi-

ness with Turks and Yugoslavs now that the Swedes are getting bored with pornography. Predrag said that, being a modern man, he wanted a modern wife who "knew things," but when Darinka agreed enthusiastically, he changed his mind and told her that she had better stop thinking about lewd Swedish things and pay some attention to keeping house for him like a decent Serbian wife and bringing up his children properly.

Nine years ago, when Slavko Jovanović promised Darinka to Predrag, Darinka said no. She cried for a week, she says. She demanded a husband from her own hamlet. She insisted that the boys she knew were good enough for her—that any of the boys she knew would do. In the end she agreed, but it was only out of fatigue and duty. She liked her life at home with her parents and her sisters, tending the family fields and feeding the cows and the goats, the oxen and the prize pigs. She says that at four she was already a farmer—running behind her father's horse plow, scattering corn and wheat seed for the next harvest. At five, she was in charge of the oxen, two cows, three calves, and a splendid sow with eleven piglets, and her father had fitted her out with a yoke that had a little bucket at each end, so that she could draw water from the well beside their house and carry it to the barn, two kilometers into the countryside. Soon she was carting sixty kilos of water to the barn three times every day. She was up at five o'clock and in bed by eight at the latest, and she says there was no time in between to daydream about a husband or a life any different from the one she led. She stayed in school for eight years, and she might have gone on to high school in the market town, but, she says, she could not bear to abandon her pigs to anybody else. She was proud of the Jovanović pigs, and she revered her father, who had managed to become such an important person in the Party and was so prosperous that he could afford to hire ten workers every August to help the family with the harvest. She has never discovered how, or why, he chose Predrag for her. She had heard from her married sisters that Predrag was vain and lazy, that he had wanted a girl in his own village and had agreed to her only as a second choice. But she knew nothing at the time about Predrag's strange father, about having to stand through dinner and having to wash an old man's filthy feet, about the clamorous piety that existed in the Ilić household.

When Predrag moved to Sweden, in the fall of 1968, Darinka was left at home as a kind of hostage to his father, who objected to his going anywhere and had consented, in the end, only on the assurance of the village priest that a boy like Predrag would miss the services of a young wife too keenly to stay away for very long. The truth was that Predrag was longing for adventure. He ignored Darinka's tears and her pleas, her new passport and her timid seductions, saying that he would be able to save more money for their villa by living a frugal bachelor life with the two villagers who already had a place in Södertälje and had got him his job contract with the telephone-component company. At the train station he embraced his father for the first time in a year. He left Yugoslavia with a week's wages in his pocket, two smoked sausages, and a bottle of fine slivovitz from the Jovanović orchard. The bottle rolled off his lap and broke during a screeching curve in Austria, and he ate the two sausages while looking out at Germany. The money went for a cab to Södertälje, because Predrag, dazed and sleepy after two days and two nights in crowded second-class compartments, missed his stop and landed in a small town he had never heard of, asking for help in a language that nobody but the Yugoslav cabdriver understood. His adventure began then. His friends from home had a room in a shabby boarding house where thirty *invandrare* waited for Södertälje's latest suburb to open, and the two of them kept a record of every krona Predrag cost them, including the food and beer that they consumed in quantity in his company. When he had worked for a month, they took his paycheck, having added to their costs some 200 kronor, which was the entire rent for the room they shared. They also took him to a tiny Yugoslav establishment that specialized in illegal gambling and in serving liquor without a license after hours. It was raided—and closed—one night while Predrag was in the process of winning a thousand kronor. And the day it opened again, under another name and at another address, Predrag walked into a fight that started when a Bosnian wanted to change television channels, and ended as a battle between Serbs and Croats that put three people in the hospital, Predrag among them.

Predrag tried discothèques next. In a cheap discothèque in Stockholm, he met the only real friend he has made in Sweden —a Finn with a job coiling tungsten wires for a light-bulb company—and the two of them made the rounds nights, gesturing wildly at each other until embarrassment forced them to learn enough Swedish to begin to talk. They were out celebrating the news that Predrag was a father when Predrag's friend introduced him to a pretty Finnish cleaning woman, who caught his fancy, and who eventually took him home to bed. Predrag was proud and horrified. By now he was certain that he was leading the most modern and manly life possible, but, he says, he was also spending all his villa money—in restaurants in Södertälje, since he could not imagine a man cooking his own meals, and in Stockholm on a Finnish girlfriend with a passion for discothèques and an apparently equal enthusiasm for marriage. Their romance lasted a month and cost a thousand kronor. It ended forever after Predrag ran into a ragged, bleary-eyed Serbian from his own village, who collapsed over a beer and explained, upon reviving, that he had just married for the third time and was consequently working day and night, at the hardest, dirtiest jobs in Sweden, to pay for *three* villas—one for each of the wives he had abandoned and one for the wife he had now.

Darinka arrived in Sweden three weeks later. Predrag's letter demanding that she come at once had taken a week to reach the village. Weaning the baby took another. Then Darinka had to carry the baby through a snowstorm to her parents' hamlet because the Ilićs, who were furious, had refused to keep the child for her if she went away. And her father had to spend a few days in the market town looking for an honest couple on

their way to jobs in Sweden to chaperon Darinka on the train
ride north. In Södertälje, at first, Darinka spent her time alone
in a dark basement bedroom of the old boarding house, which
was the only room the landlord could spare. Nothing else in
Sweden depressed her as much as the dark, she says. It was
dark inside, and when she and Predrag moved from Södertälje
to a two-room apartment in the New Town of Skärholmen, she
discovered that it was usually dark outside, too. Her first excur-
sions outside were to the supermarket—Predrag would give her
money, and she would present it at the checkout counter and get
her change back and a receipt for Predrag without having to say
a word. Her first job was a cleaning job at a motel near Skärholmen, where a crisp manager drove her to helpless tears, leading
her from room to room and pointing at mops and pails and dust-
bins, apparently convinced that no one from Yugoslavia had
ever washed a floor or emptied garbage. Darinka hated Skärholmen, which is a monstrous suburb halfway down the highway
from Södertälje to Stockholm, with nothing in sight but factories
and speeding cars. And she missed her baby. Predrag says that
she kept him awake nights sobbing and moaning over the baby's
picture, and that whenever he did manage to fall asleep she
would promptly wake him and begin again. He says that he had
no choice, finally, but to bring the baby back after their first trip
home, that summer. He persuaded Darinka's mother to come
along and help them, and Mrs. Jovanović installed herself on a
mattress in the foyer, kept house when Darinka worked, looked
after one baby and then, in a few months' time, delivered another while waiting for Predrag to get home from the factory
and take Darinka to the hospital. Having never before been
farther from her husband and her pigs than the market town,
Mrs. Jovanović was so terrified in Sweden that she refused to
leave the apartment at all—that is, until she developed stomach
trouble and demanded to be put on the next train to Yugoslavia,
with her ticket pinned to her coat and her passport sewn inside
her black kerchief. Darinka has had three jobs since her mother
left. For a while she worked as a maid in a tourist hotel in

Stockholm, commuting half an hour each way by subway and trying to make friends with a clique of Rumanian women who worked there, too. But the hours were long and erratic, and after she stayed home sick for a month once, she had to start all over again at the bottom of a complicated cleaners' hierarchy, without a regular schedule and her own rooms to clean—just filling in nights and weekends for women who were out. She worked in a Stockholm dairy next, on a line in a hot, poorly ventilated room, watching machines pour milk into cartons. That ended with a move back to Södertälje, and a third child. She says that she did not really want the expense of another child, but Predrag, after two daughters, insisted on a son. And now that he has one he wants another, in case the first turns out to be stupid or unhealthy or does anything to disappoint him later on.

B y now Darinka is used to Sweden. She watches Predrag sulk and listens to his complaints, but she has learned not to pay much attention to his moods. Little by little, she has taken over their lonely life in Södertälje and tried to make it as pleasant as she can. It was Darinka who went to the Invandrarbyrå—the Immigrant Service Bureau—in Södertälje, used its interpreters, saw its advisers and its social workers about nurseries and day-care centers and housing, and even arranged Predrag's first interview at Saab-Scania. It was Darinka, too, who found the apartment in Vikingabyn where they live now. The apartment costs 650 kronor a month, which is a lot of money for them, but they have three rooms—a living room, a bedroom, and a kitchen—and the five Ilićs sleep together on cots in the small bedroom just to keep their first living room in Sweden beautiful. Darinka is especially happy about the living room. She regrets sometimes that she does not have a walnut wall unit opposite the couch, the way Swedish families on television do. She has heard that the Teodorović family have a fine wall unit, where they display their liquor bottles and commemorative

plates from Tito's birthdays and crystal bowls of expensive wax
fruit, and that the Mlinaričs have a wall unit, too, full of important books and records, as well as a stereo set and a copper
stand, on wheels, for their plants. She would like some pictures
to go with her Walt Disney print of Snow White and the Seven
Dwarfs, which came free with a family-size box of a new
detergent, and which Predrag has referred to sourly as "Darinka's Picasso" ever since he watched the painter's funeral on the
evening news. She used to bother Predrag about pictures, but
when she came home from work one night and found that he
had hung a calendar of the Holy Family on one side of the
television set and a nude centerfold from *Playboy* on the other,
she stopped. She says now that the room is fine without pictures. It has a big color-television set that Predrag brought home
one day last year, barely used and for a good price, and two
standing lamps and a pale wooden coffee table that Darinka
herself got years ago, when the hotel where she worked was
changing furniture. And since Christmas its bare walls have
been redeemed completely by a bright new orange couch and
matching club chairs, which Darinka and Predrag bought at a
discount department store near Stockholm for a down payment
of 400 kronor, with two years, at 12 percent interest, to pay the
rest.

Darinka would like to have a friend—someone besides
Predrag's Finnish friend, who comes to drink sometimes—to
visit her in her new living room. The two Yugoslavs with whom
Predrag lived so long ago are gone now. So is a woman from
Darinka's factory who used to stop by after work, once they had
established the fact that their married sisters were neighbors in
the market town. And so is a young couple from Predrag's
village who used to come on Sundays. The women would cook
together and the men would play poker, and often, in the spring,
they would all drive off with their children for a picnic on the
lake. But last year the couple got better jobs and moved to
Tensta, on the far side of Stockholm, and since the Ilićs have no

telephone, there is no way for the two families to stay in touch. The living room is now mostly given over to the children. The little girls—Cveta and Slavica, six and seven years old and already in school, mornings, and learning Swedish—come home from Vikingabyn's day-care center, where they play, afternoons, and watch television till bedtime, and Radislav, who, at three, is spoiled and ornery, sprawls on the orange couch making a racket on his toy harmonium. Darinka spends most of her time at home in the kitchen, cooking meals for them, while Predrag, at the table by the window, counts Volvos in the parking lot and doodles in his copybook.

One night not long ago, Darinka was at the stove, stirring a paprikash of beef, peppers, and shredded carrots—flushed and plump in her plaid shirt and the let-out jeans she saves for the first months of a new pregnancy. Predrag, at the table in his pink shirt, was pouring himself a glass of slivovitz. He did not pour any slivovitz for Darinka, because he does not believe in wasting liquor on women, but he was in relatively good humor, having just come home from an encouraging meeting with the boss at the filling station where he wants to work.

"Eleven kronor," he said. "That's what a liter of slivovitz costs in Belgrade. Here, a liter costs fifty kronor." He raised his glass and gave a rueful *Skål*. "The Swedes do not know how to live. *That's* their problem. Look at Stockholm. Where are the parks in Stockholm? Belgrade has twice as many parks as Stockholm."

Darinka glanced at him. "You always tell *me* that Belgrade is so terrible. Terrible noise. Terrible traffic."

"Traffic, yes. But more parks, more nurseries for the children, more real food. Here in Sweden, you open the refrigerator and it's all frozen. Here, everything is sandwiches and coffee, sandwiches and coffee." Predrag thought for a moment. "I would like to see a Swedish wedding. Ha! I will bet a liter of slivovitz that at a Swedish wedding all you get is sandwiches and coffee."

Darinka laughed. "There is enough betting in this house already," she said. "Predrag is a Swede now. He plays the football pool. And the money we need for our villa—all gone."

"Six kronor a week—what does that mean?" Predrag grumbled.

"Don't lie. It's thirty or a hundred kronor."

"Twenty-five, maybe," Predrag said. "Besides, I'm waiting to *win* the football pool. Then I'm going home. I have figured it out in here"—he tapped his copybook—"by mathematics. Every week that I bet, I have a better possibility of winning. But if I don't bet at all, then there is no possibility."

Darinka shrugged, and Predrag, pleased with himself, reached for Radislav, who had wandered in dragging the harmonium. The boy ducked and ran to his mother, shrieking for supper.

"He comes home so very hungry," Darinka said.

"Well, what does that Swedish woman feed him? Soup. You pay, and she spends the money on her own children and gives my son soup. If I were that woman, I would give him steak." Predrag banged on his chest and then went on, "No Serbian would let a child go hungry. It would break the heart of a Serbian to see a child crying for food."

"Serbians are liars," Darinka remarked. "They promise you one thing and do another."

"Here they promise you everything and do *nothing*," Predrag interrupted. "They have no hearts, these Swedes. They try to be helpful, but in their souls they are very bad. They put ads in the paper: Good job. Easy job. Swede wanted. They don't know how it is to be a stranger. They never invite you home. They think you are an animal. They think that you never went to school, that you know nothing. I would like to take a Swede to Yugoslavia and leave him there without help, with no way to talk, no way to understand instructions."

Darinka remarked that there was a Swedish woman at her factory who was very nice, very helpful. "She had a birthday last month," Darinka said. "She gave me a piece of her cake. Now we take our coffee together, like people—like people on the same level. She talks about things like work and food and family—"

Predrag scowled. "But has she ever invited you to her home? Tell me."

"Maybe I will ask her to *my* home," Darinka said. She had picked up Radislav and was jiggling him on one arm while she stirred her stew with the other. "You see, I can understand Swedish now, but I still cannot speak so well, and she helps me. She tells me that I should go to classes at the factory, or go to night school."

"*I* would like more than anything to go to school," Predrag said. "In mathematics."

"You can begin with Swedish," Darinka told him.

Predrag ignored her. "That is my dream—to go to school. But, of course, there is no money for me to study." He sighed. "I have a family."

"We are in the way," Darinka said pleasantly, depositing Radislav on his father's lap and beginning to set the table. She has heard this before, and refuses to argue.

Predrag shrugged. "Early marriage," he said. "It's our habit. A man is a man at twenty, when he leaves the Army. It's a hard life, our Army. Not like in Sweden, where you have long hair and a beard and go home on weekends. And a *girl* of twenty. Ha! Who will want her? A man will look at her and ask, 'Why did nobody want her before?' "

"I have a friend who went home to Yugoslavia at twenty-eight, and *she* got married," Darinka announced. And then she said, "It is not so bad, the Swedish way. It's—economical."

Predrag glared. "Like animals—that's the Swedish way. Living together like animals. Waiting till thirty to get married. When you marry at thirty, you're an old man. But me—when my son is fifteen, I'll be a young man. We can chase girls together."

Darinka chuckled. "He wants to chase girls, with all the problems he has already. This morning, in Södertälje, they put a fifty-kronor parking ticket on his car—for the second time."

"I'd like to go to that Palme," Predrag said. "That Prime Minister. I'd like to ask him, 'How does it harm you if a sick man's car sits on the street for a few extra minutes?' "

Darinka laughed again. "Predrag is a sick man. He refuses to take the pills the doctor gave him for his stomach because he knows that if he takes the pills he cannot drink, and so—"

"All these problems," Predrag said, furious. "It wasn't like this in Yugoslavia. I know that always life has problems. But not like these. At home, there is always the grandmother to look after the children. Here, nobody cares about the children. They let them do whatever they want in school. They leave them alone at home, let them run around, never hit them. It's too free here, and they don't care. This Swedish woman who takes Radislav—she doesn't care for anything but the money. And even her—it took me a month to find her. I stood in a line. I said, 'You must help. My wife works, and there is no room yet for my son at the day-care center.' I almost fell on my knees to get that selfish woman."

Darinka nodded. "When I came here, I sat in that dark cellar, and I was always thinking, What kind of country is this—this *dark* country, where no one is friends? Predrag's father had told me that the life was bad in Sweden. He said that Predrag would come home a drunk, a bandit, like the Swedes. But that was not the problem. It was the Swedes who thought that Yugoslavs were drunks and bandits. I know that now. At work, there is always talk about the foreigners—how the foreigners call in sick, sit at home, do nothing, and take the Swedish benefits. I ask them, 'How do you know?' They say, 'We don't know—we just think it must be true.' And I say, 'To think is not enough.' "

"They are not the people to talk about us," Predrag muttered. "The Swedes are not so quick. The Swedes don't like to work so much." He put Radislav on the floor, poured himself some more slivovitz, and drank it down. "It's hard to live here," he said. "My best years! When I think of it, I ask myself, 'Is it worth it?' I can't stay here much longer—that's sure. I'll lose my nerve."

Darinka shook her head. "No, *I* would stay here now. Not forever, but maybe for a long while. There are no jobs for us at home, and even if you find a job it's hard and dirty. Here, I have a good job, a good flat. There, I have Predrag's parents. I get up first in the morning to make the fire, make the coffee—" She smiled suddenly. "*My* father washed his own feet."

Predrag turned away and stared out the window. "I will join the Party when I get home," he said finally. "They offered it to me. I told them that I would come when I had saved a hundred thousand kronor for my children—"

Darinka, carrying plates to the table, burst out laughing.

"Well, forty or fifty thousand kronor. Listen, I don't like to stay here, but we go home summers for a month and spend a lot of money, so we must come back, earn more—"

"We go for a month, I sit in the house, and *he* spends money," Darinka broke in. "So I get restless. I go to our villa and wipe the dust of a year off my furniture. I dust my cabinet. It is a beautiful cabinet—wood, with lacquer to make it shiny. It is a—a *display* cabinet. I keep my china figures in it. China flowers and little china people. And my platters from the seaside. Beautiful platters, all covered with corals and starfish and sea urchins and oyster shells." Darinka stopped, took her stew from the stove and set it on the table, and went on, wiping her forehead on her plaid sleeve. "Then I plant flowers in the garden. Red roses, and white and yellow asters. I plant trees—apple and pear and plum trees. But then I am restless again. It's enough for me—one month. After a month, I want to go back to Sweden." She laughed, almost merry. "I am not used to sitting at home like a Serbian wife anymore. And I tell Predrag, 'Now that we have gone through all this; now that we can manage by ourselves, express ourselves, understand things; now that all this trouble is past, trouble with work, trouble with friends taking our money—we *could* go home, but why not stay now for a while and begin to live?' "

Darinka called the girls to supper.

"It's a kind of habit—Sweden," Predrag said, despondent. "You get used to it."

THE
UGANDA
ASIANS
(1974)

Back home, in a small village of Asian families in the Uganda bush, Akbar Hassan's neighbors called him a big capitalist man. The finest shop in the village belonged to Akbar. He had built two large houses for himself, and he collected rent on two others and on an assortment of shacks and storage huts that he had picked up in the district. Three thousand Africans from the local tribe brought their produce to his food "cooperative." He had a license to transport wheat through his district to Ruanda, maize to the Congo, and coffee beans to the big processing factory in Kampala. And in all these projects he enjoyed the protection, and the referrals, of an important government minister—that is, until General Idi Amin Dada took over the country, in January of 1971, and the unfortunate minister was hacked to death and his head deposited on a post across the road from Akbar's front door. But what really made Akbar a big capitalist man were the five elegant Mercedes trucks he used for transport. Akbar loved his Mercedes trucks. He kept them parked in the family compound, guarded at night by two huge dogs and a Banyankole tribesman with a murderous past. He polished them himself and tuned their engines. Over the years, he even started to entrust his other business to assistants so that he would always be free to drive off in his favorite on safari.

When Akbar came to England, in the fall of 1972, along with some twenty-seven thousand other Uganda Asian settlers who had been given three months to leave their country, he walked into the biggest Mercedes-Benz garage that he could find in London and asked the manager for a mechanic's job. "I am calling on Mercedes people, and I am saying, 'You know, Mr. Manager, I am seventeen years your customer,'" Akbar recalls. Akbar speaks three Indian languages and three African languages, but his English is terrible. Most of the people he comes

across in London think that there is something not quite respectful about the way he talks to them. "And the manager is
saying thank you, but I am having to take test in changing
plugs. Well, I start to laughing. 'Changing plugs?' I telling him.
'I no need to changing plugs. I know too much, too much
Mercedes. In Uganda, I am called the father of Mercedes. In
Uganda, when I fix Mercedes, I am changing whole engine in
five minutes. In Uganda, I am having servant with me just to
open doors and hand me tools.'" Akbar is certain that the
manager didn't understand him. He waited a week, and then
went back to the garage. He had practiced his English, and
this time he tried harder to make the manager understand. He
told the manager that every year, in Uganda, he had traded in
his old trucks for the latest models. He told him that there were
a hundred Asians in the towns of Masaka and Kampala who
had bought Mercedes cars and lorries on his advice. He told
him that now, when he had lost everything, it was only right
that the finest Mercedes-Benz garage in London should offer
him a job. When the manager showed him out, Akbar became
despondent. He had thought till then that Allah would not for-
sake such a big capitalist man, the elected president of three
hundred and seventy-one Muslim cousins from the Gulf of
Kutch whose fathers and grandfathers had settled in Uganda.
But now he told his wife, Rabia, that his life was over. He said
that Allah gave only one chance to a man in life and that
General Amin Dada must have taken his, and used it up, in
Africa.

Rabia says that for a long time nothing cheered Akbar or
changed his mind or gave him hope. They were living then in a
run-down four-room house in the outlying London village of
Southall, along with their six children, Akbar's parents, and
nineteen of his relatives, and on the door there was a health-
department warning that some of the family would have to
move or everyone would be evicted. But even after Akbar found
a furnished house, on a tidy street, just for his wife and children

and himself, he would not believe Rabia when she said that Allah might be giving him a second chance. Akbar brooded through his first, long London winter. He put Rabia in purdah. He slept alone, on the plastic couch in their new sitting room. The children began to avoid him, because he got violent when they made noise. Then, one morning in early spring, Akbar woke up looking relatively happy. For the first time since he had come to London, he took his tea and chapatty with his five sons. He left the house, asking politely if Abdullah, the oldest, would like to join him. And he appeared that evening, with Abdullah beside him, at the wheel of a dilapidated gray 1957 Mercedes-Benz sedan. Rabia has never discovered where Akbar got the money to buy the car—it cost £ 100—but she often tells him that he should have used that money for the family. He brings home no more than £ 27 or £ 28 a week, working double shifts, six and sometimes seven days, at a service station in Hammersmith. The rent on his house is £ 18, which leaves him only £ 10, at most, for feeding Rabia and the children, paying the electric bill, and running the gas heater in the sitting room. Even Abdullah, who loves the Mercedes, told him that morning to buy a small car, a Fiat or a Mini, because a big Mercedes would use up too much gasoline. But Akbar says he *needed* a Mercedes. He still cannot afford the gasoline for it. The Mercedes sits, unused, on the road outside the house—there is a fiine view of it from the sitting-room window—but it comforts Akbar just by being there. "You know, in Uganda I am leaving everything, but I not want to be leaving Mercedes," Akbar says sometimes, at the window. "No, I must to see Mercedes. For me, to see Mercedes is to think that I am not losing everything."

The English still call them Asians, using the old imperial rhetoric that did not distinguish among any people east of Europe. They came, in fact, from what are now India and Pakistan. Some of them are Hindu, some, like Akbar, are Muslim,

some Sikh, Ismaili, or even Christian. And there are still a
million of them living in the countries of East and South Africa
that once were under British rule.* They started coming to East
Africa centuries before the British. A thousand years ago Indian
merchants lived in Zanzibar, and traders from Karachi and
Bombay were sailing regularly to Madagascar. In time, they
crossed from Zanzibar to Bagamoyo, on the mainland, and
eventually to hundreds of trading centers up and down the
coast. By 1860, 6,000 Asians had settled in the ports of East
Africa, and by 1900 they controlled the wholesale trade along a
two-thousand-mile stretch of coastline. But by then the British,
in claiming India, had also claimed the services of Indians in
Africa. Britain sent them inland, toward Uganda, in the eighteen-nineties—first as a regiment to subdue the area, and then
as coolie labor to lay a railroad from the port of Mombasa to
the shores of Lake Victoria. English settlers were already stak-
ing claims to farms in what is now Kenya, with its great, cool
plateaus and rich plantation soil, but none of them would ven-
ture up into the land that has become Uganda. It was known
then as the White Man's Grave. Europeans who went there and
managed to avoid the lions usually ended up dying of malaria.
But the British were determined, nonetheless, to build themselves a railroad, to secure their new territory and extend their
trade. They assumed at first that Africans would build the railroad for them. They discovered instead that the coastal Africans they tried to hire found the thought of such hard work
revolting—the Railroad Commission, in its reports, liked to
complain about the extraordinary unresponsiveness of the African to inducements of money—and so Asians got the job.
Asians, it was reasoned, were dark and could be considered a
people born to hardship. Asians could put up with the lions and
the fevers that had given the English so much trouble. Asians
could be shipped cheaply and conveniently across the Arabian
Sea to Mombasa. Asians worked hard, and poverty had made

* This is still true.

them tractable. And Asians could be got for far less money than almost anybody else.

Recruitment began in the Punjab as soon as a Colonial Office law against the exploitation of coolie labor overseas was temporarily abolished. Some of the Asians went willingly; some were coerced by native officials who got paid off according to the number of coolies they produced; some of the younger men were peddled by their starving fathers. All told, 32,000 Punjabi coolies sailed for Mombasa, and many of them died in the seven years it took to build the Uganda Railway. But they had succeeded in opening up the bush for thousands of other Asians, who soon followed them to Africa in the remote hope of a better life. These Asians came from Karachi and from towns and villages down the west coast of India, through Kutch and Gujarat, to Bombay—poor artisans and merchants crammed into schooners and indentured to the railroad or to rich Asian traders in Mombasa and Nairobi who were planning to send them inland to open *dukas*, or shops, as outlets for the merchants' goods. Akbar's father, who had been driving a horse cart in a Kutch village, came to Africa at thirteen, in the early days of the Uganda Protectorate, to work for a Kutchi trader. He stayed in Mombasa for a few years, at one of the trader's shops, and then he was sent off to Uganda, with 300 shillings in his pocket and instructions to open his own *duka* in a clearing some sixty miles by foot from the nearest town. When he got there, five months later, four other Kutchi merchants were already building *dukas* in the clearing, and a Seventh-Day Adventist missionary from Des Moines, Iowa, had settled down to edify the local tribe. Akbar's father spent the next half century in the clearing. Over the years he saw the missionary send to Iowa for assistants, and each of the merchants send to Kutch for a wife, who then produced a huge family. Their settlement became a thriving village. But no Africans except the household servants ever lived there. Out in the bush, the Asians kept the "color bar." They worked desperately at making money, and, in their isolation, they became narrow. The British, who managed to exploit them and ignore them at the same time, despised the Asians. The Africans despised them, because they stayed in their shops all day instead of enjoying themselves and letting their women do the work for them. Actually, the Asians shaped Uganda. They spread their *dukas* across a thousand-mile wilderness. They connected the tribes with the towns, the farmers with the new factories, the remote chieftains with the British in Kampala. They were the labor, and then the skilled labor, and then the businessmen and the contractors. They did the digging, the building, the putting together and patching up for the whole country. Their sons were the clerks and accountants in the banks and offices and the civil service. The sons of the Ismailis, who had "Westernized" themselves on the Aga Khan's orders, became the country's doctors, lawyers, and engineers.

A few of the Asians got rich. People who were able to buy property before laws were passed reserving the land for Africans developed plantations for coffee, sugar, and tobacco. The men in two Hindu families got to be multimillionaires, with plantation land and factories all over East Africa. Akbar's father, who started out with a two-room sheet-metal hut in the clearing, ended up with a twelve-room family compound, which may have lacked plumbing, electricity, and even water, but boasted a sitting room so vast that for a time it doubled as the village mosque. The majority of Uganda Asians, though, were rich by no one's standards except the standards of the Africans around them and of the starving families they had left behind in Kutch and Gujarat. They were the government bookkeepers, making £40 a month, and the thousands of *dukawallahs* with inventories stocked on credit and worth a couple of hundred pounds at most. To the Africans, however, they were the strangers who had taken the country. They did, in one sense, take Uganda. There were never more than a few thousand British in the country—people who had come mainly to administer the government and run the Army—but by the time of Uganda's independence, in 1962, there were over 60,000 Asian settlers. Asians employed some 500,000 of the country's 10 million

Africans. Asians controlled the daily commerce of the country. They managed the working capital. And they kept the towns and cities for themselves.

Still, it was the British who really owned Uganda. Three British banks controlled Uganda's commercial-bank assets. The big insurance companies, with their finance capital, were British. And the important wholesale trade in raw materials, machinery, and goods for heavy industry was in the hands of businessmen in London. The British kept most of their economic power after independence, though few Africans outside Kampala saw many Englishmen once the old district commissioners went home, and in any event British capital and international-trade arrangements had always been a little remote, as concepts, for a Baganda or a Lango tribesman to understand or contrast with his own poverty. The *bwana*—the boss—he was likely to see each day was Asian, an Asian with his shop, his driver, his native servants, his furtive women, his pruderies, and his peculiar food. Asians were easy to blame for native poverty. They were clannish and insecure. They paid their workers badly, as they themselves had been underpaid by British bosses. They drove their servants with hard work and long hours, made them pay for their own meals, and claimed that Africans were too dirty to touch the family food. Most of them refused to share their skills—and their opportunities, when they had opportunities—with anyone but other Asians, and preferably with Asians in their own families. Their politics began and ended in their pockets. They liked Julius Nyerere, in Tanzania, because he left Tanzanian Asians alone to go about their business of making money, and they liked Ian Smith, in Rhodesia, because he left Asians alone, too. In fact, most of them liked Amin when he seized power because Amin changed a new nationalization law that would have compelled Asian businesses to turn back 60 percent of their profits to the government. "I not understanding. I am thinking this Amin is very good for Asians," Akbar still says. Amin, on one of his district tours, had stopped at Akbar's house, demanding dinner, and Akbar, who not only

fed him very well but also presented him with a gold ring that
he had just bought for himself from the best goldsmith in the
town of Masaka, had assumed his future was secure until Amin
was overthrown or murdered and the next ruler came along. He
says now that Amin must have gone crazy when he decided to
expel the Asians. Akbar has never unpacked the plaid suitcase
that holds the family documents, and he admits, sometimes, that
he likes to keep the documents in order on the chance that Amin
recovers and calls the Asians back.

Most Asians still believe that they will be going home some-
day. They find it much harder to believe that they are surviving
the English climate than to believe that they will not see Africa
again. Some of them even refused to believe Amin's expulsion
order. The flights from Entebbe were almost empty for the first
six weeks of the twelve-week deadline, and most of the people
on them were unmarried girls or women with young children.
Akbar sent Rabia and the children to England at the end of
August. He stayed on with his father and left the country on the
last day of the decree. He arrived at Heathrow Airport with
£50 in his wallet—£50 was the total exit allowance for an
Asian family—and a notarized statement of his seized and
abandoned assets, which came to £51,000. He was carrying the
plaid suitcase and a bundle of eleven Japanese transistor radios
he had just picked up at a clearance sale in Kampala and had
managed to take with him by making the soldier who searched
him at departure a present of his last Mercedes truck.

No one in England, and especially no one in London, wanted
the Uganda Asians. When the Asians came, there were already 1.5 million New Commonwealth—"New Commonwealth"
is the official British way of saying "colored"—immigrants in
England, and half of them were living in London, where jobs
are scarce and thousands of people in every residential borough
are on waiting lists for council homes. Enoch Powell had been
busy making racism politically respectable—though Powell him-

self had encouraged West Indian immigration in the early sixties, when he was Minister of Health, and hospitals in London were recruiting West Indian nurses and paramedics to ease their staff shortages. And the National Front, England's neo-Nazi party, was polling good percentages of the vote in local urban elections, soothing the English worker with visions of a pure-white island from which all his troubles had departed with the unwelcome immigrants. There had been race fighting in some of the workers' boroughs, and firebombings of Asian shops and houses. Asians already living in London were afraid to walk alone at night because of the white gangs who called themselves Paki-Bashers and spent their time stalking Pakistani immigrants.

Even the law was bending to accommodate the new intolerance. The Law Lords, in the House of Lords, sat that January on the case of an Asian whose application for membership in his local Conservative club had been rejected, and ruled, in effect, that private clubs were legally entitled to bar members on ethnic grounds. And while liberals in the country claimed to be scandalized by the decision, most white Britons considered it their first victory in years. The arrival of the Uganda Asians, coming when it did, fostered a kind of panic politics. Only the National Front could pretend that some 30,000 refugees were a threat to the security of English labor. But in the rest of East Africa there were still over 100,000 Asians holding United Kingdom passports, everyone knew their days were numbered, and people reasoned that once England had taken in the Uganda refugees so quickly, Kenya and Tanzania would start sending their Asians up to England, too. The English, in fact, had been trying for years to curtail Asian immigration from East Africa. The Commonwealth Immigrants Act of 1968, written by Harold Wilson's first Labour Government, restricted the entry rights of citizens whose parents or grandparents were not United Kingdom subjects—which meant, in effect, black or Asian citizens —to a worldwide yearly quota of 1,500 families. The Conservatives, in 1971, had to expand the quota to 3,000 families be-

cause the various "Africanization" schemes in East Africa were
leaving so many of the British Asian settlers destitute.* But at
the same time the government negotiated a yearly grant of
£ 11.5 million to Kenya—55,000 Asians with British nationality
live in Kenya—which was supposed to assist the transfer and
distribution of white plantation land to Kenyan farmers but was
also apparently contingent on a pledge from Jomo Kenyatta,
Kenya's President, that as long as the money kept coming,
Asians in Kenya would be allowed to stay.†

The English, of course, suspected that in a crisis they would
have no option but to accept their own passport holders. So did
Amin, who was running out of money for his Army and had
decided to solve his problem simply by appropriating all the
Asian capital. Within a few weeks of the expulsion order—
Amin announced it, after a prophetic dream, on August 4, 1972
—Prime Minister Edward Heath said that in the case of British
citizens from Uganda he would waive the New Commonwealth
quota for the year. At the time, no one in England could estimate how many Asians would be coming, or even how many
Asians qualified. There were over 20,000 bona-fide British
Asians in Uganda, but there were also thousands of Asians who
had applied late for Ugandan nationality and were still, practically speaking, waiting to be told what country, if any, they
belonged to. The newspapers in England assumed the worst.
They started quoting a figure of 60,000, and the Uganda Resettlement Board, hastily put together by the Home Office as a sort

* There are about 180,000 "African Asians" in Great Britain
today—both the immigrants themselves and the children and
grandchildren born since their families left Africa. Margaret
Thatcher's new Conservative government wants to limit all New
Commonwealth immigration to the dependents of male heads
of household who are already legally established in the country.
† Daniel Moi, the new Kenyan President, seems to be keeping
Kenyatta's promise. And so the grants continue. From 1977
through 1978 Kenya got £15 million a year from the British,
and the estimate for 1979 through 1981 is an annual £27 million.

of clearing house for refugee problems, started getting official
memorandums from the big cities claiming that *they* had no
room for any immigrants. Local councils in the Midlands,
where there was already a history of racial tension, met to
resolve that no public housing would be made available to
Uganda Asians. The city of Leicester, which already had a
sizable Asian population, went so far as to place ads in the
Uganda Argus warning the immigrants to stay away. Finally, a
kind of admonitory map of Great Britain was produced for the
Resettlement Board officers and volunteers. It was a map with
red zones and green zones—red for crowded cities with big
immigrant communities and racial troubles, and green for what
were described as gracious, welcoming regions where an Asian
could easily settle down to a quiet and successful life. The
Asians were warned, for their safety, to stay away from the red
zones, and urged, for their future happiness, to try the green—
which meant that the first question put to Akbar by a Resettlement Board officer who met his plane at Heathrow was
whether he had ever considered the Outer Hebrides as a place
to live.

A kbar chose London; that is, by the time he joined his family
he was too exhausted from his troubles for another change.
Akbar is only forty, but he has been working hard for over
thirty years—since the day he turned seven and his father stood
him on a box behind the counter at the *duka* in the clearing and
taught him about trading thread and salt and kerosene lamps to
the local tribesmen for their skins and crops. He thinks of himself, by now, as an old man. His hair is gray, and over the years
he has got paunchy. Until he left Africa, he suffered a great deal
from malaria, but he is still strong, and he is taller than most of
his people, with a large, round face and gleaming teeth. In
Uganda, he says, everyone respected him because he had "the
English confidence," by which he means that he had a kind of
white man's confidence and that it made him generous and

easygoing, not furtive and self-seeking, like the Asians he knows who do not happen to be his brothers or his close cousins. It was the English confidence, he says, that made him cheerful and masterly with Africans. It was this confidence that impressed President Milton Obote and then Amin, and made them tell every important visitor to the district to be sure to stop for a meal with Akbar. It was the same confidence that made the three thousand farmers in his food cooperative come to him one by one, weeping, a year ago last November, and beg him not to go.

Akbar still worships the English confidence. He was born a colonial, and his own history has taught him the lesson that white men are the best possible people, black men the worst, and Asians destined to struggle somewhere in between. He cannot imagine a white man helpless, thrown out of his own country, plundered and humiliated, and forced to abandon everything to a bad African. That is why, he says, he was so ashamed when he arrived in England. He had very nearly lost the confidence. He did not want to face his younger brothers and his children until he had found work and bought a winter coat for everybody and could offer his family a decent place to live. He says now that he did not know how to explain to his sons why he had come to England empty-handed, why he had not been able to salvage anything of their old life. The children had left Uganda just before the Army started coming through their district. Two days after they arrived in London, soldiers were in the village, holding rifles to their grandfather's head while Akbar handed over the keys to his two cars and the four Mercedes trucks that happened to be parked in the family compound. The soldiers had seized Akbar's shop and his storage houses, and finally they had quartered in the compound. He had to abandon his interest in the food cooperative, signing a paper that said he would never claim anything from the company "regarding rights or loan monies." He lost his second house—he had built it, a few years earlier, in the town of Masaka, so that the children could go to town schools—when the same soldiers decided that it would make a nice home for their colonel. And by November he was a refugee in Kampala, living with his father in a tiny furnished room above the *duka* of a friend. It was impossible, he says, to meet his family so discouraged. At Heathrow, he put his father in a cab to Southall, and then he chose a long green overcoat from a pile of winter clothes that a vicar's widow from the Women's Royal Voluntary Service was distributing, and got on a bus for the nearest Resettlement Board refugee camp. He says that as the bus pulled out he heard a Punjabi airport worker calling in Hindi, over a loudspeaker, "Welcome to England, my lucky brothers. The Queen has saved your lives and wants me to tell you that you will all be happy here."

Two weeks later Akbar showed up in Southall. He had been X-rayed and examined and given shots for his malaria. He had filled out daily questionnaires about his situation in Uganda. He had been interviewed by politicians about "the Asian problem" and interviewed by reporters about how it felt to be a big capitalist man sharing the unused barracks of an American Air Force base with eight hundred other refugees. He had been advised by one government employment agent at the camp that Newcastle was the most congenial town in England, and then told by another that he should consider emigrating to the Brazilian jungle, where the climate would be just like home. He had not managed to find a job, warm clothes for the children, or the promise of a place to live. The retired colonial officers who helped run the camp had been gracious and despotic. The ladies who were volunteers there had been irritable and confused, and blamed the government because the immigrants they encountered were indistinguishable, to them, from the thousands of shabby Indian and Pakistani workers already in the country, and in no way resembled the group of gifted and genteel professionals that the Home Office, hoping to avoid a racial crisis, had led the English to expect. Nobody at the camp had seemed to want to help Akbar. The most that anyone had offered was a job at the airport, cleaning runways.

Still, Akbar says, he would have stayed at the camp longer

if there had been no problem with the cafeteria. He says that some of the Asians left as soon as they saw the cafeteria. And the ones who stayed, with all their other troubles, complained constantly about it because Asians consider it shameful to stand in line with trays, asking for their food. Akbar says that among Asians only beggars will stand in a line with their plates out, and that even beggars, hungry as they are, will think of nothing but the disgrace. "I am not thinking, in all my life, to see myself to ask for food," Akbar says whenever he talks about the cafeteria. "By my last day, I feel too much, too much shame. You see, I am big capitalist man, and I am thinking that in Uganda, at big hotels, there is always much waiters to serve me. I think, Oh, Lord, I never see this day for Akbar Hassan. I not taking any more food here. It is better to be leaving before I lose my last confidence."

Half the Uganda Asians who came to England live in London, like Akbar, despite the red-zone map and all the warnings about jobs and housing. Most of them figured that in a city already crowded enough with Indians and Pakistanis to merit such strong warnings they would find, if not distant relatives with big houses, at least the security of curry shops and Muslim butchers, mosques and khanas and Hindu temples, and people to talk with in their own languages. Then, too, Southall is in London, and every Uganda Asian who knew anything about England knew about Southall. The village of Southall lies at the end of the Greater London borough of Ealing—one of those outlying workers' boroughs whose only real connection with the central city seems to be the fact of a train to Paddington—and it has perhaps the greatest concentration of Asians of any neighborhood in the country. About 60,000 people live in Southall. By now, more than half the population is Asian, and if the English and the Irish who are still there continue to move on to other suburbs, the entire population may be Asian in a few years. It is already difficult to find an English face on Lady Margaret Road or on the other shopping streets of Southall. The Asians have colonized the village. They have taken over most of the shops and filled them with Indian spices and sari cloth and advertisements for package tours to Delhi, and the English who live there now prefer to take a bus to Ealing center rather than shop at Asian stores. A couple of pubs are all that remain of the old Southall. They survive because the Sikhs in the village like drinking; the rest of downtown Southall looks like a little Delhi, and that is what the Asians call it. They can eat dinner at the Maharaja or at the Sunny Restaurant, which supposedly belongs to a Suni Muslim whose spelling got confused when he was ordering signs for the window. They buy their linoleum at Mecca Flooring and their clothes at Banwait Brothers. Their vegetables come from Kashmir's Music House; their whiskey, if they are Sikhs, comes from Mr. Singh's liquor shop; and their meat, if they are Muslims, comes from the butchers at Moon Rose Fine Foods. They go to the Liberty Cinema and sit through long, torrid Indian epics, sung in Hindi. They fill the streets the way their fathers filled the streets of Delhi, Bombay, and Karachi—leisurely and vivid, keeping close together, bickering, gesturing, bargaining, and watching everything. There are few places left in Southall to see an English movie or to buy a pork pie or a framed photograph of the Royal Family. But anyone of a mind to can advertise for a wife of the proper caste, dowry, and "qualifications," go to a hammam for ablutions, and live in London for a lifetime without having to speak a word of English to anyone.

South Hall was the name of a great Elizabethan manor house, and the village surrounding it was once a lazy little hamlet with an inn, a vicar, and a few merchants to supply the farmers working for the South Hall squire. For centuries the only notice the city of London took of Southall involved the Wednesday Morning Horse Market—a glorious horse swap that still takes place in a field along the Uxbridge Road, not far from Akbar's house. It was the Great West Railway, out of Paddington, and the Grand Union Canal, passing through Southall on

its way to Birmingham, that finally tied the village to the city.
The railroaders and the canal workers built cottages in Southall,
and in the nineteen-thirties, when the road to Uxbridge made it
cheap and accessible for suburban living, workers from central
London bought those cottages from the families of the old railroad and canal men. The first Asians did not arrive in Southall
till 1947—ten Sikh families who had fled the war over the
India-Pakistan partition—and they were the only Asians in the
village for the next ten years. It was an Englishman, in fact, who
turned Southall into an Asian village. The story goes that he
commanded a Sikh regiment during the Second World War,
went home to run his rubber business, which had a factory in
Southall, and in 1960, faced with a labor shortage at the factory,
thought of the Sikhs and decided to recruit Sikh labor, starting
with soldiers from his old regiment. His success inspired companies all over England. Within a few years, factories in the
Midlands and the North were filled with Indians and Pakistanis,
working all-night shifts for below-minimum wages, and having
no language to complain in and no one to complain for them
because at first the English unions refused to let them join.
Oddly, among the first Asians to revolt were the Sikhs at the
commander's rubber factory. They organized their own union,
and the company, which refused to recognize it, was forced to
shut down and relocate in the countryside. But by then a dozen
small factories in and around Southall were also employing Asian
labor. Asians were stuffing sausages, packaging oatmeal, freezing ice cream, and stitching together the print dresses that rural
Englishwomen wear in summer. Asians are still in the factories
—friends and relatives of the Sikhs who came in 1960, worked
for a while to save some money, and started buying shops and
property, along with the Hindus and the Pakistani Muslims who
followed them to Southall.

When the Uganda Asians came, they took over the factory
jobs that none of the other Asians wanted. Three of Akbar's
sisters make £7 a week working full time at an underwear

factory in the neighborhood. Most of the other Asian women at the factory earn more money, but they are not interested in speaking up for the sisters. They consider the refugees from Uganda backward and unworldly—especially the Kutchis, who are so traditional and pious. Moreover, they suspect that, as refugees, the Uganda Asians are enjoying a fortune from the government. The sisters, for their part, know that the Sikhs in Southall are drunken, devious, and greedy. They know that the Punjabi Hindus are effeminate and superstitious, the few Ismailis snobbish and intolerant, and the Pakistanis noisy, brutal, and unwashed. Their father has told them so, and Akbar, their oldest brother, has confirmed it. They would be shocked to learn that there are Englishmen who do not distinguish among the incredible variety of Asian immigrants. Their own hatreds are as old as poverty in India. They inhabit, in a way, their history, and they read their own loss in the advantages of Asians who arrived before them.

Akbar, surrounded by Asians, is isolated in Southall. There are 1,500 Uganda Asians in the borough now, but not many of them are Kutchi, and if Akbar sees anyone, it is likely to be someone from his family, with whom he feels safe. His father, Hamid, refuses to leave *his* house at all except to go to the local mosque, where he suffers keenly from the presence of so many Pakistanis. Neither of them knows much about London. They are not interested. Akbar says that it would be useless to get interested in London. He will spend the rest of his life there, if he has to, but he knows that he can never turn London into a proper place to live. He remembers sleeping, as a child, on the floor of his father's sheet-metal hut, with meat and onions hanging above his mat and rats scurrying across his pillow. He can talk about that, and about the snakes and the sicknesses and the tribal fighting, and even about the lion that mangled his mother's youngest brother, with better humor than he can talk about his life in London. He says that he would happily trade all of London for his old village, because by the time he left the

village there was no one living in it (except the Seventh-Day
Adventists) who was not, in one way or another, a Hassan
relative.

Rabia Hassan thought of Southall when her plane landed, because it was only three miles from Heathrow, and she knew
that an old Koranic scholar from Masaka had moved there in
1970 to open a travel agency specializing in tours to Mecca and
excursion holidays on the Devon coast. Rabia did not think she
had the money to get much farther, anyway. She had tried to
leave Uganda with £200 sewn into the hem of a length of sari
cloth, but the guards at Entebbe Airport found the money when
they went through her suitcase. All she had managed to save
was a £10 note, which was hidden in her chignon—and which
the guards had overlooked because her daughter, Zhora, fainted
when they were both stripped forcibly and searched. *That*
money went to a London taxi driver who intercepted Rabia and
the children at Heathrow and demanded £10 in advance to take
them to the scholar's house.

Rabia still cannot believe that an Englishman would charge
£10 for a trip that ordinarily costs less than £1. She is a timid
woman, with wide brown eyes that always seem to be asking
why her life has been so disappointing, but she refuses to be
disappointed by the British. When she learned from her friend
the scholar that she had been swindled, she told him that the
taxi was new and beautiful and that the driver must have
needed the extra money to meet his payments on it at the bank.
When her next-door neighbors—the Hassans now live on the
fringe of Southall that is still mainly a neighborhood of white
families—did not invite her in on the night she rang their door-
bell with a gift of her special mincemeat curry, she asked Akbar
if something about her manner could have offended them. When
the manager of a local bank, whom she saw secretly about a
part-time job that was advertised in the bank window, told her
to get out and not come back, she decided that the man must

have been exhausted by his important work. It was only after eight months, when Akbar allowed her to take a half-day trip to central London, that Rabia finally complained about the British. She had been looking forward to her day in London. She had imagined London as something like Salisbury, Rhodesia, where she was born and brought up, only bigger, shinier, and even more splendid, but now, on her first free day in a year, she saw nothing but old houses. It was shameful, she said afterward, that the British cared so little for their capital that they did not bother to tear down those drab old houses and put up some modern buildings "in the Rhodesian style."

Rabia still misses Rhodesia, although she left it at sixteen, when she was married, and returned there only once, for her first confinement. She says that sometimes, when Akbar complains that life ended for him at the Mercedes-Benz garage in London, she will think of how her own life ended the day she left Salisbury, as a bride, in a truck caravan of her husband's relatives, for the fifteen-hundred-mile journey to the Uganda bush. Rabia says she was brought up "free" in Salisbury, by which she means that she went to school, joined the Girl Guides, played field hockey, took walks through town, wore a short, fitted tunic over her serwal, spent Saturday afternoons at the movies, and had her hair washed every other Thursday by a hairdresser. Her father was an eccentric Kutchi merchant who outlived three wives and sired fifteen children—among them nine daughters, whom he decided to "free" while he was under the influence of a white wholesaler with whom he hoped to do a lively business. Like most Rhodesia Asians, he considered the Uganda Asians backward. But he had a strong feeling for his own people, and he worried a lot about finding the proper husbands for his daughters, since there was a shortage of Kutchi Muslims in Rhodesia, and an even greater shortage of Kutchi Muslims with unmarried sons. When Hamid appeared one day at his door, with letters of introduction, a bank statement of the Hassan assets, and a lineage chart drawn up by his friend the Koranic scholar and proving conclusively that they were pater-

nal fifth cousins, Rabia's father saw at once the answer to his
problem.

Over the years, starting with Rabia, he married five of his girls
to sons of his newly discovered Uganda relatives. Rabia was
told that day that she was going to have a husband. She had just
started training at a local nursing school, but when she asked
permission to postpone the wedding until the term was over,
Hamid said that life was very difficult in his village and that his
wife had waited long enough for a daughter-in-law to work for
her around the house. Three months later, Rabia was in purdah
in the village. She says that at first she tried to make friends with
the women in her new family. She told them stories about the
Rhodes Centenary Exhibition in the town of Bulawayo, where
for only five shillings she had ridden in a rickshaw through five
square miles of pavilions. She taught them the words to "Old
MacDonald," taking the parts of all the animals herself. She
even offered to teach them how to read and write. But the
women said that she was being snobbish and only wanted to
shame her husband, who had never been to school. Besides,
Akbar's mother never forgave her for wearing a white European
gown at her wedding ceremony instead of a proper Asian costume. She complained to Akbar that the daughter of a fifth
cousin was not much of a relative, all things considered, and she
resolved to marry her second son to her older brother's daughter, even though the girl was stupid. Akbar, as was proper, took
his mother's part. He did not know what to do with an educated,
discontented wife, who thought it was hard that there was no
cinema in the village, who expected to sit down with him at
dinner, who was always trying to keep him at home making
conversation when she should have known that his place was
with the men. He warned Rabia, who tried her best to please
him. She threw away her English handbag and put her English
novels in a suitcase. She lengthened her tunics. She kept to the
women's path, behind the houses, and stopped asking why she
was not permitted to walk on the village roads. But she was
lonely in Uganda, and became cranky. When she went to her

parents, in Rhodesia, to have Zhora, Akbar did not send money for their passage home. Her father had to drive them back to Uganda, and Rabia did not leave Akbar again until the day he put her on the plane for London.

"When I had the boys, Akbar would tell me, 'Go to England, educate my sons,' " Rabia said one day last spring, in her clear, sad Salisbury voice. It was Good Friday. Just to the east, in the borough of Hammersmith, the local Catholics were dragging a great wooden cross along their end of the road to Uxbridge, but in Southall people were starting to congregate for prayers in honor of the Prophet's birthday. Rabia was in her kitchen, arranging biscuits on a 1967 Princess Anne commemorative birthday plate that Abdullah had picked up for a few pence at one of the weekly Southall auctions. She expected the women of the family to come at four for prayers and a long reading from the Koran. "Akbar would tell me, 'Go to England,' " Rabia said again. "He would promise to come two times a year to visit, but I did not trust him. I knew that if I left, I would never see him. I would be without a husband. So I would say, 'No, thank you. It is too cold for us in England.' And he would get angry and say that it was only the servants I cared about—that I stayed in Africa against his wishes because in Africa I had servants. But I would not go, and then, when Amin said that we *had* to go, all of us, Akbar beat me. 'You see,' he said. 'If you had gone when I asked you, we would have got some of our money out, at least. Now we are losing everything, and it is your fault.' " Rabia says that she settled down in Southall suspecting that Akbar would find a way to stay in Africa. It was Rabia who went out and rented the house where the rest of his family is still living. And it was Rabia who memorized the bus routes through Ealing Borough and then maneuvered her way through the maze of British social-service offices to get money for the family, schools for the children, work for Akbar's brothers, and information about council housing. Every week she wrote to Akbar about her progress, but he never answered her letters, and for over two months the only word she had of him was through the relatives who came. At times, she says, she was certain she had been abandoned. But she had learned by then—from a television set she rented with most of her first week's allowance from social services—that English husbands were devoted and adoring and could not function without their wives' company, and so she was also certain that if Akbar did come, their life would change. "I am so ignorant," she says now. "I had not been to English films in Uganda, and I did not know that English husbands and wives love each other so. But then I saw on the telly that they never fight. No, they are always hugging and kissing. And I thought, Well, life will be just like this for me with Akbar if he comes to London. But then he did come, and it is just like in Uganda. I am not allowed to walk, to talk. We never go to the cinema or eat together at the table. And now I think, Can this be true? Is it only we Asians who have so much trouble?"

Rabia still rents the television set, but now it is her four little boys who like to watch it. She is not altogether happy with her little boys, she says. She is proud of Abdullah because he is her oldest son, and she feels for Zhora because Zhora is her only daughter, but she is bedeviled by Habib, Hanif, Yusuf, and Ayub, who take advantage of her. They used to tell their father whenever she left the house without them, and now she has to bribe them with sweets and by letting them take their lunch at home rather than at school, where it is free and nourishing. Habib, who is eleven, is ruining his teeth with all the candy, but Rabia, despite her month at the Salisbury nursing school, does not believe that cheap candy has anything to do with rotting teeth. She does not believe that colds are caught, either. She believes that bad teeth and runny noses come from weak character, and she suspects her little boys of weak character, both because they carry tales to their father and because they readily accept her bribes. Rabia spends at least a pound and a half of the food money every week on sweets for the children, purchasing her time to walk. The walks are important to her. She never heads toward the center of the village, for fear of running into relatives, but plots a course around the block, hoping to meet a neighbor who could become her friend. One Uganda Asian family was already living in the neighborhood when Rabia moved there. Their name is Ramachandra, and they are Hindu and would prefer to mingle with other Hindus. But the Ramachandra women are as lonely in London as Rabia, and Rabia has struck up a wary friendship with Romila Ramachandra, who is just her age and has six children of her own. Rabia sometimes translates movie magazines for Romila, who does not speak English. Romila, in return, lets Rabia use her telephone, for tenpence a call. Apart, they insult each other. Rabia sometimes says that Hindus like the Ramachandras were responsible for Amin's order. She accuses the Ramachandra brothers, who are jewelers, of having smuggled a fortune in gold out of Uganda on business trips to London—whereas Akbar, who was honorable, kept his money in the country and consequently lost it all. The Ramachandras did salvage some of their money, as it happens, by buying an around-the-world plane ticket for every member of the family and, at their first stop, turning all the tickets in for a flight to London. But most of that money went for the lease on a shop in Fulham, and whatever jewelry they left with—spread under the false bottom of a special suitcase—is still in the shop-window, waiting to be sold. The Ramachandras are actually not much better off than the Hassans. In fact, they suspect that the Hassans brought some gold out, now that a Mercedes is parked in front of the Hassan house. Romila watches ladies from Citizens Aid and social services drive up to Rabia's house with bundles of old clothes and curtains, and she always stops by for tea afterward, trying to discover if they have given Rabia money, too.

Rabia would like another friend, but so far she has not found one. Down the street, there is a young Dutchwoman married to an Asian, but Akbar ordered Rabia not to see the woman after he learned that she was working, lunch hours, at a pub, and even Rabia agreed that it was a sign from heaven when the woman's house caught fire while she was out serving Guinness to the local Sikhs. That leaves Rabia's next-door neighbor, who still refuses to invite her in when she calls with offerings of mincemeat curry, and an old Pakistani widow who charges working mothers £2 a week to walk their children to school. Rabia says that she does not count the Sikh lady around the corner as a potential friend, because the lady is related to her landlord. Rabia has problems with her landlord. He wants Rabia to heat the house—he says that the cold, damp air is ruining his wallpaper—and Rabia refuses because there is no money to pay for coal. Last winter, after their first argument about the wallpaper, the landlord had a sack of coal delivered to the house, with a bill for £14, and it cost Rabia £2 to have the coal sent back.

It was then that Rabia decided to find a part-time job, buy coal, and tell Akbar that the landlord was paying for it. She says that she looked for a week, all told, before she got discouraged. Her first stop was a new pharmacy that was advertising for a part-time cashier; the pharmacist told Rabia that she was too old and unhealthy-looking to attract customers from the pharmacy around the corner. Then she tried the bank, where the manager threw her out, and then a big supermarket on the Uxbridge Road, where the manager told her to get six months' experience checking out groceries at a smaller market and then come back. Finally, she took a bus to the government employment office in Ealing center, and was sent to a Nestlé's chocolate factory a few miles north of Southall. But this time she had persuaded Romila, who wanted money for new saris, to come with her, and when the manager at the chocolate factory said that he could hire only workers who spoke English, Rabia had to refuse the job he offered rather than risk problems with her only friend. She says now that it is just as well she refused it because the Dutchwoman's house burned down a week later, and she began to imagine the dreadful things that might happen in her own house if she was out all morning wrapping chocolates.

Now Rabia rubs down the wallpaper each day to cut the

moisture. And she has the rent money ready on Monday mornings so that the landlord, who collects it himself, will not get
past the door. She would like to move to a council house,
where the rent would be £5 or £6 a week instead of £18, but
she is at the end of a list of nearly 13,000 families in Ealing
Borough, and has been told that English families on the list,
who have been waiting years for housing, will have priority
when the first units come along. In 1972, in Ealing, only fifty
New Commonwealth immigrants got council housing, and
they were advised to keep the information quiet, since the council could not afford to acknowledge what it called "the emergency preference." The Southall social workers assigned to the
Uganda Asians have told Rabia that they can find a council
house for the Hassans in one of the planned New Towns about
fifty miles outside London, but there is nothing they can do for
her in Southall. Rents are high in the village, because the new
Asians are exploited by the Asians who settled there before
them and bought the property, and the new Asians are reluctant
and frightened to move away to cheaper towns. Most of the
houses in Southall are actually too small for Asian families.
There are only two bedrooms in Rabia's house, and Zhora has
one of them to herself, because after puberty an Asian girl is
not permitted to share a bedroom with her brothers. Rabia
sleeps in the other bedroom, with her little boys. And Abdullah,
who spends the week now at his grandfather's, sleeps weekends
in the sitting room, with Akbar. The bathroom in the house is
close and dark, and none of the plumbing works properly. The
kitchen is freezing because the landlord once started to enlarge
it for the boiler, ran out of money in the process, and covered
the extension with torn corrugated-plastic sheets. There is an
old sink in the kitchen, a small stove, and a shelf where Rabia
rolls chapatty and paratha dough and keeps her spices, but there
is not much space for storage, since Abdullah has filled the
room with battered gadgets he picks up at the Southall auctions.
So far, he has brought home a spin dryer, which cost £1 and
doesn't work; an enormous hospital washing machine, which

cost £4 and doesn't work, either; and a broken dentist's chair, which tilts permanently backward.

Rabia says sometimes that it is just as well that there is no space left for cupboards. In Uganda she had seven English tea sets in her cupboards, and the few pieces she didn't leave behind got broken on the trip to London. It cost the family £28 to ship a crate ahead of them, and Rabia says that everything in it but a few cooking pots was ruined. Rabia's cuckoo clock; her favorite horn lamps, carved gazelles, with light bulbs coming out of each antler; her porcelain dolphin, sitting on a bed of iridescent sea-shells; and the filigree frame that held her wedding portrait—they were all broken, and the Uganda Resettlement Board, with funds to reimburse the Asians for shipping charges, refused to reimburse Rabia, who had no receipt. She says now that if she had cupboards she would only miss her lovely tea sets, and that if she had tea sets she would miss her lovely table, which was white Formica, seated twenty-five ladies for tea after a reading, and was kept spotless by two thick plastic tablecloths.

The white table was the only piece of furniture that Akbar managed to sell before Amin ordered African civilians to stop buying from the fleeing Asians. When the soldiers took over his houses, he quickly gave away the beds and mattresses and the bedroom chests to the man who had been loading and unloading trucks for him since he started his transport business, and then he distributed the sitting-room furniture among his five drivers. Rabia still thinks a lot about her sitting room. "I had everything matching, and it was so lovely," she says. "Green walls. Green drapes. Green sofas. Green ashtrays. Here green, there green, and so lovely, with green linoleum glittering like the sea." She likes to picture herself in the room, dressed in a green brocade tunic, receiving ladies for a proper reading. Her new sitting room is small and gray and, she knows, ugly. It came with the plastic couch, a bridge table, where Akbar and the boys eat dinner, and some folding chairs. The only things that belong to the family are a set of pillows with "Home Sweet Home" embroidered on them by Zhora; the family photograph album; the remains of Rabia's dolphin; and a 1972 EL AL Israel Airlines calendar—the gift of an Israeli engineer who was building roads for the government near Masaka and disappeared the day Amin gave a couple of thousand Israeli guest technicians seventy-two hours to leave Uganda, thereby saving himself the expense of having to pay them for several years of work. In the family album, there is a photograph of the same calendar on the wall of Rabia's green sitting room. Rabia has pasted it on the first page, along with a picture of her father's house in Salisbury, a picture of herself, at ten, in her Girl Guide uniform, and a picture of the table at her wedding banquet, with two bottles of Coca-Cola set at every place.

"I nearly lost my album at Entebbe Airport," she said the day of her first Southall reading, wiping her eyes with her shawl and then laying the album next to the plate of biscuits on the bridge table, for her mother-in-law to look through after prayers. "It was because the guards were angry. An African lady stripped us naked. She said, 'Take off your clothes, take off your trousers.' She seized Zhora, and Zhora screamed and fainted, and after that the guards were very angry with us. They told us they were happy to see the Asians go because the Asians were always making so much trouble. They forgot about my hair, but they searched everything that we were taking. Socks and hems —especially hems. They took my two hundred pounds, although Akbar had already bribed them twice as much to let us go through customs. Then they came to the album in my suitcase. 'Aha!' they said. 'You have money hidden under the pictures.' They ripped out every picture, looking for the money, and when they did not find it they started talking among themselves, saying that they would keep the album anyway, that there was a picture of a soldier in the album—it was a picture of my brother, when he was in the Rhodesian Army—and that we might be spies. I said, 'No.' And my little one, Ayub—he said to the guards, 'Please, give us our picture book.' You see, Ayub loves the album. He looks at it every day, with his brothers, and, oh, how he loves it whenever he is in a picture! 'Please,' he said. And one of the guards raised a hand to slap him. I saw him shivering, my little five-year-old shivering. And I said, 'Don't be afraid, Ayub. Your mother won't let them harm you.' Then the guard started laughing. He said it was so funny that *I* could protect anyone from Amin Dada's soldiers. And soon all the guards were laughing, and they let us go. It was very odd, with all of them laughing and all of us crying. Abdullah cried all the way to London, because he had wanted to stay behind with his grandfather. I cried, too. I was frightened, but I knew that I had to calm the children and I must not show it. I said to myself, 'Do not lose hope,' but I could not forget that the trip alone had cost nine hundred pounds and that here I was, on my way to London with six children, no husband to protect me, and only a ten-pound note rolled into a ball and hidden in my hair."

By now Rabia suspects that she is never going back to Uganda. She hears the news on the television set, which is always on to please the little boys, and she is beginning to understand that no one is going to ask the Asians back to Africa when Amin falls.* She misses her life in Uganda now the way she used to miss Rhodesia. When she came to London, she was still complaining about the hardships in Uganda—chopping wood to heat water for her ablutions, making ghee, pounding curries, cooking by herself for such a big family. Lately, she has been talking a lot about the good life in the village, about her gardener and her three house servants and her famous readings, to which all the Kutchi ladies in the district came. She likes to quote the price of food there. Fivepence for chilis in a big basket. Sixpence for tomatoes, wrapped in matoke leaves. Fivepence for peas—four in season. And no one would ever think of weighing produce. Food came by the basket, and all that the natives wanted for it was a few pence and a cast-off shirt or something sweet for their children. Mangoes in Uganda cost twenty pence for a sack so heavy it had to be dragged across the

* She was right.

road to the family compound, but mangoes in Southall cost twenty pence apiece, and now Rabia does not know what to tell her little boys, who are always begging her to buy them mangoes and have tantrums in the middle of the market when she says no.

Rabia does most of her shopping in the supermarket where she once looked for work. It is more expensive than the shops that compete along the main streets of downtown Southall, but it is just a few minutes from the house, and Akbar has forbidden her to go farther. She used to send the boys for meat from Moon Rose Fine Foods or fish from one of the Asian fishmongers, but they inevitably stopped for sweets and then came home with bones or fish heads. Now Rabia does without meat unless Akbar remembers to buy it on his way home from the service station. He usually forgets, and Rabia is relieved that he does. Electricity for their house costs £8 a month, even now that they have disconnected the refrigerator and put it in the back yard; gas for the sitting-room heater costs £5; and the supermarket takes all the household money that is left.* Rabia does not know how to shop in England. She would know how to bargain with an African who came to the door with a basket of beans or chilis, but she is dazzled by the packaging in the English supermarket and keeps coming home with packaged pink cakes to serve with tea to Romila, damaged fruit camouflaged in cellophane and cardboard, and multicolored tissues in tiny and expensive boxes. She says that she wants to be a perfect and efficient English wife, like the wives she sees on television, but she has no one to talk with about it, no one to help her except an occasional social worker, or Romila, or the women in Akbar's family, who know less than she does.

Rabia is still looking for the woman who will be her special friend and tell her English secrets. She keeps a long list of questions that she will ask her friend, over tea and pink cake,

* Gas and electricity in England cost nearly $2\frac{1}{2}$ times more today than they did in 1974.

when they do meet. Some of the questions are about marketing.
And some are about the children—which English medicines are
good for sore throats, and which English fruits will appease
small boys who cry for mangoes and matokes. But the most
important questions on her list concern Akbar. Last winter she
ordered a book called *Secrets of Marriage*, which she had seen
advertised in the back of one of Romila's movie magazines. But
the pictures embarrassed her, the text alarmed her, and she
threw the book out in a few days anyway, after dreaming that
Akbar found it under the mattress and beat her up. She suspects
now that there are other, easier ways to console Akbar. She has
tried being meek and uncomplaining, talkative and full of jokes.
She has made his favorite curries. She has rubbed his back at
night with Vicks VapoRub until her hands burned. Nothing she
has done has made a difference. Rabia is disappointed in herself, and desperate to learn the secret that keeps eluding her.
She knows from television, she says, that it is not the custom in
this happy country for a husband—even a husband who has lost
everything and is despondent—to spend a whole year sleeping
on the sitting-room couch.

Every morning at eight, Zhora puts on a regulation blazer
over her Kutchi serwal and tunic and leaves the house for
school. A few blocks on, she meets two Sikh girls and, a little
farther, a girl from Gujarat. Zhora does not care much for the
girls—especially the Sikh girls, who wear lipstick—but she
walks with them anyway, for reinforcement. She says that the
English schoolgirls turn away and whisper when they pass, and
the boys run up to them, laughing, and yell "Woggies!" or
"Black pigs!" or "Black cows!" Zhora does not mind much
when they call her a Woggie, but she is angry and confused
when they call her black, because "black" means "African" and
is a terrible thing to say to a nicely brought up Asian girl. When
Zhora came to London, she started school in downtown
Southall. Most of her classmates there were Sikhs and Pakis-

tanis, and *they* teased her because she was not allowed to walk with boys or go to the Liberty Cinema after school. One of the boys, on a dare, delivered a love letter to her house, begging her to sneak out and meet him in the balcony of the Liberty, and when Akbar saw the letter he beat Zhora and kept her at home for the next two weeks. Zhora was glad to move to the new house and the new neighborhood, and to start over at a school where most of the children would be English. Now she is lonesome, and spends a lot of time writing to her old friends from the village and from Masaka, who are scattered around England, and whom she never sees.

Zhora is tall and graceful, and she has deep sloe eyes, like the eyes of the film stars in Mrs. Ramachandra's magazines. She is already beautiful, at thirteen, and Rabia, in spite of herself, is jealous. It was Rabia who read the love letter and showed it to her husband. She watches her daughter walking off to school in her blazer, and she suspects that Zhora's life may turn out a little better, a little less disappointing than her own. The injustice rankles Rabia. "She doesn't like me" is the way Zhora always begins a conversation about her mother. She says that every time she starts to do her homework, her mother comes in with orders to make chapatty or wash the floors, and she worries that she will not do well enough in school to study nursing —which is what she wants to do, now that her vocational adviser has said that in England even Asian women have professions. She already has trouble with "English History Since 1700," and with her geography lessons, which are all about England, Canada, and Australia and have nothing to do with Africa. But she is good at mathematics and English, and "very keen," she says, on biology, not counting the principle of osmosis. Her science teacher, in fact, has told her to forget nursing and think about studying, later on, to be a doctor. He even asked Akbar to come to school one day and talk about her future, but Akbar said no because as far as he is concerned Zhora's future is to marry one of her cousins, bear sons, and stay at home like a decent Muslim wife. Akbar worries a lot about Zhora, though they have barely spoken since she reached puberty and it became shameful for them to be in the same room. He has said that if she must work before she marries, she will work as something modest—say, a bank teller—and he has specifically forbidden nursing, since nurses deal so intimately with men. Zhora has asked her mother to persuade Akbar, but so far her mother has said nothing; she has not got over the fact that *she* wanted to be a nurse once and was refused. The matter is settled for Akbar anyway. He would marry Zhora off now, or send her to the bank, if the law allowed it. He thinks that school in England will make her discontented and demanding, like her mother. Moreover, he is afraid that one day one of the boys at school will follow Zhora and try to talk to her while she is walking home.

Even in Uganda, the idea of a daughter's walking to school alarmed Akbar. Zhora says that when the family stayed in Masaka for the school year, he bought a special Ford, with blinds on the windows, and hired a driver to transport her the quarter mile to her school and back. She always opened the blinds, she says, as soon as the car had turned a corner. She was fascinated by Masaka, which had thousands of Asians and was a big city to her. She discovered a library at the school and started reading. She took out *Oliver Twist* and "all the tales of Shakespeare," but when she was only halfway through the comedies, her mother told her father that Shakespeare was full of lewd stories. Akbar took the books back, furious at her teacher for encouraging Muslim girls in wanton thoughts. "My teacher was an Ismaili, and, oh, my daddy hates the Ismailis," Zhora says. She is a dutiful, wise child, and would never contradict her father, but she thinks about it constantly, now that she has seen Masaka and London, and thinking about it makes her merry and talkative.

"My daddy says that the Ismailis want too much to be Europeans, that they have no habits of their own, but I say that the Ismailis have freedom from the past and it is we Kutchis who have been left behind," she tells people. "On Sundays, in

Masaka, the Ismailis go for a walk, every family together. My mother would say to my father sometimes, 'Let's go, too.' But my father always said no, we would see things on a walk that were not good for us. I saw them anyway. I saw boys and girls laughing together, talking together. I saw it. And I started to pray to God that we would go to London, where everybody laughs, and get some freedom. I said to myself, 'If we stay in Uganda, I will be locked in a house all my life.' You see, my daddy is strict, very, very strict, and in Masaka I was not even allowed to go to the ladies' films, Sundays, with my aunties. My daddy didn't know that I was wanting to come here. He didn't know how happy I was when Amin said that horrid thing about the Asians. My daddy had wanted my mother to come here, with my brothers, because he says they must have an English schooling, but he never wanted me to come here. People in Uganda would go to London and they would come back and say, 'London is nice for visiting but not for daughters. The girls are too free in London. We have seen girls walk down the streets with boys in London, holding hands.' So, of course, I thought I would be free in London—free like my brothers. I thought I would have a different life. But it was not true. My daddy is more strict than ever. The oldest Ramachandra boy— he is in my class at school, but when he comes to my house for cake I am not permitted in the sitting room. I am not permitted to take the long way home from school. I am not permitted to go downtown on the bus. I am not permitted to visit my classmates. I am not even permitted to see the circus when it comes. The circus was right here once, on the Uxbridge Road, and my mother cried until my father agreed to take the family, but when the time came he would only take my brothers. He said to my mother, 'You two ladies are not coming. I am a religious man, and I would be embarrassed if you were there.' "

Actually, Zhora would never enter the sitting room when the Ramachandra boy was visiting. She has no intention of taking the long way home—even the short way is a trial for her. And no classmates have invited her home to visit after school. Once she did take the bus to downtown Southall. Her mother let her go after she begged and begged and finally threatened to tell her father about her mother's walks. But Zhora started back after some Pakistani boys standing on the corner of Bridge Street and Lady Margaret Road whistled at her and made strange comments. She stood at the bus stop trembling until her bus came. The streets of Southall still fascinate Zhora. Walking home from school in the afternoon, she sees the Hindu women, their eyes lowered, trailing behind their husbands, and she sees the teenage English couples standing in doorways kissing shamelessly. She does not know why her father, who admires the English so, says that their ways are not good for Asians, but she does know that even now her life has to be full of secrets from him. She hides her biology textbook so that no one will see the drawings and take the book, the way her Shakespeare was taken from her. She hides the novels she borrows from the school library. She hides the money she has been making baby-sitting, and she will hide the English skirt and sweater that she is going to buy with the money as soon as she has saved enough. Zhora baby-sits once a week for a woman from the London School of Economics who appeared at the house one Saturday morning, with an address list of the local refugees, asking questions about life in Southall. She invited the woman in, and Rabia found them together, eating cake from the Princess Anne plate, when she returned from a walk around the block. Rabia was distressed that Zhora had found the friend who by rights belonged to her, and it took many visits and many discussions before Zhora was allowed to drive off with the woman to central London. Now, on Sundays, Zhora eats her lunch at a big table where men and women sit and talk together, and then she wheels the woman's baby through a big park where English families walk. Her friend, who thinks Zhora is very clever, wants to talk to Akbar about letting her take up nursing, but Zhora knows that her father has already written home to Kutch inquiring after young male cousins he may have overlooked. "What can I do?" she sometimes asks her friend when they are driving back to Southall, Sunday nights. "I am always asking God to help me, but nothing happens. Who do *you* ask to help you? Who do the English ask when they want help?"

Abdullah would never complain to anyone about God. He is rigidly, pitilessly pious—a fourteen-year-old scourge, tense and fat, who stalks judgmentally through Southall wearing a Bulova wristwatch and a tight pink paisley shirt. Abdullah has a nose for transgressions. Whether he is roaming around Southall or sitting in his history class, he is always busy sniffing for a transgression, ready to catalogue it, condemn it, confront it with the example of his own goodness. Zhora and even Rabia are a little afraid of Abdullah because they feel him watching them. He has seen Rabia leave on her secret walks, and he has stood at the door to Zhora's room and listened to her conversations with the Englishwoman who claims to be a professor at a big university in London, but in fact he would never report them to his father, the way his four little brothers do. He does not believe that women are worth saving. He watches women only as a kind of object lesson in the weakness of some lower spiritual order, and reserves his energy for men, of whom he naturally expects more. In Masaka, he was outraged when he had to go to a school with girls in it. In Southall, his first project was to find the only boys' school in the village and apply for admission, and he refused to go to any other school, even after he was told that there were three hundred names ahead of his name on the boys' school waiting list. Instead, he talked his way into a job, at £4 a week, with a Sikh who owned a fruit-and-vegetable shop on Lady Margaret Road, and when the Sikh began to demand that he put in a thirteen-hour day unloading produce crates, he found an Englishman with a fruit-and-vegetable shop around the corner who stayed open only eight hours and would pay him £7.5 for the same work. He has never forgiven the British for forcing him to enroll at another school, four months later, when the waiting list at the boys' school was already down to two hun-

dred and thirty-seven names. But he did manage to avoid the
disgrace of going to school with Zhora, and chose a school in
central Southall, a couple of streets away from Hamid's house.

Abdullah prefers spending the school week at his grandfather's. It means that he has the satisfaction of seeing his
grandmother, who otherwise rules the family, abandon her half
of the bed to him and sleep in a room with her unmarried
daughters. It also means that he can save on bus fare and add
his small weekly allowance to the £30 he put away while he was
working for the greengrocer. Abdullah wants to get his own
passport—a passport costs £5 in England—and run away to
the west of Canada, where one of his uncles lives, and where, he
has learned at the movies, men lead celibate and pious frontier
lives. His English teacher, whose father is in the travel business,
has promised Abdullah a one-way ticket to Canada for a down
payment of only £7, and Abdullah plans to reserve a seat on a
plane that leaves the day school lets out for the summer holidays. He prefers to wait till then, so that he will have a couple
of warm months to work as a cowboy and earn money for the
fur-lined parka he is going to need next winter. He has heard
from Akbar that the cold in Canada is dreadful—worse even
than the cold in London—but he is willing to endure it.

He wants so much to go to Canada, he says, that he is even
willing to endure the fact that most of the Ismailis from Uganda
will be there, too. The Ismailis went to Canada because, unlike
the other Uganda Asians, only a few of them had kept their
British passports. While the British were busy trying to stall the
Asian immigration, the Canadians were offering visas to some
five thousand refugees, on the basis of education and professional background, and they chose, predictably, Ismailis, de-
priving the volunteers at Akbar's resettlement camp of the kind
of people they expected to receive. Abdullah, however, says that
the relative absence of Ismailis is one of the few things that
please him about London. He claims to have had a great deal of
trouble with Ismailis in Masaka. The Ismaili boys, according to
Abdullah, hated the Hindu and Muslim boys who had come to

town from the bush villages, and used to waylay them on the streets at night to fight. Abdullah says that at first he and his Kutchi friends were always beaten. But then they had the idea of hiring Africans to do their fighting for them, and the next night, as Abdullah puts it proudly, "the Kutchis won."

"It cost us ten shillings for twenty-five Africans, but it was worth it," Abdullah says. "The Ismailis were so angry that they told their fathers. And on the *next* night their fathers came to fight our fathers and our uncles. Our men won, because my Uncle Osman is such a very brave fighter. One Ismaili was hurt so badly by my Uncle Osman that he called over an African major to stop the fighting, but my grandfather saw the major coming, and *he* called an African lieutenant colonel. The colonel said to the major, 'Look, we have never seen Indians fighting before this moment. Why stop them? It will be more interesting to watch.' " Abdullah admits that after that night he had no real problems with Ismailis—except, perhaps, with the headmaster of his school in Masaka, who favored his old pupils until his new Kutchi boys followed him to a pub one afternoon and broke his nose. Abdullah says, in fact, that the Ismaili boys in Masaka could even be considered friendly compared to the Pakistani boys he has to contend with in Southall. The Pakistanis at his school torment him. They have been toughened by the city, and they take their cues from the gangs of Paki-Bashers who torment *them*. There are only nine Uganda boys in Abdullah's class at school, but there are a good many Pakistanis. On Abdullah's first day at the school, some of the Pakistani boys backed him against a wall and took twenty-two pence from his pocket, and the first time he went to a Southall movie a gang of Pakistanis and West Indians cornered him in the lobby and threatened to kill him unless he gave them £2.

Now that Abdullah sleeps at his grandfather's house and can walk to school, he doesn't need to carry pocket money, but he still likes going to the movies, and so far, at the movies, he has had to hand over more than £10. He still cannot believe that the Pakistani boys are truly Muslims, although each evening he

sees their fathers in the mosque. He has heard from some old
Uganda friends who moved to Birmingham that Pakistanis
there have made the city loud and filthy. His friends write to
Abdullah that Pakistani women in Birmingham never clean
their houses, and Abdullah writes back that the same is true in
Southall, though he has never entered a Pakistani house—and
never would. He has visited one of the Sikhs in his class, but he
left the Sikh's house in a temper after he came upon the boy's
mother pouring herself a glass of stout. As for Hindus, he used
to play ball with the oldest Ramachandra boy, Prakash, but he
stopped playing when Prakash started to talk about smoking
cigarettes and kissing girls. By now the only boys he sees regularly are two Kutchi boys who have rescheduled their afternoon
marble game so that Abdullah can join them and still get to the
mosque in time for early-evening prayers. They never go to
mosque themselves, and Abdullah says that it is only a matter
of months till they succumb totally to English ways. He swears
to Hamid that *he* will never be corrupted. He is proud, he says,
that his hands are scarred from beatings by his old teacher in the
village. He likes to describe in detail the proper method of hand-
beating—twining one stick over and under the fingers to hold
the hand rigid and then taking another stick and striking sharply
—and to complain that Asians become lax and irreverent in
England because they are not subjected to the discipline of a
strict, pious man.

Abdullah misses his Uganda village. He misses the boys'
weekly picnic at the water hole, and the baskets of meat and
mangoes and matoke. He misses catching snakes on the end of
his hockey stick, and watching the Tarzan film, in Hindi, that
came to the village once a month, and playing at night with
twenty or thirty of his cousins. He uses the word *"paraz"* whenever he talks about Uganda. He says that it means a special
kind of respect. It means that a boy stands up when his teacher
enters the classroom. It means that a young man obeys his
father and always accepts a wife of his father's choosing. It
means that a lady never contradicts her mother-in-law or enters

the place where men kneel down to pray. *Paraz*, he says, is what is missing in Southall, along with elephants and lions, and sitting rooms that always stay the same color and do not confuse people with a new wallpaper every year. Abdullah hates change and he hates confusion, and Southall, for him, is full of both. He keeps a schedule now to fortify himself against them. He walks to school in exactly fourteen minutes. From 3:30 to 4:15 in the afternoon, he plays marbles. From 4:15 to 4:29 he walks to his grandfather's house, and then he eats his lunch, since he will not eat it at school, where the meat is not properly slaughtered. From 5 to 7 he is at the mosque, reading the Koran. At 7 he prays alone. At 8 he does his homework. And at 9 he crosses out the date on his calendar and checks his schedule to see if he has lived his day on time. He knows now that it has been eight months and two days since he last ate lunch at one, with his classmates, in the school dining room. And he knows that in exactly three months he will be able to pack his Koran and run away.

One afternoon last spring Akbar was on the street polishing his Mercedes with a special wax, which his boss at the service station had given him as a sort of Easter bonus. Akbar was still working a double shift, seven days a week, and normally would not have been home on any afternoon, but his boss's mother had died the day before, and the station was closed for the funeral. It was a warm day for London. The sun was out, and the four little boys, watching their father at a safe distance, were in their favorite Amin Dada T-shirts, but Akbar was bundled up in a winter parka from the station, complaining about the cold. Akbar would find it hard to believe that his oldest son is planning to run away to the west of Canada. He still cannot believe that his brother Musa, who left for Vancouver two years before Amin's order, plans to stay there. Musa keeps sending the family pictures of himself throwing snowballs, building snowmen, standing up to the waist in snowdrifts, and Akbar puts them away in the album, certain that Musa is making a joke he somehow doesn't understand. Musa is twenty-five—three brothers and an assortment of sisters younger than Akbar—and his life is as different from Akbar's as the life of any Englishman. Akbar, who helped bring Musa up, watches with a kind of anxious pride the boy he nurtured and encouraged and unwittingly freed from the family. He feels responsible for his youngest brother's conduct. He knows that Musa is serious because Musa is teaching school and studying hard for a master's degree in economics, but he also knows that in Canada students drink liquor and go with women, and that there is not apt to be a mosque in Vancouver, or other Kutchis to set a good example for him. These things worry Akbar, but none more than the thought that in Canada, Musa might be tempted to abandon his duty to his people and take a wife from outside the family.

When Akbar got to London, he wrote to Musa asking him to come as soon as he could for a family conference. Musa got on a student charter flight during his spring vacation. He stayed for two weeks at his father's house in Southall, and on the last night of his visit he listened respectfully while Hamid and Akbar told him that he would not be welcome in the family if he refused to accept the wife his parents chose. Musa, who is engaged to a blond Presbyterian girl he met in his advanced-statistics class, promised that his first loyalties were to his faith and his family. He flew home, leaving his father £1,800 of his own savings as a sort of good-will gesture, and, having seen his oldest brother so unhappy, leaving Akbar the £100 for the Mercedes-Benz. He sends more pictures now, and fewer letters, and he has stopped insisting that the family emigrate to Canada. But when Akbar writes to him apologizing for the delay in tracking down a female cousin, he answers promptly, saying that he understands. Akbar, in fact, does not know how to find the right cousin for his brother. In Southall, he is suddenly more than six thousand miles from his ancestral town in India, which would normally have been a source of wives. Most of the

Uganda Asians share his problem. None of them would think of moving back to India—sacrificing British welfare to confront the same poverty their fathers fled—but still they complain a lot that the business of marrying off their children is getting too bothersome and expensive to manage properly.

Akbar finds it odd that the English are so lackadaisical about their children's marriages when for everything else in life they have so many rules to follow, so many forms to fill out, so many people to convince before anything can be accomplished. He says sometimes that he started filling out forms the moment he landed at Heathrow Airport and has not stopped since. He claims to have filled out fifty-seven job-application blanks alone before he found work at the service station. On his second day at the camp, he says, he was trying to complete a form in English—it was an application for a job at a British Leyland plant and for a council house to go with it—when a Hindu walked past him, bribed the employment officer, who was a Hindu, too, and got the job and the house. And just lately a woman from the local Citizens Aid office has been urging another form on him—this one comes from a trucker in Uxbridge who needs a driver and will pay £150 for ten driving lessons at a government training center, provided that Akbar indentures himself, at a salary of £20 a week, for the next three years. Akbar has already said no to the man in Uxbridge, but he would still like to know why the British insist that a man who has been driving trucks on African roads for over fifteen years needs to take lessons. He says that he came to London expecting simply to exchange his old lorry license for a new one. He was given a test instead, and failed it three times because of his language problems, and now he is not permitted to reapply until he can prove that he has completed an accredited ten-lesson truck-driving course. He did try some lessons for a while last winter, with a Sikh who owns a clothing shop in Southall and has been running a driving school as a sideline since he took over a Ford dump truck from a customer with a large unpaid bill. But Akbar says that after the first lesson the Sikh decided to raise his rate to £4 an hour, and after the second lesson the truck broke down.

"You know these British," Akbar said after he finished buffing the Mercedes and was sitting on his doorstep admiring the way the car gleamed in the sun. "They have these rules coming from I don't know where. The man who is testing me for my license—he is telling me to answer questions on a form for changing gears. And I am saying, 'You know, we are just driving together for forty miles and I am not making mistake. Why am I having to fill out forms now? You are seeing yourself that I am champion at changing gears. In Uganda, there is so many hills. I am always changing gears in Uganda. And here, here is busy road for forty miles, much traffic. I am always changing gears here, too.' But I see the man is not listening. So I am changing conversation. I am telling him how easy it is to doing business in Uganda. I am telling him story of how I am getting Obote's very important minister for my business partner. You know, this minister, he was a child near my village, and he was having white father at the mission who is helping him too much, too much, because his real father is big district chief. So I am knowing him and all his family. And when he is making his campaign in the district, he is coming to me, taking my petrol, money, trucks—taking all he is needing for getting his people from one place to other place to vote. He is saying, 'Help me, and when I am elected I am helping you. But if you are not helping me it will be very bad for you.' So I am saying, 'O.K., I help you. And when you are getting elected you are making sure that I do not have to give up my business, like all other Asians in the district.' And he is laughing and saying, 'O.K., Hassan, you are giving me half of your business and I am promising to protect us both.' You know, I am telling all this to the pure-British man who is giving me driving test. I am showing him how easy it is to doing business in Uganda. And how I am pro-tected in my business until Amin's soldiers take my partner and chop him up. But this British man is saying, 'That is nice story,

Mr. Hassan, but you are still having to fill out form.' I tell him, 'You know, Mr. British Man, now I am having to go to toilet. Maybe it is rule in England that I am having to fill out form for going to toilet, too.' "

Akbar has given up by now on his license. He still wants a better job, with good hours and a good salary, but he does not want to work for an Asian, and so far his only offers have come from Asian shops. When he arrived in Southall he tried to explain to the people at social services that he had lost his English confidence and therefore needed to work for a "pure Englishman," who would tell him his mistakes, man to man, in private, rather than for another Asian, who would shame him, by custom, in front of clients. He knows now that unless his English gets a great deal better he will probably have to stay at the service station or take a factory job. There are adult classes in English at night at one of the Southall schools, but Akbar claims that he is too old, at forty, to go to school for the first time. He says that he has had bad luck with schools, anyway. When he was eight he wanted to go to an African school a few miles from his village, but the district health inspector told his father that all the African children had terrible diseases, and Hamid kept him home. Two years later, when Hamid had more money, he tried to enroll Akbar in an Ismaili boarding school in Kampala, but that was impossible, Akbar says, because the Ismailis were then permitted to restrict their schools to Ismaili children. Akbar eventually taught himself to read and write in Hindi and Gujarati, but there was no one around to help him with English until he married Rabia, and he never thought of asking her. Now Rabia has to read the mail and the papers for Akbar, and Akbar is embarrassed to have to depend on a woman for his news—especially since most of the news he gets is so discouraging.

Early last spring a letter came from the English company that holds Akbar's life-insurance policy, saying that he had not met his premiums, which amount to £160 a year, since the trouble in Uganda started, and that he was in serious danger of forfeit-

ing his benefits unless he paid soon. The next letter he got was
from the Standard Bank of Uganda, Ltd., where he had left a
savings account containing £17,000, and that letter informed
him that all his money had just been seized by the Uganda
government.* Akbar decided to save the letter from the bank in
the suitcase with the other family documents, inasmuch as it
sounded so respectful, ending the way it did: "We regret that
our association has had to be terminated in this manner and
without your specific agreement, but trust that you will understand that the action we have taken was not of our instigation."
But the £17,000 he lost was the last of his assets in Uganda,
and represented his savings for over twenty years. Akbar says
that when Uganda got its independence he kept his British passport for the sake of British protection in the new country, and
so he is confused and disappointed that the British, only ten
years later, would let someone like Amin walk into a British
bank and take away a British subject's money. He knows that
the British look after their white subjects—people in Southall
tell him that white refugees from Egypt and the Sudan have
been indemnified for their property—and he has concluded,
sadly, that the British do not worry as much about citizens who
are colored.†

There is a small group of Uganda Asians who go to meetings
at the Foreign Office and write letters to the newspapers demanding that the government retrieve their money, but they are
all rich and important Hindu and Ismaili businessmen, and
Akbar doubts whether they are much concerned about anybody
else's claim. He says sometimes that Rabia and the children are
his last possessions—which is why, perhaps, he guards them

---

* There is no way for Asians to get back their money, even if
Uganda should suddenly decide to offer it to them. By the time
Idi Amin was overthrown, in March of 1979, he had spent every
pound of the Asians' bank assets.
† The British claim that New Commonwealth immigrants are not
entitled to any indemnification by the London government.

closely. Rabia has been begging him to give her back a little of her girlhood freedom now that they are in London, but he will never do it as long as she is all he has. It is hard for him, then, to understand the changing life in England, with West Indians who drive into the service station and call him "brother," and, at the same time, professors who take an interest in his daughter. The England he approves of is the old England, where a servant esteems his master, a black man an Asian, and an Asian a white professor—just as a wife esteems her husband, a son his father, and a family its head. He says that one reason he stayed in Uganda until the last moment was his responsibility, as head of his Muslim cousins, to see his people safely out. He is proud of, even nostalgic about, his last days in Uganda. They were his last days of authority and respect.

"You know, I am last man out," Akbar said as he sat on his doorstep and watched the sun set. "I am speaking the African languages, and the soldiers, they like this, and they are always talking to me. They see me, for a month, every day, taking my people to planes, getting my people passports, sending away their luggage, and they is saying to me, 'Hassan, is getting too much dangerous in Kampala. What you doing here so long?' I am saying, 'I stay to help my people to leaving. I am not letting you kill these, my people. First you must to kill me.'" Akbar laughed, and then he shook his head. "Now all my people is in England. I am hearing is in Birmingham and Manchester, and some in London. I am hearing about their progress, about the good jobs they have to getting. But none of them is thinking to ask how Akbar Hassan is doing. None of them is writing to me. None of my people that I am helping is saying to me now, 'How you doing, Hassan? Can I help you?' So I am saying to myself, 'O.K., this must to be the way it is with people in England. Nobody is coming to ask how you are doing except the ladies the government is paying to ask you.'"

Akbar stopped talking and looked down the street of red-brick workers' cottages, each with its pointed roof and its double chimney and its drab facade. "I am deciding now I want too much, too much to stay in London," he said finally. "Is settled here. The children are in school, and they not be having to change their uniforms. And is near my family, is much Asian people. And I am getting my reputation. People is coming to my station now, and they know Hassan. So I am saying to myself, 'Maybe soon the government is giving me cheap house, and I am staying.' I am saying, 'Why go to where is more cold, to where is maybe no Asians?' I am better to be making my life for my children here in London. But, you know, I am all the time thinking about Uganda. You know, is not bad people, these Africans in Uganda. Is even getting clean now. Before, is wearing skins with butter and if you pass by, you want to hold nose. But now is getting clean and is getting Mercedes, is going from skins to Mercedes. No, is not a bad people. But I am thinking too much about Uganda, and I am wanting to tell them, 'Listen, you Africans is very lucky to get such nice country.' "

LES
PIEDS NOIRS
(1972)

M me. Martin's suitcase has been in her family for a hundred years. It is more of a satchel than a suitcase, really —a plump, black gros-point bag with faded yellow flowers and leather fittings, the kind of bag that women used to take traveling. Mme. Martin's great-grandmother bought it in Béziers just before she married, and in 1873, when a cruel phylloxera epidemic ruined the local vineyards, she packed her best trousseau linens in it and left for Algeria with her husband to start a new life. The bag was passed from oldest daughter to oldest daughter, down to Mme. Martin. In June of 1962, the month that over a quarter of a million French *colons* were fleeing from Algeria, Mme. Martin brought out the satchel, which had not been used since she took her four children on a pilgrimage to Notre Dame de Lourdes de Misserghin. She put in the family photographs, her husband's Croix de Guerre from the Second World War, a change of socks and underwear for each of the chldren, and all the documents that she had time to get notarized—a paper, stamped at the *mairie* in Algiers, stating that Paul, her oldest son, had passed his *baccalauréat*; an inventory of the household; a list of the vines and fruit trees in her garden and the rabbits that she raised to sell; bills for the equipment that M. Martin, who was an electrician, had bought for his workshop. The socks and the underwear were stolen on the boat that took the family back to France, but the papers and the pictures are intact, and they are still in the satchel, which sits on the cracked stone window sill in Mme. Martin's new kitchen, ready for the next emergency. She does not have confidence enough, she says, to put the satchel away, although she doubts that she will ever leave the little peasant village where the family lives now. She claims, sometimes, that she is going to die of sadness

there, the way her mother died, at eighty, in another strange
village, near Marseille. "You take a sapling and replant it, and
it thrives," she often says, talking about her children. "But an
old tree like me, a tree with roots—out of its own soil that tree
will die." She would like to leave the satchel to Yvette, her
only daughter, but Yvette thinks it is shabby and old-fashioned.
Yvette is married to a *métropolitain*—a *French* Frenchman
—and for her own honeymoon she bought a new white plastic
suitcase at the Prisunic in Marseille.

In June of 1830 the first French soldiers marched into what is
now Algeria "to avenge the honor of the flag of France."
Actually, the flag had been insulted for centuries by the Barbary
pirates, who used to relax between their escapades at sea by
pillaging along the French coast, but now, it seemed, the flag had
been definitively insulted—the Dey of Algiers had hit the
French consul with a flyswatter during a discussion on the price
of grain. It took the French five years to seize the major coastal
towns, and seventeen more to occupy most of the rest of Algeria, north of the Sahara. At the time, however, there was no
Algeria—in the sense that there was a Morocco or a Tunisia,
subject to a ruling dynasty—and the French who came set out
to organize the land into a sort of overseas *département* of
France. They were the poor of France, and they came by the
hundred thousand, even before a good deal of the land was
pacified—the political refugees of 1848 and 1852; the Alsatians
of 1871; the Corsicans, and then the peasants from Languedoc
and the Cévennes and the Basses-Alpes whose vineyards had
been destroyed by the same long phylloxera epidemic that
forced Mme. Martin's great-grandparents to leave their land.
Spaniards came to Oran, Italians and Maltese to Constantine,
and *they* were Frenchmen for just the price of an official nat-
uralization stamp. *"Français à douze sous,"* people called them.
A decree in 1870 naturalized all the Jews in Algeria, and after

1889 any European born there was automatically a French citizen. Around *métropolitains*, they would refer to themselves grandly as *les Français d'Algérie*, but at home in Algeria they called themselves *pieds noirs*, which was what the natives called them, though by then no one knew whether this old epithet referred to the shiny black boots on the first French officers in the country or to the bare, blackened feet of the first French immigrant farmers to dig their toes into the rich Maghreb soil. Some of the *pieds noirs* were rich—big landowners, whom the French call *gros colons*—and all the *pieds noirs* were unquestionably richer than the 9 million Arabs and Berbers who worked to keep them that way. But most of the *pieds noirs* were simply farmers turned workers in the big cities of the colony. They had gone to Algeria as a peasantry in exile, and in 1962, when Algeria won its independence, they left the country as an exiled proletariat. Twenty-four families immigrated to Australia, 14 went to Canada, and 100 settled in Taiwan. No one else wanted them—except, apparently, the Shah of Iran, who offered land to 2,500 *pied-noir* families and was turned down. The French certainly didn't want them—but a million *pieds noirs* went "home" to France.

Most of the *gros colons* had seen the trouble coming, for the good reason that they were the cause of so much of it, and they got their money out in the late fifties, with the result that almost everyone who was rich in Algeria in the nineteen-fifties was just as rich, or very nearly so, in France in 1962. All 200,000 civil servants who were in Algeria at independence were given jobs in France or were retired with pensions because, as the *pieds noirs* like to say, France may abandon her colonies but she will never abandon her *fonctionnaires*. And as for the *vedettes de clandestins*, the superluminaries of the Organisation de l'Armée Secrète who had not been captured by the Algerians, jailed by the French, or welcomed, when they fled, to Spain or Paraguay or Argentina—many of them found a congenial new life in Marseille, smuggling heroin, or in Paris, in "assistance" rackets, extorting money from other refugees.* It was the *petits pieds noirs*—the ones like the Martins, who had stayed out of the fighting, as well as the ones who had carried the *bombes plastiques* for the OAS and had run through the streets of Algiers and Oran shooting Algerians—who arrived in France without a franc and without a future. Some of them, like Mme. Martin, were obviously French, but the great majority of these *Français d'Algérie* returning destitute to the motherland were the Spaniards, the Corsicans, the Maltese, and the Italians who had helped settle the colony in the nineteen-hundreds.

The French in Paris called these new arrivals *hyper-méditerranéen*, because they were brash and insular and volatile, extravagantly pious, and violent in their hates. They were the Ulstermen of Africa. They had learned their politics from the rightist, demagogic newspapers of the *gros colons*, and they had learned their responsibilities as Frenchmen from the secret broadcasts of the OAS. The French, who had effectively abandoned Algeria to violence and had then sent soldiers in to keep the peace, blamed them for the war and for the death of soldiers who had gone, unwillingly, to save Frenchmen they did not consider French at all. The *pieds noirs* were despised in France in 1962, but they came anyway, while their protectors in the OAS bombed trains and docks and airport towers to stop them. They arrived in Marseille—10,000 of them almost every day that June—and the first of France that most of them saw was the legend SALES PIEDS NOIRS, which the angry *Marseillais* had painted on the walls of the old port. They lived at the port there—families without food, sick children without medicine— while the government, which seems to have never really counted on their arrival, tried to administer their future from a dockside office that it called a *centre d'accueil*. Eventually, a small subsis-

* They are still trafficking in drugs, and they are still extorting money, though the "assistance" business has been dropping off now that their old clients are a little more established and a lot wiser.

tence allowance was settled on them, and—for as long as the beds lasted—families with young children were guaranteed free lodging for a week or two in Marseille's hotels. Over 100,000 *pieds noirs* settled in Marseille, but the rest soon moved on. Many went to Paris, where the chances of finding work were better, but most of them scattered to towns and villages across the south of the country where the *mairies* had reported empty rooms.

The village where the Martins have settled is in Provence, about two and a half hours' drive from Marseille, and the family went there after two months in Marseille, when the *préfecture* reported that the village had a large empty house, which had once been used for local orphans. There are 700 people in the village. Most of them work the fields, the vineyards, and the orchards in the dry, sparse valley that the village overlooks from its perch on the south face of one of the steep little mountains that ring the area and have protected and isolated it for centuries. Before Parisians came looking for old stone farmhouses to buy as country places, most of the strangers who crossed those mountains were escaping from something. Roman soldiers hid in the mountains. So did Albigensians, and the Resistance fighters of the French Maquis. The peasants like to complain that their village is a place that the young leave, coming back only when they get in trouble. The peasants themselves rarely leave it, except to go to the nearest town on market day. They do not like strangers much. Once, they say, an old man from their village went off in his cart to paint a picture of the village that sits on another little mountain, ten kilometers across the valley. They saw him off at dawn with much advice for his conduct and his safety, and they were waiting up at night when he came home. "Well, how did it go?" the mayor asked him. The peasant spat. *"On ne peut pas travailler chez les étrangers,"* he said.

The house where the Martins live now is on the Rue de la Libération, which is a dirt path that starts at an old stone church at the top of the village and winds down to a new church at its foot. Most of the house was built by a farmer in the fifteenth century, and all of it was in ruins when the Martins bought it, four years after they arrived in France. No one else in the village wanted the house—it was huge and crumbling and full of scorpions, and it opened, in the back, onto the fierce mistral. The Martins bought it for 20,000 francs, which was about $4,000, from an old peasant who did not know when he signed the papers at the *notaire*'s office that he was selling to *pieds noirs*. They got the money by borrowing—half from one of Mme. Martin's brothers, who had left Algeria in 1958 and had set himself up in a hardware store outside Marseille, and the other half from the government—and they fixed it up with a *déménagement* loan that the state had made available to *pied-noir* families. M. Martin, who by then had found some work at an electrical-repair shop in the market town, put in plumbing, heating, and electricity himself, on his Sundays off. Mme. Martin scrubbed the stone walls with disinfectant and set off little bombs in every room to kill the scorpions. When the house was ready, she knocked on the neighbors' doors and invited them in for an after-dinner drink and coffee. She bought a new dress for the occasion—her first new dress since she had left Algiers —and M. Martin, who had been shattered by the war and the move and his own homesickness and had started drinking, stayed sober all day long to greet the company. No one came to Mme. Martin's party. And no woman in the village has ever asked the Martins to coffee in her own house.

M me. Martin is fifty now, and she is used to the solitude. She spends most of her time in her kitchen, cooking and washing clothes and worrying about her children—and sometimes looking at the pictures in her gros-point bag. She is a bitter, tired-looking woman in a brown nylon housedress, and she is heavy and getting gray. The village children who see her in the morning at the grocer's, complaining volubly about the prices, still point to her big gold teeth and whisper to each other that she is an African, but they have at least stopped asking to inspect her feet, which they are sure are black. They see more of M. Martin, who has been spending most of *his* time drinking wine behind the blacksmith's shop since he was burned at work in 1969 and had to leave his job. He was ill for a year with the burns. For a while, he was getting 400 francs a month in workmen's compensation from the government, but this was based on the assumption that he could not work as an electrician anymore. When the other electricians around the valley discovered that he was taking odd jobs on the sly to earn some extra money, they sent an anonymous letter to the social-security office in the *département*, and, after an investigation, M. Martin's pension was reduced to less than 150 francs a month. Now, when he is not drinking, he makes a few francs looking after the garden of a Paris banker who has a farmstead in the valley. M. Martin, in fact, can take on almost any job he finds —the *pieds noirs* are smart, he says, and have the frontier spirit, which the peasants lack—and his wife thinks that the local electricians got together and wrote their letter because they were jealous of his skill.

Mme. Martin says they were all out watching on the day, ten years ago, that M. Martin repaired an old truck that everybody else had given up for ruined. It happened the morning after the Martins arrived. Mme. Martin was in the old orphanage, trying to clean the room the *mairie* had assigned the family, and listening to her two youngest children cry. The children were hungry —Claude was nine then and Jean-Jacques eight—but Mme. Martin had no money, and, besides, the three grocers in the village were closed, because a saint's-day fête had kept them open late the night before. M. Martin was sleeping in a corner, but he woke to the crying and then went out to find a way to feed his family. At Pierre's café he met an old farmer who said that he could use a man to drive his melons to the market but that his only truck had broken down a year ago and no one in the village could make it run. M. Martin fixed the farmer's truck in less than half an hour, and he drove for the old man until he

found his job in town. He is sixty-one now, and looks much
older because of his drinking, which the village doctor says is
going to kill him. His hair is white, and his skin is brown and
leathery—in fact, he looks a little like an Algerian. He says that
once, during the fighting in Algeria, when the Front de Libération Nationale made a reprisal rampage through his quarter, he
escaped by posing as an Arab with a French wife. Actually, he
is more Spanish than anything else; his great-grandparents came
to Oran from Alicante Province in the eighteen-sixties, and the
family married other Spaniards until his mother took a husband
from Algiers who was half French. He says that it is the Spanish
in him that enabled him to get along so well with Algerians,
whom he tends to regard as testy, impressionable creatures, like
women and children, and he often talks about his old Algerian
assistant, who once told him that in the best possible world a
man would marry an Arab, live next door to a Spaniard, and go
to court before a French judge. Martin is not bitter about the
Algerians; he reserves his rancor for De Gaulle and the other
métropolitains. He is querulous and boastful, and gallant around
a pretty woman, but his eyes are nearly mad with loss and help-
lessness. He laughs and swears a lot when he is drunk, and once
he scandalized the villagers by squeezing his wife's breast as they
stood by themselves in a corner of the schoolyard during Bastille
Day fireworks display. His wife complains that France has
ruined him, and has made him lecherous. "It is the sorrow," she
says. "At home, he was proud. Every *pied noir* is proud. He
does not like to see his wife go out where men can look at her.
He is very possessive, very loving when she is young and pretty.
But later he respects the fact that she is not young. He knows
that it is even written in the Bible—the life of a woman my age
is not for love; it is caring for her grandchildren, caring for her
old husband. But my old husband—here my husband has become evil, like a Frenchman. He has worked and fought for
France—seven years he fought for France, and no one then
called him a *sale pied noir*—and now he is old and he has nothing. So he is jealous of the young, jealous of his own children.

He drinks and dreams of being young, and then he brings me lipstick and perfume and tries to kiss me at the fêtes. It is not respectable. He comes to me mooning like a boy, and we fight, because he is crazy. I say to him, '*Laisse-moi seule. Je me fous de ton amour.*' "

The war in Algeria made them all crazy, Mme. Martin says. Paul, who married a *pied noir* and left the village, works for an insurance company in Marseille and poses as a *métropolitain*. Yvette still wakes at night, screaming, from nightmares about the day she took an apple tart to her great-aunt's farm and found the old woman with her throat slit and stuffed with a warning from the Liberation Front. Claude, who is nineteen now, wants to be a martyr, and he prays each morning in the village graveyard and decorates his room with shrines to the Virgin and with old snapshots of his dead relatives. And Jean-Jacques—he goes to a *lycée* and should be sensible, his mother says—is insolent and headstrong and so fierce in his hatred of the French that even his parents are afraid of him. One day Jean-Jacques will leave the village. In fact, he will leave France, if he can, as soon as the family is indemnified and he can stop working during his school vacations to help pay off his parents' loans. His parents, like the million other *pieds noirs* in France, have been waiting ten years now for compensation for their abandoned property. They were guaranteed it in the Accords d'Evian, which established Algerian independence, but the guarantees were an empty, placatory gesture, since the Algerians were clearly not going to reimburse them, and the French, after years of fighting in Indochina and then in Algeria, had no money in their treasury to indemnify a million refugees. Even Mme. Martin will admit that France was poor then. "Certainly," she says. "Once the port of Marseille was busy for Indochina, busy for Algeria. Now what does France have left? A few worthless little colonies. *C'est rien.*"

De Gaulle had had to devalue the franc in 1958 to save it, and for the rest of his life he ignored the *pieds noirs'* pressure for restitution, claiming that such a huge expenditure would

plunge the country into an even worse economic crisis than
before. It is probably true that the French, anti-*pied noir* to
begin with and still smarting from their involvement in the long
and idiotic Algerian war, would have resisted any scheme to
divert money from the economy to indemnify the *pieds noirs*,
but De Gaulle's postponements only confirmed the *pieds noirs'*
feeling that they had been betrayed. They blamed De Gaulle,
because he had campaigned for the presidency in 1958 on
what they interpreted as a "Keep Algeria French" platform, and
they had believed in him, and, in fact, had done more than any
other bloc of voters to elect him—which meant that they had
forced the Algerians, who by then had the right to participate in
French elections, to go to the polls and vote the Gaullist slate.
Less than a year later, De Gaulle offered his cooperation to the
Algerians and announced that Algeria would be decolonized.

Some concessions were made to the *pieds noirs* in 1962, if
only to avert another sort of economic crisis, which was sure to
follow if a million extra people stayed permanently on the public dole. The subsistence allowance was small—450 francs, or
about $90 a month per couple, with 50 more francs for every
child—but it was guaranteed for a year or until the head of the
family found steady work. The *déménagement* loan of 20,000
francs was more generous—although it was extended only to
families who had bought a house or an apartment, and fewer
than 25,000 of the *pieds noirs* could qualify. And there were
also loans—of up to 200,000 francs, at 3 percent interest—for
businessmen, professionals, and farmers who needed financing.
A few of the *pieds noirs* who took these loans went bankrupt.
Nearly every *pied noir* who took one *pretended* that he had. In
fact, forging bankruptcies was probably the major occupation
of most *pied-noir* businessmen until the end of 1969, when the
government, confronted with a 70 percent bankruptcy rate and
under pressure from the *pied-noir* assistance syndicates, declared
a moratorium on all repayments.

By 1969, too, the era of De Gaulle was over, and every
important and ambitious politician in the country had produced

a plan to indemnify the *pieds noirs*. President Pompidou's plan, which is now a law—it had been intended as a *loi d'indemnisation*, but the *pieds noirs*, who did not consider the terms sufficient, had protested, and it was finally written as a *loi de contribution nationale*—provides 500 million francs a year for fourteen years for purposes of restitution. Its terms probably *are* sufficient. It does not, for instance, allow for devaluation and inflation—the franc now buys half of what it did in 1962. Eighty thousand francs is the maximum "contribution." And, even so, a contribution will almost always amount to only a percentage of a claim. "A *fonctionnaire*'s delight" is what M. Martin calls the new law, because in each *département* it is up to *fonctionnaires* to evaluate every *pied noir*'s papers and settle on the percentage he will get. Martin himself is unlikely to profit by the law for at least a few years.* The process is slow. In July of 1971, the first month of the contribution, only 1,000 *pieds noirs* in all France received any of the money, and they were over sixty-five or destitute or had four dependent children in their households. Still, the Martins put their dossier in order. Mme. Martin, in fact, did it—with the help of an eccentric old baroness from the valley, whose only son had been an OAS colonel and who likes to drive around in a 1947 Citroën, distributing food and medicine to *pied-noir* families. At first, Mme. Martin had hoped that an assistance syndicate would help her. She took her papers to one, in the market town, but the man at the office there announced that he would help her only if she gave him money and signed a note committing herself for life to

* Only a very small percentage of the *pieds noirs* got money through Pompidou's *contribution nationale*. Giscard d'Estaing revised the law in 1978: 34 billion francs were set aside for the *pieds noirs*, who were then entitled to "reimbursement certificates"—negotiable bonds, with a maximum value of 500,000 francs, to be redeemed in stages. People over seventy have evidently got their certificates and can redeem them over a five-year period. Everybody else has to wait until 1982 for a certificate, and it will take fifteen years to redeem it fully.

yearly dues. Then she went to Marseille, to see the people at the
Association Nationale des Français d'Afrique du Nord d'Outre-
Mer et Leurs Amis, or ANFANOMA, which is considered the
most respectable of all the *pied-noir* syndicates. Mme. Martin
had heard that the people there were honest, but the office was
full when she arrived, and everyone was arguing about the blacks
in Paris, saying that Paris would soon be overrun with Africans.
She left at once and consoled herself with a bowl of Marseille
fish soup, and she was too frightened to return. She had heard
about gangsters in the syndicates, and Jean-Jacques came home
from school one day with the rumor that the syndicates were
planning a revolution and that every *pied noir* who was a member would be rounded up and forced to fight. Mme. Martin
stopped taking her papers to the syndicates. She said that she
did not want any part of the revolution—which turned out to be
a demonstration in Paris that did not come off.

   Mme. Martin has put her dossier in the gros-point satchel,
along with her old papers and the family photographs. It includes a list of the Martins' own assets in Algeria as well as the
assets of their fathers, who are both dead. Martin will get a
share of the money for his father's holdings as soon as his older
brother, who is sixty-four and lives in Lyon now, is indemnified.
He doubts whether it will amount to very much, though, since
his father, who had a vegetable farm some twenty kilometers
outside Algiers, was forced to sell it at a loss and move his
family to the comparative safety of the city at the beginning of
the war. Mme. Martin's father had a bigger farm, with cows and
goats and chickens, and five hectares of vineyards and three of
grain. Her brother who lives outside Marseille sold half of it in
1958 to raise the money to take their mother out of Algeria.
The rest was abandoned after Mme. Martin's aunt, who had the
farm next door, was murdered. Mme. Martin, however, has
seven sisters and brothers living in France now, and they are all
entitled to a share of the reimbursement for their father's farm.
At best, she says, she will get enough to cancel the rest of her

debt to her older brother, who is a shrewd businessman and charges her bank interest every month.

"I will believe in this contribution when I see the money," Mme. Martin announced one morning when she was feeling homesick and was going through her satchel looking at the old pictures. "They are waiting for us all to die, so they will never have to pay. They say that a hundred thousand *pieds noirs* are dead in France already. Fourteen of my friends—fourteen people from my own quarter of Algiers—are dead here, and they never touched a sou of what was owed them. But, ah, the promises! First De Gaulle and now Pompidou.* When Pompidou needs our vote, he goes on television and says that it is disgraceful that the Accords d'Evian were not respected. But then when he has the power he does nothing. So I do not believe in this contribution—in this money he has promised. Listen." Mme. Martin hurried to the window and closed the shutters. The window in her kitchen opens onto the mountain, where there are no more houses, but, even so, she always closes the shutters when she talks. She does not trust the people in the village. She worries that they will hear her talking and tell the government about it—and that then she will never get the contribution she does not believe in. She has only one confidant in the village—Mme. Duclos, who is the gendarme's wife. But Mme. Duclos is not a villager. She comes from Alsace, and lived in the colonies when her husband was in the Army, and according to Mme. Martin, she "understands." Even so, they talk in the grocery or on the steps of the church at the foot of town. The gendarme's wife does not want gossip, and Mme. Martin has never been asked to visit her in her own house. As

---

* And now Giscard. Giscard d'Estaing made his own promises to the *pieds noirs* during his presidential campaign. When he took office, he announced that he was doubling the annual amount of compensation payments. Later he introduced the revised reimbursement law.

for the other women in the village, Mme. Martin will nod when
she meets them on the road or in the market; she has rarely
spoken to them since the night of her party, in 1966. She used
to see them in the new church, where they liked to gossip,
mornings, on their way home from picking up their bread. But
now they have all stopped going to the church. The village is
Communist, and it never had much use for churches anyway,
even in the days of the papacy at Avignon. The women had
always used their church as a place for chatting and for getting
married properly, and Mme. Martin, with her prayers and her
piety, always crossing herself and smiling at the Virgin, frightened them away. Only Mme. Martin and the three village sorcerers go regularly to the church on weekdays anymore. Occasionally, the baroness, who supplies the candles, goes. So do the
women of the two other *pied-noir* families in the village, but
they are from Oran, and Mme. Martin knows that people from
Oran and Algiers can never get along. She says that the *Oranais*
are loud and vulgar, and give the *pieds noirs* a bad name. Mme.
Martin tends to overlook the fact that most of her husband's
family came from Oran, and she is always startled to hear that
the *Oranais* say the same thing about the *Algérois*.

"Listen," Mme. Martin went on. "They are peasants here.
Imbeciles! They are jealous because we are a little educated and
are from the city and know how to live. It is their mentality.
They are rich, these peasants, but they are misers. They put
their francs in their mattresses and dress in rags. And they
whisper that *we* are rich because we have a toilet—because *they*
would never spend the money for a toilet. Before the doctor
came, they emptied their chamber pots onto the street at night
and then wondered why there was so much sickness every
summer. But a *pied noir* is smart. A *pied noir* will always have
a toilet and a washing machine, and a television set to let the
world in." Mme. Martin pointed to her own television, which
she bought on credit in 1967 and is still paying for. It was the
first television in the village. The man who delivered it warned
her that it might cause trouble with the neighbors, and even now

Mme. Martin makes certain that the sound is low whenever the family watches. She keeps it in the kitchen, where it sits on a little table by the icebox, its screen, like a mid-Victorian piano leg, decorously covered by a little gathered skirt. Mme. Martin thinks that it is more respectable—and certainly more elegant— that way. She said that she had learned about making skirts for furniture in a Parisian women's magazine that she subscribed to in Algiers, but that she herself had thought of covering the screen.

"In Algeria, we knew how to live decently," Mme. Martin went on, pulling a picture of Paul in his First Communion outfit out of the satchel, and then a picture that her husband had taken at the Communion lunch. "Our house was always filled with friends. Everybody eating and talking. In that, the *pieds noirs* are like the Arabs—they love to talk, to entertain. The Arabs were our friends—we understood each other. What did the *pieds noirs* care who had the country, as long as we were left alone?" Mme. Martin stopped, embarrassed. She had never thought of that before—that it didn't really matter whether the French or the Algerians had the country. "When the fighting started, it was different. Nine million Muslims to a million *pieds noirs*. It was like my father's chickens—if you have ten chickens and one is black, the others will kill it as soon as there is fighting. And there is nothing that the poor black chicken can do. After a while we never left the house without a military escort. If the children were sick, I called the soldiers to take them to the doctor. If I needed food and my husband was out working, I had to wait until the soldiers came. We bolted the doors, and for two years we lived like that—with the courtyard boarded over. We lived with mattresses against the windows to stop the bullets from coming in the house. Whenever there was a knock, my husband or Paul would take a gun and wait behind the door, thinking it was Arabs who had come to kill us. There was nothing to do but wait. If you went with the OAS, the FLN would kill you. If you helped the Arabs, the OAS would kill you instead. So we kept the gun, but we kept it hidden, because the

French soldiers were always searching houses, and if you had a
gun they called you OAS and put you in their jails. *Ils sont
bêtes, les Français.* They thought they understood the Arabs,
but that was not true. They would never have understood that
many times when we had trouble it was an Arab who saved us.
At the Marseille port, an Arab woman shared her food with my
children. Once, in Algiers, an Arab who had worked for a while
with my husband saved our lives. He came to our house one day
and said, 'Listen, I am coming with my men tonight to kill the
people in your quarter. Take your children and hide, because I
have my orders, and if I find you here, I will have to kill you,
too.' So we went to my father's farm and spent the night. And
the Arab was right—when we came home, we saw that there
had been fighting, and many of our friends were killed."

Mme. Martin sighed and went on looking through the satchel.
The shrine at Misserghin, where Claude was cured of colic by
the Virgin. A comic book of the life of Notre Dame de Fátima.
A picture postcard of the Virgin, looking a little like Betty
Grable, that her husband had carried in his wallet all through
the Second World War. His letters from the front to Mme.
Martin. And the Croix de Guerre, with palm, that he had been
awarded after the six-month battle that led to the liberation of
Alsace. M. Martin was a *premier canonnier* in the Groupe
d'Artillerie d'Afrique. When he got the cross, he was cited as a
libérateur de la patrie—the Algerians like to say that a Frenchman who fights for France is always a *libérateur de la patrie*,
but an Algerian who fought for France is just an *ancien com-
battant*—and so, in the course of the two world wars, were four
other men in his family. He and his wife have lost thirteen
relatives in France's wars. The *pieds noirs* were proud to die for
France, Mme. Martin says now. Her husband was drafted in
1938, stayed in the Army until France fell, and immediately
reenlisted with the Free French. One of his first jobs in the
Army, according to Mme. Martin, was rounding up deserters
from Provence and marching them, at bayonet point, to join
their companies. She says that the men of Provence, who claim

that the *pieds noirs* are not true Frenchmen, were too cowardly to fight for France themselves. The mayor of the village, whom she likes, was a Maquisard and a Resistance hero, but she refuses to acknowledge the possibility that anyone else around the valley ever risked his life in the Maquis. The village, after all, sent only one soldier to Algeria in the fifties; all the others who were drafted managed to get themselves deferred. Still, she admits that she owes her life and the lives of her children to the French soldiers. They came to her house one night in June of 1962 just ahead of a band of FLN terrorists who were raiding the quarter in reprisal for the death of an Algerian boy. M. Martin and Yvette, in fact, had seen the killing. The boy had been riding his bicycle through their quarter and had been shot by their next-door neighbor on the off-chance that he was carrying a *plastique*—which he was not. The neighbors had expected a reprisal, but the Algerians did not appear until two weeks later, and caught them unprepared. The Martins were saved by the fact that they lived in the last house on the last street in the quarter. Everyone else on their street was dead by the time the soldiers came. Mme. Martin was glad, she says, that she had changed her mind about the next-door neighbor, who had phoned the day before with an offer to crate her furniture for the voyage for 500 francs. He was dead now, his crates were burning on the street, and Mme. Martin had the 500 francs in her satchel when the soldiers, in armored trucks, drove her and the children to the Algiers port. Thousands of *pieds noirs* were camping at the port then, helpless to leave the country, because the OAS had said that anyone who fled would be considered a deserter, and terrorists had been bombing the boats the *pieds noirs* tried to take. The boat the Martins finally took was an old freighter that normally made the run between Algiers and Haifa; it got lost on the way to Marseille and had to turn back to Algiers for readings and begin again. Mme. Martin bought third-class tickets for the family—second class was too expensive, and she spat at a French soldiers at the port who offered to get her second-class accommodations cheaply for a 50-franc bribe.

The trip still cost most of the money in the satchel; the family
arrived in Marseille with 20 francs, or roughly $4.

"I will tell you a story," Mme. Martin said, folding the old
letters from her husband. "I was alone at the Algiers port with
Yvette and the two little ones. Paul had gone to find his father,
who had been working late that night in the city, and I was
trying to find the building where the French soldiers were guarding the *pieds noirs*. I came to the place I thought was right, and
I asked a soldier at the gate to let us in. The soldier looked at
me, with the children, and then he pointed to a street and said,
'Go there. That is where the *pieds noirs* are waiting.' I started
toward the street, and I was almost there when another soldier,
who was a captain, stopped me. '*Bon Dieu!* What are you doing
here?' he asked me. I turned and pointed to the first soldier.
'*He* sent me; he said that the *pieds noirs* are here,' I told the
captain. 'Then he is an assassin,' the captain said. 'Down that
street is the FLN quarter. The soldier sent you there to die.'"
Mme. Martin shook her head. "A year later, here in the village,
I went to the *tabac* to buy cigarettes for my husband, and whom
should I see at the counter, talking to the owner, but the same
soldier who had sent us to die at the Algiers port. I said to him,
'Tell me, weren't you in Algeria?' And he said yes, he was the
son of Blanchot, the farmer, and had been the only village boy
to go. 'Do you remember, by chance, a night in Algiers when
you sent a poor *pied-noir* woman and her children off to the
Arabs to be killed?' I asked him. He looked at me then, and
then he turned away quickly, but I saw in his eyes that he
remembered. 'It is destiny,' I said. 'Now we are neighbors in
this little village. We are here to remind each other. Live with
your conscience now, and I will live with mine.'"

Mme. Martin would say that nothing else of any interest has
happened to her in the village. She lives in the past, like
most of the older *pieds noirs* who came to France. Her life, she
says, ended on the freighter; there is nothing to hope for any-

more. She could have moved to Paris with her family, as one of her sisters did in 1962. She admits that life is much better for the *pieds noirs* in Paris, but she chose Provence because the sun was hot and the weather dry and the country looked a little bit like home. So did half a million of the *pieds noirs* in France now. "What could we do?" Mme. Martin says often. "We *pieds noirs* were so accustomed to a fine climate." There was Aix, of course—or Marseille, with its raucous, polyglot population, its Service des Rapatriés in every paper, and more public housing for its people than any other town in France. But Aix sounded expensive, and there was no work in Marseille for M. Martin when they arrived. They still talk, sometimes, about going to Marseille to settle. The *pieds noirs* are strong there. They live together in huge apartment houses. They make up 15 percent of the city's voters. And Gaston Defferre, the mayor, has installed the president of ANFANOMA as one of his *adjoints*.* M. Martin has said that they can sell the house and move there, but Mme. Martin says no, that it is too late now to start again in such a big city. Carnoux, she thinks, is better; it is a busy little town, a new town, just north of Cassis, that was settled by the French who left Morocco and later by the *Français d'Algérie*. In fact, everybody in Carnoux is from North Africa, and even the houses look it—with flat roofs, and courtyards, and bougainvillea at their doors. Still, Mme. Martin is much too fearful now to leave the village for a *pied-noir* town. She says that if there is ever a war between the French and the Algerians, the Algerians will bomb Carnoux even before they bomb Paris. And she would rather die of sadness in the village than die happy in Carnoux of an Algerian bomb.

So the Martins stay on in the village, dreaming about the past and sometimes bickering about their new neighbors, whom they tend to distinguish according to whether or not the neighbor likes the *pieds noirs*. The mayor likes the *pieds noirs*—by which

* Gaston Defferre is still mayor of Marseille, and apparently he still has a *pied noir* as one of his deputies.

the Martins mean that he has never reported to the tax collector that M. Martin gets paid in francs as well as in produce for looking after the Parisian's garden. For that, they have forgiven him for being a Communist, although they blame the Communists for turning the French against the *pieds noirs* during the Algerian war. They do not believe that the mayor is a Communist, anyway. He is a rich old peasant now, with several vineyards and a flock of sheep that summer in the Alps; he goes to church on Sundays, and M. Martin thinks of him as a good, conservative, Catholic farmer, not so very different from a *Français d'Algérie*. He says that the mayor is clever, and was merely being diplomatic when he joined the Party, which has been supplying mayors to all the villages around the valley since the time of the Maquis. According to Martin, the peasants have no idea what Communism is, anyway, except that it is dead against the government in Paris—a position with which they heartily agree. They have a stubborn sense of independence— all the people from Provence have it—and, moreover, they are insulted by the fact that some of the politicians in Pompidou's party keep their mistresses, and not their wives, in converted valley farms. They are proud that the village voted 98 percent against the government in the last elections. They say that the vote was so satisfying because of the mayor's fine campaign posters: "Vote Communist—the Party of the Small Property Owner."

M. Martin has kept one of the posters, and he likes to look at it and laugh when he is in a good mood. He says that the mayor is a better Catholic than any old woman in the village—better, even, than the curé, who comes from the market town to say a Mass on Sunday mornings and, as is the village custom, to marry people in the new church and bury them from the old one. Everybody in the village gets married in the new church and expects to have his funeral at the old church, but not many of them go to Mass. Even the Martins stopped going after the curé refused to marry Paul and his girlfriend, who was an *Algéroise* from the next village and was four months pregnant at the time.

He insisted that they post their bans and wait out the time that the state requires—and the Martins took this as a sign that the curé definitely did not like *pieds noirs*. Mme. Martin had a loud fight with him in the churchyard, during which she called him a frog in the holy water and he called her an African devil who had come to France to spread debauchery. Mme. Martin, who takes a practical view of youthful passions, decided that the curé must be a Communist, and not a Catholic, to be so puritanical. Paul and his fiancée were married by another curé in the church in the girl's village, and Mme. Martin then sent a note to her own curé, wishing him a transfer to a French colony.

After the curé, the Martins complain most about the village doctor. The doctor came to the village only a year or so before the Martins did, from a small city in the next *département*. The Martins, however, consider him a *pied noir*, like themselves, because he spent his first five years of practice in North Africa. The doctor considers himself a Parisian because his wife was born only seventy-three kilometers outside Paris. And the villagers consider him a scandal because he got the carpenter's wife pregnant, and the carpenter, who was a villager, had to sell his shop and move his wife and family to another town. Everyone in the village agrees that the doctor is incompetent, but everyone goes to him, although the peasants do try to avoid him until they are very old and, theoretically, have less to lose if they happen to die while he is treating them. The Martins blame the villagers for the doctor, since the villagers prefer gossiping about the doctor to signing a complaint against him and sending it to the government, which pays most of their medical bills. Mme. Martin once started to compose a letter—after the doctor left Yvette, who was in the middle of labor, to keep an assignation with the carpenter's wife—but she tore it up the next morning. No one would have listened to a *pied noir*, she says now. Besides, the family needs the doctor. Mme. Martin has asthma —she had her first attack in Marseille, getting off the freighter. Claude, who goes on fasts, is always fainting. Jean-Jacques gets beaten up fighting with teen-age *métropolitains*. And Yvette's

twin babies keep falling down the steep stone steps in Mme.
Martin's house. The doctor, who lives a few doors down the
Rue de la Libération, will always come at night in an emergency,
but the Martins resent him, not so much for his incompetence
as for the fact that he never speaks to them in public and always
keeps them waiting in his office until all the villagers who wander
in have gone.

Mme. Martin does not suffer the doctor calmly. The villagers
still talk about the day he kept her waiting over three hours and
she grabbed him by the stethoscope and called him a *sale pied
noir*. They talk about all of Mme. Martin's scenes, because they
are people who keep their shutters and their mouths closed, as
they like to put it, and would never think of asking a family in
for coffee before it had been in the village for a century and had
intermarried with their own at least ten times. The mayor says
that this is just "the peasant mentality"—that the other villagers
talk against the *pieds noirs* because they enjoy gossip, but that
they mean no harm. He likes to remind the Martins that in June
of 1962, when he called a meeting of the village council, all
thirteen members agreed to his plan to open up the old orphanage. Still, the villagers managed to discourage four of the
seven *pied-noir* families who tried to settle permanently in the
village. They found the refugees noisy and pretentious, and very
high-handed—a quality that the more educated villagers at-
tributed to their having so recently had nine million Algerians to
boss around. The older peasants made no such distinction between the *pieds noirs* and the Algerians. They still call them
both *les Africains*, and they are shocked by the young Parisian
women who summer in the valley and carry their babies on their
backs, exactly the way they have heard the Africans do. Yvette
was careful, when she had her first baby, to buy a proper baby
carriage and wheel it daily up and down the Rue de la Libération. But the carriage merely irritated the old village women. It
was too big and too shiny, and they said to each other that only
a *pied noir*, showing off, would ever buy such a vulgar contrap-

tion. No one knows exactly what they mean by *pied noir*. The three sorcerers mean that there is new and powerful magic—North African magic—in the village and that they fear it, whereas the two respectable widows who sell groceries mean that something not quite proper, not quite French, has come to the village. Mme. Martin no longer patronizes either of the widows' shops. One of them refused her offer to share the transportation when they both had children at the Catholic day school in the market town; the other once offered her credit and then spread word that Mme. Martin would never pay her bills. Mme. Martin is resigned to shopping with Rimbaud, the third grocer, although Rimbaud cheats in his addition and, as a theoretician of the local Party, feels politically obliged to shortchange his *pied-noir* customers with Belgian francs, which he keeps for that purpose in a small glass jar on his counter.

Mme. Martin still misses her old grocer, and her old butcher, who knew her parents and could remember her as a small girl. "Who knows me here?" she says whenever she talks about them. "Who is there here who can greet me when I go shopping and tell me that Yvette's babies have their great-grandfather's eyes?" She says that the villagers are bitter because their own children go to the towns to earn a living and they are left to die alone. According to her, the children of the *pieds noirs* are different. Yvette, Claude, and Jean-Jacques are still with her, "like chickens around a mother hen." Paul is gone, of course, but Paul is special. He has his *bac* and is an insurance accountant, and she says it is only right that he should make his own place in the world. She is very proud of Paul, even now that he has stopped sending a monthly contribution home, but she says that she doesn't expect the villagers to understand. She says that the villagers are not ambitious for their children, as the *pieds noirs* are, and she tells a story about a village woman who met her on the road and asked her what her oldest son was doing. "My son is an accountant with a big company," Mme. Martin said proudly. The woman, hearing this, looked

smug. "Well, my son has a *very* good position," the woman told
her. "He is second apprentice to a man who bakes croissants in
Aix."

Yvette lives in a little rented house at the bottom of the village, but she spends more time at the Martins', visiting her
mother, than she does at home. Mme. Martin says that Yvette is
her only consolation. Yvette comes in the morning to help her
with the cleaning; she leaves her children there most afternoons
in summer, when she goes to the valley to work as a maid for a
Parisian couple, and at night, when she picks them up, she
always stays awhile to help her mother with the family's supper.
She is a rosy, buxom girl of twenty-four, and resolutely cheerful. *"Il faut vivre"* is Yvette's favorite phrase. She says *"Il faut
vivre"* to her husband when she sits up late in bed, with her
glasses on her nose, studying the dresses in her favorite mail-
order catalogue, and she says it to Mme. Martin when she
leaves for work and sees her mother crying because the Martins
once had servants of their own. Yvette is not a bit ashamed of
having to be a maid now, although she says that she hated
working for the villagers before the Parisians came and bought
houses in the valley. The Parisians pay 5 francs an hour, and
like to talk, and have all the best appliances, but the villagers,
she says, were stingy, and they were rude to her because she
was a *pied noir*. They would look for dust in corners, and if
they found it, they would shake their heads and say, "Ah, so
this is how you sweep in Algeria." Or they would hold their
wineglasses to the light to look for smudges, saying, "We are
very particular about our rinsing here in France."

Yvette says that it galls the village women now to see her
working happily for the Parisians. And this amuses her, because
she is the only young woman in the village with pocket money
of her own. She has been working, and saving, since she first
came. She had lost the habit of school, she says, having left it at
twelve, after Algerians raided the school in Algiers where she

and Paul were students, and slit the throats of some children from the country who were boarding there. Mme. Martin decided then that even in the daytime, when the schools were guarded, education in Algiers was too dangerous for her children. They never went back. Paul took correspondence courses —Monday mornings, soldiers drove to the house with a week's lessons, and Saturdays, at noon, drove back to pick them up— and got his *bac* that way, but Yvette, who hadn't liked lessons to begin with, retired to console her mother and help care for her two small brothers. She can count the times in the next two years that she was able to leave the house. The first time, she found her great-aunt murdered. The second time, some soldiers took her downtown to the dentist. And the third time, she saw her neighbor shoot the Algerian boy. Yvette went out for the last time less than a week before the family fled. She wanted a pickle, she says. She wanted a pickle for her lunch and was too eager to call the soldiers to take her to the grocer's or to wait for her father and Paul—who usually did the marketing together, the gun hidden in Paul's pocket—to come home. While her mother was busy with the children, she unbolted the door and tiptoed out, toward the Berber grocer's down the road. She was just at the door to his shop when someone behind her opened fire. The grocer pulled her in, and, for lack of a better place to hide her, shut her in his big icebox. Yvette was nearly frozen when the soldiers cleared the neighborhood.

Yvette says that by the time she came to the village there was no use in starting school again. Besides, the boys and girls her age teased her. They wanted to see her feet, and they called her names because she was covered from head to toe with hives for the first few months she was there. It was the calm in France that gave her hives, she says. It made her nervous. She was always waiting for something terrible to happen. The sound of the farmers' shotguns during the hunting season would send her running to her mother, crying, "Mama, Mama, the Arabs are attacking!" And the sound of their trucks backfiring made her think that the OAS had come with *bombes plastiques* to punish them. The stillness at night when she woke from a nightmare frightened her more than the dream itself, she says.

Yvette had no friends at the beginning—the peasants had warned their children to stay away from the *pied-noir* children —but she laughs about that when she talks now. "They were so young," she says. "And I was a big, well-developed girl, you understand—a *pied-noir* girl. I would see these kids running through the village, giggling and shouting and playing games, and I would think, *Sauve-toi!* These children will give you a complex if you let them." What Yvette wanted most then was a husband. She got a job cleaning for the wife of the *notaire*'s assistant, and gave half her salary to her parents and stashed the rest in her "trousseau" piggy bank. By the time she was sixteen she had a long white nightgown from Marseille, and eight pink sheets and four pillowcases waiting to be embroidered. She also had a dress for dancing. Yvette loved dancing—she says that all *pieds noirs* love dancing—and she knew that every Saturday night there was bound to be a dance or a saint's-day fête at one of the villages not far from home. The boys and girls in her village always went to them. The girls went with their mothers, looking for husbands, and the boys went together, looking for fights and for the lovely, legendary girl who would come to a dance without a chaperon. Yvette would hear them talking Saturday mornings at the fountain by the blacksmith's barn, and sometimes she would join them, hoping that someone would think to offer her a ride. "They would say afterward, 'What a nice dance we had last night, Yvette. What a shame that you weren't there with us.' And I would always say, 'How would I have known about it?'—because *pieds noirs* are clever and we always have the right answer. But then I would run to my mother crying. I wanted to kill them all." Finally, Yvette got Paul to take her to the dances. They met the children of the Italian farmers who had come to Provence before the war. And they met other *pieds noirs*, who had been resettled in little villages like their own. Yvette says that the *pieds noirs* were always attracted to each other at the dances. "You would meet a person who was warm and friendly and who danced well—not like the peasants here, who jump around and think that they are dancing. And later he would say, 'I think I should tell you—I am a *sale pied noir*.' And you would say, 'Me—I am a *sale pied noir*, too.' And then you would both laugh, because you knew then why you had got along so well. The boys from the village were all jealous. The boys would ignore me on the street at home but they would always flirt with me at dances. They were like that. Once, I had a boyfriend in the village. He was the blacksmith's son and he was very handsome, but his friends made fun of him for seeing me, so he dropped me. For one month, I didn't see him. And then, one night, he came to the movies in town when I was there with Paul. He passed right by me and didn't even say *bonsoir*, but when the lights went out he sneaked over and sat down next to me. So I said in a loud voice, 'What? Are you ashamed to be sitting next to a *pied noir*? Are you going to sneak away before the lights go on again?' And I stood up and left the theatre, but as I left I heard that everyone was laughing at him. 'Ha!' they said. 'The *pied noir* has made an idiot of Henri.' After that, I never had a boyfriend in the village. *Chat échaudé craint l'eau froide*."

Yvette met Georges, her husband, at a summer saint's-day fête in another village, when she was twenty and he was seventeen. She had gone to the fête with her family, and as soon as she saw Georges she told her mother that she loved him. He looked like Nino Ferrer, the singing star. Georges did look something like Ferrer, apparently, scrubbed for a fête and in his slick brown suit. Yvette says that she was a little disappointed, three days later, when he came to see her at her own house. Georges was working in a tile factory at the time, and he arrived in his boss's truck, with some roof tiles for the village mason, completely covered with grease and dark-red dust. He was wearing new overalls, but he had forgotten to put his shirt on for the visit. Moreover, Yvette noticed in the daylight that most of Georges's teeth were gone. Georges was a brawler. He had spent his first six years in an orphanage in Paris, and had finally been taken on by his maternal grandparents, who lived in the village where Yvette had met him. They put Georges to work when he was eleven. He made his way, digging in quarries, picking cherries in season, and working here and there in tile factories and on road-construction crews, but he was a scrappy sort of boy, and very simple, and when he met Yvette he had never kept a job for more than two months.

Yvette liked Georges because he was young and she was used to looking after boys, she says, and she reasoned that it would take her only a year or so to earn the money to replace his teeth. Her younger brothers liked him because he was close to their own age and could become their friend. Even her father didn't seem to mind him, and that pleased Yvette, who had heard that Pierre, the café proprietor, always took a shotgun to the beaux *his* daughters brought home. As for Mme. Martin, she was happy, since Georges had managed to arrive at lunchtime, and anyone who came at lunchtime qualified as real company. She set an extra place at the table, and Georges joined them. No one mentioned to him that day that they were *pieds noirs*.

"When he discovered where we came from, he was very angry, and shouted, *'Moi, je n'aime pas les pieds noirs!'* " Yvette says now. "And then he brooded. But that was nothing, because I knew that it would pass. I knew by then that he already loved me. And, besides, Georges is very supple. I have a stronger character than he has, and if he broods, what of it? He is always brooding about things he doesn't understand. You see, he had nothing of his own before he met me. No real mother. No father. No friends. The day he came for lunch, he and my brothers went upstairs and played and fought with pillows, and later he came down to me and said, 'Now I have a family.' Even now, he is still jealous. He comes to me and says, 'I never had anything. Now I have you and the children and your family, and I am always frightened that I am going to lose you.' And he hits me. Or he threatens to tear up all my pretty clothes and throw them out the window so that no one else will want me and try to take me away from him. But I am stronger. I hit him back. I say to him, 'If you throw that dress away, I'll go to the store and buy *two* just like it.' So there is really nothing he can do.' "

Yvette and Georges were married in October, after she had embroidered her eight pink sheets with hearts and lilies and Georges's name. Georges, by then, was already living in the village, sharing a room at the Martins' with Jean-Jacques and Claude. In fact, he had not been home since late in August. His grandparents had thrown him out when he told them—they had just signed papers permitting him to marry—that his girlfriend was a *pied noir*. They came to the village twice, though—once to ask the Martins about a dowry, and then to attend the wedding, because they didn't want to miss the wedding lunch.

Yvette was married in the new church by the curé. She had hoped to wear a miniskirt, but Georges had protested that he wanted her to look like a moving-picture bride, and so she wore a long white net gown from her mail-order catalogue. Four of Georges's friends from the tile factory came to the wedding, and ten girls, six of them *pieds noirs* and the rest Italians whom Yvette had met at dances and at saint's-day fêtes. No one from the village came except the doctor's wife, who wanted Yvette to work for her, and the wife of the *notaire*'s assistant. Yvette says now that the villagers were jealous, because she, a *pied noir*, was marrying someone who was *presque Parisien*.

Georges is twenty-one now, and he is almost as much of a stranger in the village as Yvette. He is on his fourth job since the wedding—this time he is working for the plunber—but no one knows how long he will keep it, since he alarms the villagers by standing on the roofs of his clients' houses and joyfully flinging down old pipe parts. Yvette says that he loses his jobs because he happens to be married to her. Mme. Martin, who is rather down on Georges now that he has taken to storming out of the house when he hears her criticizing Frenchmen, says that he loses them because he is *"un peu stupide."* Georges is good-hearted, in a random, uncomprehending sort of way, and when the Martins complain about the French, they hurt his feelings. Some of the people in the village like him. The mayor likes him, and got him his third job there, driving for a farmer, when Yvette was pregnant with the twins and he needed work. But Georges is always dropping pipes, and racing the plumber's truck up narrow roads and into the front of people's houses, and the villagers think that he is probably a little crazy. Why else, they say, would anybody with the congenital disadvantage of not being from their village ever compound his problems by marrying into Yvette Martin's family?

Lately Georges has been talking about leaving the village. He says that maybe he will move, as an indentured plumber, to Australia, where he has heard there are a lot of bathrooms being built. But Yvette refuses to talk to him about Australia. She wants to be near her mother, like a good *pied-noir* daughter, and, besides, now that she has her husband and her own children, she is beginning to feel a little more at home. She likes to go dancing with Georges on Saturday evenings, and to stroll through the village on Sunday, showing him off to all the farmers. She will always dress him up when they go out together, and she sees to it now that he washes carefully with laundry soap. People who meet them at the café sometimes complain that they cannot understand Georges, who speaks with a mushy, toothless kind of sound, but when they do, Yvette will simply look at them and smile. She knows that what they have heard is his Parisian accent. She is proud to have captured Georges. *"Pour moi, il est impeccable,"* she likes to tell her mother, and her mother agrees that Yvette has certainly shown the village that she did not need any of its own young men.

Claude, his mother says, was always delicate and moody, even before the family left Algiers. At six, he caught a bronchial infection—he says now that he got it from the Algerians—that must have developed complications because he was in bed with fever for a year and was still too weak to walk when the family fled. Mme. Martin held him in her arms throughout the two-day crossing on the freighter, and Yvette took over in Marseille when her mother collapsed from fright and fatigue and her attack of asthma. Claude is still usually a little feverish, though it is difficult to tell now whether the fever comes from his illness or from his religious enthusiasms, or from a combination of the two. His cheeks are flushed, and his wide black eyes are always wet and glittery, but Claude is a handsome boy, and these things make him look less like an invalid than like a sort of overheated cherub. "Handsome, but too thin," his mother says whenever she talks about Claude. She thinks that he is thin because of the fasts he undertakes, and she nags him constantly about his diet, which for the moment consists of half a tomato and a piece of dry toast a day. She blames his religion, which she says is morbid and conceited, not natural like the Catholicism of the *pieds noirs*. She knows that he would like to be a martyr, or at least a saint, but she wants him to take the medicine she buys for his digestion, and she tells him that being a martyr or a saint is a gift from the Virgin, and that there is no use planning and practicing and fussing about it now. Claude himself swears that he is not fasting—he says that suffering has ruined his liver and that this is the cross he has to bear. But Yvette, who has a big healthy appetite and no patience at all with deprivation, claims that, stopping by at night, she has come upon Claude, in the dark, at the icebox, gobbling down leftovers from the family supper. She says that he is showing off, with his dry toast and his tomato, and that he wants attention because he is having romantic problems with his *chérie*.

Claude works for a carpenter—not Maurice, the new village carpenter, who does not like *pieds noirs* and refused to take Claude on when Mme. Martin asked him, but another carpenter, five kilometers along the road to town—and he met the girl Yvette refers to as his *chérie* when he went to work there. She is a melancholy Italian from the valley, and is very diligent about her job, which consists of keeping the accounts for Claude's carpenter. Claude says he decided that, given their combined talents, he and the girl could have a fine atelier of their own one day. He announced to his parents that he had a

fiancée—a word that he prefers to *chérie*, because it sounds
more spiritual—and he started taking the girl to Saturday
dances, and even to the cemetery, where he stands on Sunday
mornings with three tin cans marked "Blind," "Crippled," and
"Aged," collecting money for the favorite causes of the
baroness. Their problems began in the cemetery one Sunday
when the girl, who had eighteen francs in the can marked
"Aged," told him that she would like their atelier to make
beautiful modern furniture, like the furniture at the Prisunic.
Claude knows one thing about his future atelier, and that is that
it will produce "antiques." He loves old furniture. To Claude, a
piece of old furniture is something sacred, like a dead relative
or his Algiers home. He has been learning about antiques by
mending the furniture that the Parisians in the valley find on
their farmsteads. He used to practice on his family's furniture,
but now he confines his experiments to his own bedroom, which
is the biggest bedroom in the house, and which he appropriated
from his parents when he went to work and became, officially,
the head of the family. He takes care of the room himself,
scrubbing the floors, waxing the chests and chairs that he finds
on abandoned farms around the valley, and keeping his favorite
pictures of the saints' temptations laid out in an aesthetic and
offhand fashion across the bed. He says that he considers the
ambience crucial for his meditations. He cannot tolerate dis-
order and is afraid of change. His mother says that he was
screaming when the soldiers in Algiers arrived to save them—
but not so much from the shooting as from fear that the family
would leave without the little knife and fork he always used.
She put them in her satchel at the last moment, and Claude still
refuses to eat with any other silver. He feels the same way about
his room, he says. The last time that Mme. Martin cleaned it,
she moved a picture, and Claude, who couldn't find the picture
for an hour, had a tantrum, after which he went on a diet of
melons—it was the melon season—for two weeks. Mme. Martin, who called him a *vieux garçon* and then regretted it, does
not enter his room anymore. Claude has barred the whole

family. "It is all mine," he says. "And no one can touch a thing there. No one can even sit down without asking my permission first." No one in the family wants to, really. The room is decorated with pictures of the Crucifixion, and there are three small shrines to the Virgin, where Claude can kneel and say his prayers. The wall over the bed is nearly covered with the pictures of his dead relatives, framed in lace paper and velvet ribbons, but there is a space left empty in the center, which Claude is reserving for his parents' photographs. He says that "after God calls them" their pictures will complete the room. Mme. Martin, who likes to see a wall filled properly, has to agree with Claude, but the empty, waiting space above the bed is disconcerting to her husband, who sometimes sneaks into the room to have a look around the closet. Claude's closet is his secret. It is papered with pinups of Italian starlets and with glossy pink nudes that he clips each month from girlie magazines.

Claude did not start school until a year after the family came to the village. At first he was sick, and then there was no money for books and clothes. He was ten by the time he did start, and then he hated the village school so much that before the term was over, his mother had to move him to the Catholic day school where the grocer sent her sons. He says that he liked the new school because everybody there was pious and the teachers told the local children that Jesus apparently loved the *pieds noirs* and they should, too. When he had been there a year, he punched a teacher who had slapped one of his classmates. "Do you see the cross you wear?" Claude asked the teacher. "It will pay you later for your sins now." The teacher repented. He blessed Claude for his "intention," and promised to say a Mass for him that evening after school. It was then, Claude says, that he knew for certain that he had "the power." He says he must have got it from his great-grandmother, who laid hands on the sick and prayed and made them well. His grandmother had the power, too. And so has Mme. Martin, although she has never used it. She prefers the medicine she buys at the pharmacy— she says that medicines are as good as prayers and hands for most things, and just as cheap, now that the government pays for them. But before she dies she will pass the prayers and incantations that she learned from her mother on to Claude, and maybe to Jean-Jacques, though not to Yvette and Paul, who, according to Claude, are too frivolous to have the power. Claude is already practicing on dogs and cats and crippled pigeons, but he says that animals, like babies, are innocent, holy creatures, and so are much easier to cure than adults. Last summer he tried out his power on Yvette's small bedside table, which was her wedding present from Georges's grandmother and was so full of the old woman's malevolence that it jumped around at night. Yvette had made a practical assessment of the situation. "If it wasn't the table, it would be the armoire," she told him. "And who could sleep at night with a jumping armoire in the room?" But Claude was determined to resist the table; he was very confident that day, having cured his carpenter's dog of blocked tear ducts. He put a church candle on the table, sprinkled it with holy water, and waited for an hour, with his hands trembling over the offensive furniture. The table did stop jumping for a fortnight, but then it started again, and Claude was forced to have a consultation with a hand trembler from the next village, an old man who had once cured him of a sprained arm. The curer came and looked things over, but then he told Claude that Georges's mother had already established her malign presence in the house. He agreed with Yvette, he said. If it weren't the table jumping, it would be the armoire, and no one can sleep at night with a jumping armoire in the room.

The curer is Claude's hero. The old man likes the *pieds noirs*, who he says are "the true Catholics and believers," and who have done a good deal to revive his practice, which had fallen off before the Algerian war. He is licensed by the state, keeps office hours, like a doctor, has a waiting room with the latest *Jours de France* and *Paris-Match*, and cures by drawing crosses on his patients with oil from an old ink bottle and then lifting their afflictions into his trembling hands. Claude first met him at a quarry in the valley, where he worked for a while before he joined the carpenter and where the curer likes to moonlight in his slack seasons. He says he knew at once that the old man had *"le fluide magnétique,"* which is what Claude often calls the power. He invited the curer home that evening for a glass of *pastis*, and asked his advice about the village sorcerers.

Claude knows more than anyone else in the village about the three sorcerers. He sees them every morning at the cemetery, scraping up the dirt around the tombstones to use as an ingredient in their magic charms. One of them is an old spinster named Berthe, who raises chickens in a hovel, and who even the villagers will admit is more miserly than they consider proper. The second sorcerer is the widow of an old mechanic who spent seven years in prison for collaborating with the Germans and dropped dead of a stroke not long ago by the Martins' front door. The third sorcerer is the mad daughter of the butcher, but people in the village rarely trouble themselves about her because she makes most of her magic against the Parisians in the valley who take their business to the supermarket in town. No one knows whether the sorcerers are particularly angry at the Martins because of Claude's magnetic fluid, or because he spies on them, mornings, in the cemetery, or because they hate the *pieds noirs*. Berthe certainly hates the *pieds noirs*. She spits when she talks about *les Africains*, and she even sacrificed a chicken and left it, stuck with pins, on the Martins' doorstep on the day Yvette replaced her as maid to the *notaire*'s assistant. The *notaire*'s assistant had dismissed Berthe after he ran out of clean white shirts one morning and his wife confessed that Berthe would do the laundry only under a full moon. Berthe blamed *les Africains*. She and Claude had a confrontation near the graveyard, and Claude, who was not yet ten then, called loudly on God to punish her. Unhappily, a funeral procession was coming toward them at the moment, and the sorcerers, who consider themselves exemplary Catholics, never forgave Claude for the disgrace. They keep sprinkling cemetery dirt on his mother's doorstep. They got into the house one day and put a ball of copper wire, laced with spices, behind the television set, which then broke down. Last spring, when Claude was complaining of fainting spells and blindness, his friend the curer said that one of the sorcerers must have bought a camera, taken Claude's picture, and pricked the eyes with pins. It is true, certainly, that the sorcerers, like the curer, have been very busy since Claude arrived. Claude, in fact, says they are so demanding that he hardly has time left over for his true vocation, which is being the conscience of the whole village. No one in the village believes this—Claude is relentless in his prayerful, admonitory pursuit of villagers he thinks have been unfriendly to his family. There is Pierre, who tried to kiss Claude's mother and then, when she slapped him, shouted, "So the *pieds noirs* are savages! Then what I have heard is true!" There is the grocer with the Belgian francs on his counter, who once gave the Martins a tank of Butagaz for their oven and, after they almost died, protested that he had not known the gas tank had a leak. There is a farmer who told the baroness that if she let a *pied noir* make her collections in the graveyard he was certain to keep the money for himself. There is the doctor, of course. And the new village carpenter, who explained to Mme. Martin that he could not take Claude on as an apprentice because Claude went out too much to be *sérieux*. Claude ignores the *notaire*'s assistant, who would probably qualify as the biggest scoundrel in the village, having taught the plumber's idiot son to sign his name in order to use him as a silent partner in a number of odd but very profitable land transfers. But then the *notaire*'s assistant arranged to buy the Martins' house for them after the farmer who owned it had refused to sell to *pieds noirs*. The house, which a visiting *fonctionnaire* from the Beaux-Arts noticed, is classified now as a historic monument and is worth seven or eight times what the Martins paid for it.*

Claude has more than enough to keep him busy anyway. He

---

* At last offer, the house was worth nearly fifty times what the Martins paid.

works a six-day week, from six in the morning till eight at night, for his salary—200 francs—and he has to bicycle to the carpenter's and back at least twice daily, since, fasting or not, he will eat his lunch only at home. Claude will stay in the village, and he will have his atelier one day, if not his *chérie*. He is determined to stay. He says it is his calling as a Catholic to remind the villagers of their own and France's sins against the *pieds noirs*. "It is better to have a true enemy than a false friend," he tells his mother, who takes credit for having taught him that herself. "I know the people here now, and I am going to stay here always because they want so much for us to go."

Jean-Jacques is the smart one in the family. He knows it, and the rest of the family knows it—he was the child who would stay in school and one day go to the university to study law. It is doubtful now whether he will ever get there—there is not enough money, since Paul stopped sending part of his salary home. The government gives Jean-Jacques a little over 60 francs a month toward his expenses at the *lycée* in the market town, and Mme. Martin says that last year she spent twice that on his books and lunches and transportation to the town and back. She wrote to the Minister of Education last spring and even enclosed a stamped envelope, but no one answered her letter, and now she says that the government is treating its students the way it treats its *pieds noirs*. "Anyone can pick a cherry tree or hoe," she said in her letter. "But not everyone can be a student. When someone is smart, as my Jean-Jacques is, you must open doors for him." The mayor apparently agreed, because he offered Jean-Jacques a job last summer, helping a crew that was going to dig the gutters for the first sewerage system the village has ever had. The mayor had been waiting nine years for Paris to authorize his sewerage project, and there were debates all spring in the village about the way the project should be carried out. The district administrator, thinking about the tourists who would be driving through in summer, said that the dirt from the digging should be trucked away and not left to make the roads unsightly. Some of the villagers, such as Pierre and Beratti, the proprietor of the other café, agreed with the administrator. But most of them said the mayor was right when he argued that trucking the dirt away would cost too much in time and money and that, anyway, if they left the dirt, it could then be used to fill the holes. Finally, after months of talking, the mayor and the administrator compromised: they announced that the dirt dug up would be carried exactly twenty centimeters off the road. Jean-Jacques, who had been waiting since June to earn some money, went to work on the twelfth of August. That morning a rock fell on his foot and crushed a toenail, which had to be removed. The doctor did it, for twice what would have been his first week's salary, and Mme. Martin, with visions of accidents and bills, ordered Jean-Jacques home till school began.

Jean-Jacques is tall and gaunt, and he looks like a student, with his round steel-rimmed glasses and a little beard that he has just grown. He reads a lot, and already speaks Spanish, German, Latin, and Italian. He has two obsessions—his education and the French. Jean-Jacques loathes the French with an intensity that even his family tells him is excessive, although his mother is proud of it, really, and when she complains about the French she will often say, "But this is nothing. You should ask Jean-Jacques." His first memory of Marseille is of an abandoned hut, with no beds and no water, where the family stopped for several days. His first memory of the village is of his mother, at the bus stop, crying, while the peasants, at their fête, danced in the schoolyard and a band played. He will never forget that night, he says. "My memories are bad, but they are stronger than I am. You see my father. Seven years of war in France. Then seven years of war at home. And now the French spit on him. So he drinks and he is crazy, but no wonder. His suffering has made him fanatical—and I fear the same thing is happening to me. To understand me, you must think of Aznavour's song about *les enfants de la guerre*. A child of war grows up too fast. I grew up too fast. I grew up, in a way, against myself. And

I am still divided. Sometimes now I am an adult. I can recognize my hate and understand it. But then, suddenly, it takes me over, and my thoughts are the thoughts of a boy who is lonely and bitter and afraid. The child is always there. You are wounded, and suddenly the child in you will say, 'They are wounding me because they do not love me.' And you become *méchant* then, like a child. You draw yourself up and you fight back. You do not want to fight, but you know that if you do not draw up, without fear, then you are nothing, you die. And so I fight the French. I am accustomed to hitting and getting hit. And I fight them in my mind, always. The wounded child is always in my mind. When I came here, I tried. I wanted to be friends. But the children here avoided me. They treated me as if I were a sort of germ—a dangerous germ to be avoided. I felt it. I felt that I was not loved. So I fought, and I tried, and then I fought again. Even now it is the same, though maybe it is worse here, in this village. The *esprit* is small here. My teacher—she was small because I was a *pied noir*, and so she said to my mother that I was an imbecile. She said that sending me to school was just a waste of time. That is the French spirit. The French do not say no. They never say no to anything, but if they don't like you, they make whatever it is you want to do impossible. At the *lycée* it is better because the intelligent always understand. But in the village nothing changes. It is not politics or pride that makes them hate us—it is the peasant mind. The peasant says that you are French if you are from his village. If not, *sauve-toi, tu es mal tombé.*"

Jean-Jacques has made himself two promises. One is that he will leave the village, and the other is that he will never fight for France. He says that he is disillusioned with nationality and politics—that he would rather die in prison than fight for the country if it goes to war. He is eighteen now, and very certain. The French, he says, are never certain. "They do not know why they hate. They hate the *pieds noirs*, but if you ask them why, they cannot tell you. And they hate the Arabs, too. They say they're for them, but they are scared of the Arabs. And why?

The Arabs did nothing to them. I tell them, 'Well, I hate the Arabs too. I know it is wrong, but at least I know my reason. You—you hate with no reason at all.' "

When Jean-Jacques goes dancing Saturdays, his mother waits up with bandages and a bottle of iodine ready on the kitchen table. He hitchhikes when he has to—he says that no one from the village will take a *pied noir* with him—and if he is lucky, a *pied noir* from another village drives him home. Otherwise, he sleeps in a field and waits for a bus that circles the valley Sunday mornings—and then his mother knows that he has had a fight. Jean-Jacques is always getting into fights at fêtes and dances. Usually the *pieds noirs* will fight the French boys, but sometimes it is the *pieds noirs* against the Algerians who work in factories around the market town. The French will never join in when the Algerians and the *pieds noirs* are fighting. And the Algerians go home when the *pieds noir*s are fighting the French. Jean-Jacques says that the only time a *pied noir* gets any chance to dance at dances is when the French and the Algerians are fighting one another. That happens often, but not often enough, apparently, to have prevented Jean-Jacques from losing three teeth, cracking a rib, and dislocating a finger—not to mention getting assorted cuts, black eyes, and bruises—over the past year. He says that the way he cracked his rib is instructive, because it happened at a fête that he went to with a French friend. The fight started after the disappearance of his friend's sweater, which Jean-Jacques discovered on the back of a boy from the village just across the valley. Jean-Jacques says that he asked the boy politely to give the sweater back but that before he could even finish, the boy had called his friends. They started beating Jean-Jacques, who was not in particularly good condition to defend himself, haviing lost his toenail only the week before. There were boys from his own village watching, but none of them stepped in to help him. Neither, for that matter, did the friend whose sweater he had found. "But why didn't you help? It was for your sweater that I did it," he asked his friend when the fight was over. He says that his friend was ashamed at first and din't answer. But later he came up to Jean-Jacques and whispered that he hadn't wanted to be seen fighting for a *pied noir*.

One night in September, M. Martin sat at the kitchen table, finishing supper, while Mme. Martin stood at the sink, rinsing out a set of new wineglasses. It was an occasion for Mme. Martin—her husband is rarely home for supper anymore. He comes for lunch, which is his big meal, but by suppertime he has usually started drinking, and because he is embarrassed—lecherous, as Mme. Martin puts it—he prefers to wait until she is sleeping to come back. Mme. Martin had made some cookies for him, and she had bought the glasses and a bottle of Asti Spumante. Her husband had already opened the wine. He was at the table in his undershirt, and he hadn't bothered to shave for days, but he was in a good humor and in the mood to talk. He said that he missed talking with friends, evenings, in Algeria —he still found it curious that *métropolitains* should be so cold.

"Individually, I would always take an Arab over a Frenchman," he said, slapping his knee because the thought amused him. "I have nothing against the Arab. I embrace the Arab. I want to share my bread with him, the way we used to do."

Mme. Martin shuddered. There are more than 100,000 Algerians working in the south of France, and, while she finds it extremely satisfying that Algeria has been so poor since independence that all those people have had to come to France to earn their living, she is always afraid that her husband will get drunk one night and bring an Algerian home.

M. Martin laughed. "You worry too much. Believe me, the Arabs are like the Germans. Alone, they are fine. It is only when they are together, with a leader, that they go mad."

"I say that the day an Arab comes into this house I leave it," Mme. Martin told him.

"And *I* say that you have the habits of a timid, fearful woman," her husband said, and then he turned. "My poor wife. She has had too much fear in her life."

Mme. Martin put the glasses on the table. "I'm frightened of getting killed," she said. "You're telling me not to fear the dog that has already bitten me."

M. Martin shrugged. "You see, she does not understand the psychology of crowds—that is her real problem."

"It isn't true. I remember the Arab who came and said to hide the children. He said that he had orders to kill us and that if he didn't his friends would get angry and kill him instead." Mme. Martin thought for a minute. "Still, when I see an Arab now, I think, Does this man want to kill me? It's the very first thing I think of."

'You think that because you were always in the house at home. You didn't have the experience of human contact with the Arabs, the way I did. I tell you, if an Arab saw you now, he would be ashamed," M. Martin said, and added, "Five times the Arabs tried to kill me. Twice with pistols, once with a knife, once with Army rifles, and once with a crowbar. It was my assistant who saved me when the man with the crowbar came. An *Arab* saved me. The assassin ran away, and when I saw him on the street later, he couldn't look me in the eyes. He was ashamed." M. Martin sat back with his glass of wine. He said he was thinking of the time an Algerian really almost killed him. The man was a Harki—the Algerians who took the side of France were called Harkis—and a soldier in Algiers with the French Army.

"This man—this Harki—he knocked on our door and asked my husband to come with Paul to fix a power saw," Mme. Martin said. "My husband agreed. But *I* knew, inside, that there was something wrong. I said to my husband that the man was a traitor, but my husband laughed and took the boy."

"You cannot always be listening to a fearful woman," M. Martin protested.

"Still, I went to the Army to ask about this man, and just as I arrived I saw him in the street, outside the barracks, whispering to a group of Arab men. There was a French captain at the gate, and I pointed to the man and said, 'I want to talk to you in private because that man you see there is a traitor. He is going to kill my husband this afternoon.' 'Madame, that is a grave charge,' the captain said, but I told him that it was better to be mistaken than to see my husband and my son dead, and so we went with some soldiers to the place they had been told to go." Mme. Martin shook her head, looking at her husband. "We got there just in time," she said. "The Arabs had them both surrounded. They had their rifles drawn. 'So you have come for nothing, have you?' I said to the captain. And I was right. Later the Harki confessed that he had orders to kill three Frenchmen every week."

"Last month, I saw the man in town," M. Martin cut in. "He is working here in a factory. Not a bad sort, really. It was simply the psychology of crowds, as I have told you." The man, he said, had spent some time in prison, but M. Martin had told him that in the long run he was better off than the true Harkis. After the war, M. Martin said, the Algerians seized the Harkis and kept taking their blood until they died, to give to the wounded FLN soldiers. Thousands did die, and some of the eighty thousand Harkis who managed to flee the country under French protection are still living in wretched little refugee camps and villages, in the Alps and in the Massif Central, where the French put them. They are out of sight in the mountains, and most of the French have forgotten all about them now.*

"It is just like the French to abandon their children," Mme. Martin remarked. "It was the same thing with the OAS generals."

M. Martin nodded. He worships the generals—Salan and Jouhaud and the others who led the Secret Army—and still refuses to believe that they had anything to do with the terror

---

* The Harkis are not much better off now, although their children have tended to migrate to towns and cities, looking for work.

that the OAS spread. He says that they were good, loyal soldiers, and that when they confessed in court they were acting in the best military tradition, taking responsibility for the bad behavior of their men. None of the evidence has changed his mind or shaken his faith in the generals. The fact that they, like everybody else, betrayed him is too much for M. Martin to bear. He blames the Communists—all the *pieds noirs* blame the Communists—for the feeling that exists in France against the generals now.

"There are always a *few* extremists in a revolution," Mme. Martin said. "There are always a few who do bad things."

"The generals were good soldiers, *French* soldiers," M. Martin repeated, getting teary. "And what did De Gaulle do? He sent them to prison. Even the baroness's son he sent to prison."

"They say that the baroness's son was part of the plot to kill De Gaulle," Mme. Martin whispered, jumping up and going to the window. She had forgotten to close the kitchen shutters.

"Why do you say that?" M. Martin asked her. "That's cinema."

"It is *all* cinema," she said, and she refilled his glass because she saw that he was crying.

"It is the warmth we miss here," M. Martin said suddenly. "There is no warmth. And it is not just us. There is no warmth among the villagers. Even among themselves, they are not *gentils*."

"And they say they are Communists—even the mayor says that he is Communist," Mme. Martin said.

"The mayor? Ridiculous!" M. Martin wiped his eyes and grinned. "The mayor is different. If you scratch the paint off the mayor, you find a true Frenchman."

Mme. Martin laughed and pointed to the plate of cookies. "Communism! At the store they charge you two francs ten for two francs' worth of flour. That is their Communism."

M. Martin sat up. "The government is worse. I will tell you, I don't know any logic that will disinherit a second generation." He touched his leg, and then his chest. "I am pierced, here and here and here, by bullets for the French, and now I cannot even take my own inheritance."

"It is their jealousy." Mme. Martin nodded sadly. "Last week I went to the social-security office in town to see about my husband's money, and a man there took me for a *métropolitaine*. He stopped me at the door and pointed to a group of *pied-noir* women who were waiting in the line. 'Look at those women,' he said. 'I'd like to throw them out. They are worth nothing. They are taking the place of *French* women.' "

"It *is* their jealousy," M. Martin said. "You have heard about the Israelis, who took a desert and made a garden. Well, that is what the *pieds noirs* did. We took a desert and made a garden. And when we came to France we came with our ingenuity, we came with the habit of working in a wild country. We looked around Provence and said, 'Ha! There is something to be done here.' And after a year we began to have melons in January. Pears in November. Even mandarin oranges in Isle de Rhône. The French were jealous because *we* did that and they could not."

"They do not know how to live," Mme. Martin broke in. "They say to me, 'But you have *two* toilets in your house. Imagine!' " She chuckled. "Two toilets, and the first washing machine in the village. It is unthinkable to the people here."

"Plus the first television," M. Martin added, and then he said, "What do you expect? The peasants—they are hippies in their fashion. They need the *pieds noirs* to get things done. A *pied noir* will come in as a worker and in two weeks he is the director. And then the peasants, who have done nothing, will complain that he has taken a Frenchman's job."

"Oh, they are babies," Mme. Martin said. "They are idiots."

"But they are *méchants*," M. Martin said. "The first *pieds noirs* who came here, the ones who had the first taste of it— they were obliged to leave for Paris."

"But we survived," Mme. Martin said, sighing.

"Because we were the strong ones," her husband said. "The

pieds noirs who came here first were not strong. If they had been strong, they would have stayed in Algeria until the end, as we did. We stayed till the blood, till the last shot."

"The villagers here had heard that in Algeria we were charging the French soldiers a hundred francs for a glass of water," Mme. Martin said. "They read *La Marseillaise* and they believed it." She shook her head. "And they listened to the politicians. To De Gaulle. To Defferre. Even Defferre, who says now that he is such a friend to the *pieds noirs*—I tell you that in 1962 he would have liked to see us all dumped into the ocean—"

"I gave wine to the soldiers when they came," M. Martin broke in. "I said to my wife, 'Wine for the soldiers!' And then they went home and told their mothers that we charged for water."

"Well, they will live with their consciences," Mme. Martin told him as she passed the cookies. "The soldier who lives here—the one who tried to send us to the Arabs. I saw him yesterday. I went to his grandfather's funeral. I embraced his wife, and then I took his hand and shook it. He was ashamed and turned his head away."

"That young man—he knows now that the world is small," M. Martin said and slapped his knee again. "We have a good thing, we *pieds noirs*. We are bigger in spirit than the people here."

Mme. Martin nodded. "He is right. And Jean-Jacques is right. The people in France are small. I remember, in Marseille —we were at the port, and someone had made a fire, and I said to myself, 'Good, I will buy a pot and some rice with my twenty francs and cook a dinner for my hungry children.' So I went to a store, but no one at the store would sell me a pot after they heard my voice and knew that I was a *pied noir*. Then I went to another store. I asked for the pot in a Marseille accent. The man there looked at me, suspicious. 'You are a *Marseillaise*?' he said. 'Where do you live?' So I named a street—the fanciest street in all Marseille."

"She got the pot," M. Martin said, laughing. And he tried to embrace his wife. *"Bonne camarade.* She is a *bonne camarade*, even in the worst times."

Mme. Martin ignored him. "I heard later that the man in the first store was killed when a tree fell on him. I said to myself, *'Dommage pour l'arbre.'* "

"Dommage pour l'arbre! That's good!" M. Martin shouted, and he added softly, "You see, we have become cold here. In the beginning, no. But then, after the first Christmas—The children were very homesick that first Christmas, but we had heard that it was the custom here for all the children in the village to take a house and have their own party, and so we told them that, to make them feel a little happier. Then Christmas came, and no one asked my children. They walked home from church and heard the music from the party. It was at that moment that I said to myself, 'Now it is over, it is finished.' I became cold."

"We are cold, but we have not made peace," Mme. Martin said. "When Yvette was getting married, Georges's grandmother came to our house to ask about a dowry. She said that it had to be a big dowry, with many sheets and tablecloths and towels, because of the disgrace that Georges was marrying a *pied noir*. But then, after it was settled, she looked at my table, which was set for supper, and said, 'Good, now we will eat together *en famille.'* I thought to myself, She insults the *pieds noirs*, but now she is hungry and wants to eat, and she says that it is for me, a *pied noir*, to pay. No, thank you. And I said, 'No, we will each eat supper at our own house.' I opened the door, and I handed her the sheets and tablecloths she wanted. *'Le linge, madame,'* I told her. *'Le linge, madame, et bonsoir.'* "

M. Martin raised his wineglass. *"Le linge, madame, et bonsoir."*

ABOUT THE AUTHOR

JANE KRAMER has been a writer at *The New Yorker* since 1963 and for the past several years has written its "Reporter in Europe" series. She is the author of *Off Washington Square*, *Allen Ginsberg in America*, *Honor to the Bride*, and *The Last Cowboy*. She was educated at Vassar College and Columbia University and now lives in New York City with her husband and daughter.